knitting yarns

knitting yarns

WRITERS on KNITTING

Edited with an Introduction by Ann Hood

W. W. Norton & Company

New York • London

For information about special discounts for bulk purchases, please contact
W. W. Norton Special Sales at specialsales@wwnorton.com or 800-233-4830

Manufacturing by RR Donnelley, Harrisonburg
Book design by Judith Stagnitto Abbate / Abbate Design
Production Manager: Devon Zahn

Library of Congress Cataloging-in-Publication Data

Knitting yarns : writers on knitting/edited and with an introduction by Ann Hood.—First Edition.
pages cm
Includes bibliographical references.
ISBN 978-0-393-23949-2 (hardcover)
1. Knitting. 2. Knitting—Miscellanea. 3. Knitters (Persons)—Miscellanea. I. Hood, Ann, 1956– editor of compilation.
TT820.K727 2013
746.43′2—dc23
2013021938

W. W. Norton & Company, Inc., 500 Fifth Avenue, New York, N.Y. 10110
www.wwnorton.com

W. W. Norton & Company Ltd., Castle House, 75/76 Wells Street, London W1T 3QT

1 2 3 4 5 6 7 8 9 0

for Jen Silverman

contents

knitting yarns

introduction

WHEN I PICKED UP KNITTING NEEDLES FOR THE first time in October 2002, I had no idea that I was jumping on a hot trend that had started to sweep the country after 9/11. All I knew was that for six months I had been trying to pull myself out of the grief that had taken hold when my five-year-old daughter Grace died suddenly from a virulent form of strep that April. A professional writer and avid reader, in the aftermath of Grace's death I found that words—those magical things that had been my source of comfort since childhood, had lost their power. Unable to read or write, I found myself gripped by a seemingly never-ending grief.

One day, on a walk with friends, I confessed how lost I was without words. "Get out of your head," one of them said. "Do something with your hands instead." As a person who had never learned a craft, had never even learned how to properly sew a button back on, I couldn't imagine what I might do *with my hands*. "Learn to knit," she said. Looking back on that now, the fact that I seized on that idea shows me just how desperate I was. In no time, I was driving along the East Bay of Rhode Island to Sakonnet Purls, a knitting store in an old barn in Tiverton, about forty miles from my home in Providence.

I was a terrible knitter. So foreign was the very notion of knitting that I didn't even realize I was simply transferring stitches from one needle to the other. As I sat and clumsily dropped stitches, dropped the needles themselves, split the yarn, and even somehow added new stitches where they didn't belong, I could not imagine that this pile of wool would transform into a scarf—by *my* hands. But right from the start, even on that first autumn afternoon of knitting, its healing powers began to work. When I picked up those needles and began to knit, my sadness dissipated. During the hours I knit, I was calm and focused. Time, that thing that had become my enemy, passed. And as I moved those stitches from one needle to another, I could lose myself in the sounds and textures and rhythms of knitting.

Since that October day, I have met thousands of knitters and heard their stories. Stories of how knitting helped them through all kinds of things that life throws in our paths: divorce, depression, deaths; chemotherapy, loneliness, despair. But I've also heard stories about the sheer joy of knitting. In fact, according to the Craft Yarn Council of America, in a recent survey of 5,000 knitters the number one reason people knit is because it's enjoyable. Forty-two percent of those surveyed said they knit because it's a great stress reliever. Others said they liked it as a creative outlet.

When I was a new knitter, I was surprised that unlike my stereotype of a knitter, the women and men I sat with and knit beside were not elderly grandparents. Most were middle-aged or younger. The CYCA survey supported that; almost half of those interviewed were between the ages of thirty-five and fifty-four, and 18 percent were eighteen to thirty-four, proving that the knitting demographic is younger than some assume. Right at this moment, the online knitting social group Ravelry.com has 3.091 million people on it, sharing patterns and knitting stories. Knitting is hot, and shows no signs of cooling.

My novel *The Knitting Circle* became a bestseller when it was published in 2006. Now optioned by Katherine Heigl and soon to be an HBO movie, the book continues to sell in bookstores and knitting stores. But I'm not the only knitting writer. Far from it. Since I've learned to knit, as I take my latest knitting project to my seat in the back row of readings and writers' conferences everywhere, I've noticed other writers knitting too. They knit while they listen to lectures and readings, on airplanes and trains, during meetings and writing breaks. Over time, not only did I share favorite patterns and yarn stores with my fellow writers, but we also shared knitting stories. Why we do it, how we began, and the magical powers of yarn and needles.

This idea for an anthology of writers writing about knitting presented itself when I realized how many writers had told me their own knitting stories. To share those stories with knitters and readers seems not only exciting but necessary. I soon realized that the problem wasn't going to be getting writers to contribute, but rather to find a way to keep so many knitting stories from flooding my inbox. What you have now is a collection of original essays written by some of the most prizewinning, bestselling, beloved writers writing today. Elinor Lipman asked if she could write a poem instead, and so you have "I Bought This Pattern Book Last Spring," in which she tackles the stash of yarn and unfinished projects that fill a knitters' life.

Some of these essays are practical: Alison Lurie gives us a history of knitting, Sue Grafton tells us how to teach a child to knit. Others explore our emotional landscapes. Ann Patchett traces her life through her knitting, and writes about the scarf that knits together the women she's loved and lost. Taylor Polites knits for his teacup Chihuahua Clovis. Andre Dubus III learns to knit so that he can give his aunt a homemade gift, but also knits his way across the bumpy territory of love and money; and Lan Samantha Chang tackles the question of whether our knitted gifts are even wanted or appreciated. Suzanne Strempek Shea brings us back to the Crafty Critters of her childhood. Elizabeth Berg, John Dufresne, and Marianne Leone write about the frustration of trying to learn how to knit, and each of them does something very different with their failing. But knitting teaches Bernadette Murphy how to fail better. Mothers and daughters are explored here. When Hope Edelman's daughters learned to knit, it connected them to the grandmother they never knew; when Janice Eidus's daughter asked to learn to knit, the writer faced her own childhood memories; knitting connects Joyce Maynard to her mother who, she writes, could "spin straw into gold"; Anita Shreve and her daughter collect their unfinished knitting projects and set out to complete them in a weekend. And then there are the writers who found solace in knitting after loss—Martha Frankel lost her best friend to a cult, Jennifer Lauck's marriage fell apart after just a year, and Kaylie Jones sets out to repair what she lost as a young woman. Knitting forced some writers to ask themselves tough questions: After a boy teaches her how to knit in Kathmandu, Jessi Hempel examines her lesbianism; when Anne D. LeClaire cannot become pregnant, she turns to adoption and knitting. High-strung Elissa Schappell and nervous Elizabeth Searle explore the calming properties of knitting. Jane Smiley finds the link between writing novels and knitting. Ann Shayne admits that although knitting can't literally save lives, it can save the day. And Barbara Kingsolver tells us why and how it starts.

I also thought: What is a knitting anthology without knitting patterns in it? Every Friday at noon, I go to Fresh Purls on the aptly named Hope Street in Providence to get knitting guidance from

Helen Bingham, whom I refer to as my knitting guru. Not only can Helen fix every knitting problem thrust into her waiting hands, but she can decipher complicated patterns, pick up stitches, and un-knit mistakes. She designs patterns too, often offering evening classes to teach us how to re-create that slouch hat or cabled shawl. Helen's designs have appeared in *Vogue Knitting*, Ravelry.com, and many other knitting sites. For this anthology, Helen has designed five original patterns: the shawl she designed after losing her best friend to cancer; coffee cozies to keep your java warm while you knit; toasty socks for winter nights spent reading or knitting; finger-less gloves that make texting, typing, and knitting possible even on the coldest days; and a head wrap if you decide to put your knitting down and go outside.

The impressive collection of writers here have contributed essays that celebrate knitting and knitters. They share their knitting triumphs and disasters as well as their life triumphs and disasters. Some of the essays are about the role knitting plays in the lives of these writers, or of their close family members; some essays are about the curious phenomenon of their interest in knitting but their inability to do it and what that means; some are about the importance of a knitted gift they gave or received; others illuminate the magic of knitting. These essays will break your heart. They will have you laughing out loud. But they will all leave knitters and non-knitters alike happy to have spent time in the company of these writers writing about knitting.

"banks"
fingerless mittens

by Helen Bingham

These fingerless mittens have beaded cuffs that add a touch of class. There are over 250 beads knit into the fabric for each mitten which uses the magic loop method of knitting in the round. Mae Banks, my grandmother (and a knitter), was a woman who taught me to enjoy the little things in life that bring you happiness.

MATERIALS:

1 skein Silky Wool by Elsebeth Lavold (45% wool/35% silk/20% nylon with 185 yards)
color: #124

OR

2 skeins Magnolia by Classic Elite Yarns (70% merino/30% silk with 120 yards)
color #5454

504 size 6 seed beads (3 vials of Miyuki color = berry-lined light topaz) (252 beads per mitten)

US 4, 40″ circular needle or size needed to obtain gauge

SIZES: one size

FINISHED MEASUREMENTS: Width: 7.5" hand circumference, Length: 8"

GAUGE: 24 sts = 4" in 2×2 rib slightly stretched; 22 sts = 4" in stockinette stitch

PATTERN NOTES & ABBREVIATIONS:
—This pattern uses the magic loop method of knitting (YouTube has how-to videos on this technique).
—This is a tight knit to allow the beads to stay in place.
—String extra beads onto the yarn in case you miscount.
—To string the beads onto the yarn, use a sewing needle or an eye needle (sold at most bead stores).
—How to slip a bead: put the right-hand needle into the next stitch to be knit, slip the bead close to the stitch just knit, and continue to knit the stitch.

Kfb = knit into the front and back of the same stitch (increase)

K2tog = knit two stitches together (decrease)

P2tog = purl two stitches together (decrease)

DIRECTIONS:

RIGHT MITTEN
—String 252 beads onto yarn.
—Using long-tail method cast on 42 sts.
—To divide for the magic loop method, pull cable out after the first 21 sts. Now there are 21 sts on one half and 21 sts on the other half of the needle.
—Join into the round, making sure the sts are not twisted.

—Using the magic loop method, work the next four rounds:

Round 1: Knit 1 (slip a bead, knit 2)20 times, end with slip a bead, K1

Round 2: Purl all stitches

Round 3: (Slip a bead, Knit 2)21 times

Round 4: Purl all stitches

—Repeat these 4 rounds a total of 6 times ending with a Round 4 (there are 12 rounds with beads).

—While working the bead rounds the beads will pop on the inside of the mitten and the purl side (WS) will be facing you. Do not panic; when the beading is finished you will be flipping your work so the beads will be on the right side of the mitten.

Transition Round: *Flip the mitten inside out so the beaded side is now on the outside of work with the RS now facing. You will work back across the stitches that were just purled. There will be a small hole that appears after this next round is worked but you will use your tail at the end of the knitting to close this small gap.*

—Work the following rounds:

Round 1: (K1, SSK, Knit 18 sts) repeat once more (40 sts remain)

Round 2: Knit all stitches

Rounds 3, 4 & 5: Repeat Round 2

Round 6: (K2, P2)10 times

Rounds 7–12: Repeat Round 6

Rounds 13–17: Knit all stitches

Round 18: (K1, P1)20 times

Round 19: (P1, K1)20 times

—Repeat Rounds 18 and 19 a total of 7 times so there are 14 seed stitch rounds.

THUMB OPENING:

—Work back and forth in rows instead of in the round.

—Start on the WS by working across the sts that were just knit as follows:

Row 1 (WS): K2, P2, Kfb, (P1, K1) till 5 sts remain, Kfb, P2, K2 (42 sts) TURN

Row 2 (RS): P2, K2, (K1, P1)17 times, K2, P2 TURN

Row 3 (WS): K2, P2, (P1, K1)17 times, P2, K2 TURN

—Repeat Rows 2 and 3 a total of 7 times (14 rows have been worked).

—Repeat Row 2 one more time.

—Once Row 2 is finished, join to resume working in the round as follows:

Round 1: K1, P1, K2tog, (P1, K1) repeat till 4 sts remain, P2tog, K1, P1

Round 2: (P1, K1)20 times

Round 3: (K1, P1)20 times

— Repeat Rounds 2 and 3 a total of 5 times (11 seed stitch rounds since thumb opening).

—Work the following round:

Round 1: (K2, P2)10 times

—Repeat this round a total of 5 times.

—Cast off all stitches in the rib pattern.

—Weave in the ends.

—Make the second mitten!

For pictures of this pattern, go to www.helenbinghamdesigns.com.

the pretend knitter

by Elizabeth Berg

Can someone who loves everything about knitting—the yarn, the tools of the trade, the knitted projects—actually learn to knit?

OH, I GO TO KNITTING STORES, WHERE I TAKE A VERY long time to look at everything. "Can I help you?" some helpful person always asks, and I always say, "No thanks, just looking," in a very busy, maybe even slightly hostile way so that she won't come over and expose me for the pretender that I am.

I go to knitting stores because I wish I were a knitter. I like the colors and textures of the yarn, the brushed suri that is a blend of bamboo and merino and comes in turquoise and brick red colors and the softest shade of pink you ever saw, it's like white, blushing. I like the alpaca silk and the sparkle yarns, the worsted wool and copper metallics and superwash merinos, the aran cotton blends, the silk and angora blends, the Harvest Fields brand in colors of mulberry and olive. I think about buying skeins of yarn to put around my house in baskets like practical bouquets. I think about using the yarns that are fat as the rope clotheslines of yore to wrap big presents, and the yarns so thin they could double as dental floss to wrap little tiny presents. And sometimes I buy them to do just that.

It's not just the yarns I like to look at in knitting stores. I also enjoy looking at tools of the trade: carrying cases, repair hooks, gauges, tape measures and stitch counters and markers and needles made of bamboo or the Signature needles, made of finest steel. There are circular needles and double-pointed needles and there are cases for holding them. I like the whimsical things: all manner of buttons for putting on a sweater, a wineglass with levels marked off for pouring: a line for lace knitting at the bottom, where you'd get the least amount, then progressing upward to Fair Isle, stockinette stitch, and finally ripping out, and the line marked here assures that you get a full glass of wine indeed.

I look with envy at the beautiful finished products on display: sweaters and hats and mittens and ruffled rose scarves and throws and toys for young children—elephants and teddy bears and rabbits and Uglys.

There's a long wooden table with ladder-back chairs in the knitting store in my town, and one of the chairs is all decked out in ... guess what? Knitting! I like to sit at that table and hear the advice given to this woman making a gunmetal gray pullover, to that one making a shawl. I like the quietly industrious sound of the needles, of the low chatter of women who come not for advice at all but for the camaraderie. On the card that lists the hours for the store I go to is a friendly invitation: *Come knit anytime!* I would like to come and sit and knit, but I had a traumatic knitting experience. Think of it as having hit the bottom of the pool at my first diving lesson.

I grew up an army brat, and when I was a little kid, in the years 1951–54, we were stationed in Germany. While we were there, the postwar economy made it possible for us to have the luxury of a full-time maid. Gerti was her name. She was a curly brown-haired woman whom I recall as having a pleasing constellation of moles on one side of her face and an equally pleasing disposition. She had no problem with me following her around as she did her chores, lying at her feet when she ironed, or sitting practically on top of her when she knitted. She was a skilled knitter, Gerti, and I was mesmerized by the flash of her needles, the finished products ever emerging from them, and most of all, the way she rarely even looked at what she was doing. It was all in the attitude, I decided, and I tried to knit using attitude, which was just about as successful as you might think it would be. Gerti did manage to teach me to cast on, and she taught me a simple garter stitch, and I never forgot it. But what could you do with *that*? I wanted to be a knitter extraordinaire: I had visions of making sweaters like my Aunt Kate sent me every Christmas, my favorite being a navy blue one that featured a clown holding balloons. I wanted to make soft pink and blue and yellow baby blankets and hats and mittens and socks that would make the recipients go all soft in the eyes. But in all the ensuing years after Gerti taught me the garter stitch, all I ever knit were scarves of varying widths, full of holes from dropped stitches because I didn't know how to fix dropped stitches. Finally, I gave up.

But then when I was a sophomore in college, I lived with a woman named Lois whom I adored. We had no money but we had our guitars and our cowgirl boots and our Boone's Farm wine and our boyfriends and we had *fun*. I got it in mind, one winter, to knit her a scarf. It would work this time; it would be beautiful. And it would be warm, which, in Minnesota, moves right past being a blessing into the territory of survival.

Lois's eyes were a rich brown color, and so I endeavored to find a shade of yarn I thought would match. I came pretty close, and I bought several skeins and a pair of needles and hid them away. When she wasn't around, I worked on her scarf. Garter stitch, of course. And soon there were the usual dropped stitches, which I thought could be made up for by making the scarf long. Very long. Then longer. Then perhaps a bit too long. No. Not perhaps. Definitely too long. It looked like something you might give someone to tie around a bedpost and then use to escape a burning building. And here is my tip given to all knitters everywhere: making something longer does not make up for dropped stitches. Rather, it accentuates them.

Next problem: I had forgotten how to cast off. But I did it, eventually, and then I used the yard I had left to make some fringe, which was not lush and attractive but thin, like a near-bald man's remaining hair raked hopefully over the top of his head. Or, more accurately, like the cilia on a paramecium, if you've ever had the good fortune to see a paramecium, and if you have not I invite you to Google "paramecium" right now and you will have a very good idea of what my friend's scarf fringe looked like. And that wasn't even the worst of it. Somehow the thing had gotten really crooked, so it went first to the left, then to the right in really a rather hectic way, as though the scarf was having an argument with itself about which was the right way to get *out* of there.

Well. I held my gift up before me and I just wanted to weep. Never had such glorious intentions come to such a sorry end. I had wanted to give my friend a gift not only from my heart but from my hands, I had wanted to make her something that made her full of gratitude, and all I had made was a mess, even by the most lenient of standards. Nonetheless, I presented it to her the next day with a thousand and one excuses. She lifted the scarf from the box and gamely wrapped it around her neck. And wrapped it around some more, and then some more, which, if you've been paying attention to this story, you'd know she would have had to do in order not to trip on it. She stood beneath the kitchen overhead light—one of the few lights in the apartment that worked—to show me how it looked. And then, as if I had not suffered enough humiliation, I saw that the color was not a deep and rich brown, but rather a color like something you take Imodium for.

I shrugged. I said, "I'm sorry." I said, "I wanted to give you something that I made." And you know what she said? She said, "But you did. And I love it."

She did indeed seem to love it. The next day, she wrapped the scarf around her neck where it peeked odiously out from the top of her rather nice winter coat. She wore it that day and the next and the next. She wore it all winter. For all I know, she still has it. I would ask her, but I'm embarrassed to.

But here's the thing. The lesson in all this, which I did not learn then, is that so much of the joy of knitting is not in the creation of a perfect product. Rather, it is in the act of using one's own bodily skills to make something for someone else's body. The gift is not so much in the end result (although the end results are often if not usually spectacular), but in the way that something made with one's own hands says a few things of utmost importance:

I made this for you.
I thought of you while I made it.
I guess I kind of love you.

Last time I was busily browsing in my local store, this time venturing to say, "What's *this*?" and then exclaiming over its beauty, or ingenuity, or sly humor, the owner, whose name is Sue, said, "You know, you really should learn to knit."

Busted. But oh so happily. I said, "I know," and I got a schedule of classes. "But I'm not taking a class in the summer," I told her. "I'm taking it in the *winter*, that's when *I'm* doing it," I said. And Sue said, "O-*kay*."

I don't think I've ever said this before, but I can't wait for winter.

the perfect gift

by Lan Samantha Chang

Is it possible that we need and like to knit so badly that we don't really care if the recipients of our knitted goods find them aesthetically pleasing or even bearable?

I AM KNITTING A SCARF FOR MY HUSBAND. I'VE CHOSEN A deep green, hand-dyed yarn, with a wonderful springy heft; I'm working in two-by-two rib with pleasure and absorption. The scarf is like a magic thread connecting me to him. Now and then, as I measure its length, I envision him wearing it.

These weeks when I secretly knit the scarf are a precious time for both of us. They create the best of all possible worlds. I have the pleasure of feeling my affection, of touching it with two hands, of fashioning an object that will warm and hold him. *He* is also lucky. Because he does not yet know about his gift, he need not yet pretend to like it. Soon, he will receive the scarf, wrapped carefully in tissue. He may be pleased or he may not be, but on certain winter mornings, he will feel obliged to wear it. If he doesn't like the scarf—if the color or texture or length is somehow wrong—he will wrap it like a leash around his neck.

KNITTING A GIFT for a loved one is akin to creating a special meal. Imagine making a hearty stew for family and friends on a cold night. Cheerfully you add the spices, perhaps following a recipe or perhaps inventing from scratch, a pinch of this, a pinch of that. You hover near the stove as the stew bubbles away, feeling warm with the anticipation of feeding your loved ones, of satisfying this primal need. They gather at the table, chatting comfortably, lured by the promising aromas coming from the kitchen. There is a suspenseful moment when you place the steaming dish upon the table to *oohs* and *aahs* and ladle it plate by plate. Then everyone takes a bite. The meat is hard and stringy, the sauce thin and poor, the dish inedible. There is a prolonged period when you imagine everyone struggling with the question of whether to say the truth. But they need not say a word: the disappointment on their faces, the puckering of their lips, tells everything. There is a silence as they steel themselves to keep on eating.

OF COURSE, IT'S POSSIBLE to feel wretched over failed presents that are *not* homemade: a poorly chosen restaurant meal, a scarf in the wrong shade of blue, purchased, unreturnably, on a trip to Paris. But there is something especially fraught in the presentation of a knitted gift. If it's the thought that counts, then knitters are among the most righteous of all gift givers. If the recipient dislikes the gift, is he, in essence, damning the effort that went into it? Yes, he is.

.   .   .

YEARS AGO, I KNITTED a scarf for a man who seemed to wear only brown. His two coats, his trousers, his hat and gloves and socks and shoes, were all in that color. I chose a gorgeous, soft yarn the color of coffee beans. I presented the scarf as we left town for our respective winter vacations.

Three weeks later, when he returned, he had a new winter jacket—blue. It had been a Christmas present from his mother. "But the scarf—" I blurted. "I'll wear it," he promised me. Loyally, he wore the scarf, every day that winter. Did he pray to move to a warmer climate, or for one of us to leave town so he might put the scarf aside? Luckily, one of us did.

I'VE HEARD PLENTY about the pleasure and creativity and even the ecstasy of the knitting process. What I hear less about, but have experienced more times than I care to count, is an awkward gap between the fulfillment to be found in the process and the satisfaction taken in the product. I know that I am not alone. I remember reading an article before the Christmas holidays in which those polled revealed the nation's most unwanted gift: a hand-knit sweater.

All people who make things face the question of whether the world will accept what they have made. And all people who make things, if they are to keep on, must feel that it is the making itself that matters, more than the product or its reception. We knitters love the reassuring, meditative pleasure of making things, but do others love the things we make? Is it possible that we need and like to knit so badly that we don't really care if the recipients of our knitted goods find them aesthetically pleasing or even bearable?

.　　.　　.

WHY, YOU MAY ASK, did I not involve my husband in the creation of his gift? Why not let him choose the yarn, the pattern? The sad but true answer is that even if I were to show him, even if he were to choose the pattern and the yarn, something might well happen to it while I made it so that it might, or might not, turn out as he expected. I think of a friend who for some time now has been knitting a blanket with materials chosen by her granddaughter. It is a thick, square blanket made from bright red worsted. Most of it is worked in garter stitch, with turned corners. My friend has labored with innocent doggedness for many seasons, and the blanket, still unfinished, is now about four years old. Like any four-year-old knitted object, it is rather the worse for wear. It has been tossed repeatedly into a basket, its stitches caught and pulled on the wicker edges. It has been left there over the summers to gather dust. It has been knit and reknit, so many mistakes pulled out that in places it has taken on a ravaged aspect. By the time my friend is finished—and I suspect that this will likely happen when her granddaughter has fallen into the most unforgiving throes of puberty—how will the blanket be received?

I LEARNED TO KNIT as a child, from my own grandmother, but I forgot about it as a young adult, only to pick it up again in my forties, knitting baby sweaters after my daughter was born. My grandmother, born in Shanghai, knit brioche turtlenecks for the harsh winters of Wisconsin. She knit mohair cardigans in pale blues and in peach shades with matching buttons. My mother, sisters, and I wore and loved the things she made. Our family was short on money and purchased clothes so rarely that any breath of newness and prettiness in our lives was a treasure. She was a wonderful knitter. She never used patterns, but she had an eye for fashion; she studied the catalogues and newspapers for trends in collars and sleeves. We all knew that she spent every penny she had on yarn for us.

My mother loved my grandmother's sweaters. This is a testament to the knitting, or to my mother's love, since she is notorious among her daughters for being absolutely incapable of pretending to appreciate a gift she doesn't truly like. How many times have my Mother's Day and Christmas presents been set aside with a shrug? How many times have I leaned closer as wrapping paper was torn off, only to be confronted with her severe and absolutely disinterested expression? I am not alone in my failure to please, or in the lengths I'm willing to go in order to try to please my mother. One Christmas, one of my sisters presented her with a brand-new, state-of-the-art desktop computer, and she has never opened the box.

A FEW YEARS AGO, I set out to make my mother the perfect sweater. I was inspired in a wonderful knitting shop in Sheridan, Wyoming. My daughter was a year and a half old, and I had only been knitting in earnest for six months. I glimpsed a pattern for a jacket with an intricate basket weave pattern and a collar, and I was seized by the bright certainty that it would be perfect for my mother. She loves clothes with some shape to them, but never anything tight. She always wears collared things because she believes her neck is too long. Although women of her age in China have traditionally worn dark colors, nothing warmer than lavender, my mother loves colors such as reds and pinks; she is particularly fond of a beautiful rosy coral shell-pink, and when I was in Wyoming I found a few skeins of lovely yarn in this exact shade. The proprietor tried to help me. There weren't enough skeins left to make the sweater and I was leaving Wyoming in a week. Wouldn't I be satisfied with this scarlet yarn instead? No—I had a vision of my mother in the exact shade of that light bamboo silk merino. I asked the proprietor to order the shell-coral color and send it to me in Iowa. For sixteen skeins of sport-weight yarn at fourteen dollars a skein, it would be the most expensive Mother's Day gift I'd ever given her. More than a month later, the yarn arrived in the mail. At this point, I had never knit an adult sweater. I had never knit anything so complicated, never knit a fabric with a texture, and rarely ventured to a finer gauge than worsted. Buoyed by my bright certainty, I took a deep breath, and cast on 240 stitches.

I CAN STILL REMEMBER that casting on, unraveling, recasting, and recounting; but I have forgotten, I think, the worst parts of making that sweater in the same way that women often forget the worst parts of childbirth. To this day, I'm surprised I finished the sweater. I assume my determination had something to do with the hormonal upswing from breastfeeding. The exhausted tedium of new motherhood, the need for something to do while sitting still, had to do with it also. Or chalk it up to the gorgeous and expensive and unusually forgiving yarn, which kept its pretty sheen and delicate shade of pink despite my repeated mistakes and ripping out. My husband, a woodsy subdued-hue type, was no help at all. "Are you sure she's going to like that *color?*" he asked skeptically, half a dozen times during the process. But I was determined to finish; through all my errors and unravelings, I barely paused, for I could not shake my vision of the sweater as the perfect gift for my mother. I grew tired of it, but I don't believe I ever once hated it. The body, knitted in one piece, took months to complete. The sleeves were easy by comparison, and the collar—well, I knew that without the collar, my mother would never touch it, so I painstakingly counted out the short rows, and turned, again and again. When I was finished with the sweater, I took it to a local yarn shop with a workroom in the back, and patiently blocked and steamed my creation into shape. In another store, I found eight beautiful carved mother-of-pearl buttons. When I tried it on, I was certain beyond a doubt that my mother would love it.

She did love it. When one of my sisters answered our mother's phone that Mother's Day, I could hear her admiration, even envy, that I had given such a perfect gift. My mother's thanks were light and musical. I could hear her pleasure in being given a gift no one had given her ever since her own mother had died. I could hear her pride in the fact that I would go through such hell for her. In the following years, she wore the sweater on Mother's Day and on all special spring occasions.

Last winter, I made my mother a long, plum-colored cardigan. I was inspired by the softness of the yarn and by the complex pattern up the placket, yet it didn't quite work out. She set the box aside disinterestedly. I had to remind her to even try it on. It was *not* the perfect sweater. But because I know that, just once, I've made the perfect gift, I will keep trying.

blood, root, knit, purl

by Andre Dubus III

Knitting becomes an unexpected avenue to a Christmas gift for his aunt, and a way to knit his relationship with his young, rich girlfriend.

I T WAS DECEMBER 1986, AND I HAD LESS THAN THREE WEEKS to make my Aunt Jeannie a Christmas present. She was eight years older than my mother, had lost her husband in her forties, was done raising my two older cousins, Micky and Eddie, and at fifty-six was going blind. She'd always been a large woman, and lovely, with long graying hair she held back with silk scarves or pinned up with tortoiseshell combs. She preferred silver earrings and bracelets, wore minimal makeup, and had a much stronger Louisiana accent than my mother, who'd fled the Deep South when she eloped with my father in 1958. They ended up in New England, and their marriage lasted less than ten years.

That winter I was twenty-seven years old, living with my girl-friend on the Upper East Side of New York City in an 8-by-13-foot room. It had a kitchenette and a tiny bathroom, the ceiling high enough I built a loft for us to sleep in. Beneath that was my desk looking out the barred first-floor window to 82nd Street, and every morning before going to work as a bartender down in the garment district, I would work on the novel I was writing.

My girlfriend was two years younger and had found a job working in a bookstore on Second Avenue. She was kind, charming, and athletic, and she had also grown up rich while I'd grown up poor. This created a chasm between us we tried to pretend wasn't there, but daily I was writing myself backwards into the ugly mill town I'd been raised in by my overworked and underpaid single mother, and at night, sharing a meal on the new sofa my girlfriend had bought us, wearing the Irish wool sweater and cowboy boots she'd bought me, too, her five-speed convertible parked in a garage not far away, her $2 million trust fund in a bank downtown, her sweet disposition and good skin and straight teeth, her perfect grammar from private schools, her family's five homes here and abroad, it would all become too much. I would accuse her of not knowing what the real world was really like. She would deny this, and I would start yelling. I would yell that she was from The Land of Yes while the rest of us were from the Land of No.

"Do you understand what I'm saying to you!?"

"Yes! I fucking *understand!*"

She'd be crying, and I'd feel like a bully for she'd always been loving and generous to me. If I could summon the nerve and the will, I'd apologize. But more times than not, I wouldn't, even though I knew I should. And because our apartment was so small, there was no place for either of us to retreat to except the mattress up in the loft or the new sofa below.

That night in December, Christmas looming, I lay up there

feeling small. How was it her fault she'd been born into wealth and privilege? How was it her problem that I saw the world as hard and unjust and anyone who did not was naïve?

Outside it was snowing. I could hear it ticking against the window glass, the taxi cabs and delivery trucks passing by in the street. Down on the sofa my girlfriend flicked on the TV and picked up her knitting. Her fucking *knitting*. It was another thing that made me feel far away from her. Who knitted but sweetly oblivious old ladies? To me, it seemed the busywork of people who were happy to *watch* life, not take part in it. But more than this, it was a domestic art from before the freedoms of feminism; my girlfriend was twenty-five years old, her adult life just beginning, and here she sat with her legs curled under her, her eyes on the TV, her fingers working the needles and yarn without having to peek. She looked like some young wife and mother from a hundred years ago; she looked to me like a woman who relied on her man to take care of everything.

But there was something deeply comforting about this image of her. I did not know what it was, but I also could not deny it. Nor could I deny that I was drawn to that comfort. A few months earlier my father had been run over by a car and crippled for the rest of his life. Every other weekend, if I could get time off at the bar, I'd take a bus up to Massachusetts to see him. He was no longer broad-chested and robust, his beard neatly trimmed, his cheeks pink. Instead, he was a one-legged man I didn't recognize. He lay in great pain on his living room couch, and his beard was long and bushy, his cheeks pale, his chest narrow, his arms withered. When I bent down to hug him he smelled like old bandages and dead skin and dried blood.

He was fifty, but his third wife was pregnant with their second child, and their five-year-old daughter, my half-sister, was running around the house nearly crazy with all these changes. And more changes were coming. Just weeks after her mother would give birth to her sister, they'd move away from my father, and he would be divorced for the third time.

As I watched my girlfriend knitting from up in the loft, I don't know if I was thinking about any of this though it was probably the deeper root of my distance from her, not some working-class outrage, but envy that she was the youngest of five children to a mother and father who clearly still loved one another and who would stay married the rest of their lives. I did not believe lasting love was possible. My girlfriend did.

But I craved the warm solidity of family, something I was not conscious of until I was among my own—not my mother and brother and two sisters, not during those years anyway—but the larger clan our parents came from down in the Deep South.

Fishville, Louisiana, was no more than a break on Highway 8 in the pines of Grant Parish in the heart of the state. It was little more than two Texaco gas pumps in the gravel lot of a roller skating rink, and across the highway, a narrow two-lane of cracked asphalt, lay Big Dean's creek, a watering hole locals would swim in, the teenagers swinging off a tree rope into the warm murky water, its banks slippery red clay. It was fed by streams running into it from the woods where men fished and caught gar and crayfish and trapped loggerhead turtles, and half a mile up the road lay the camp built by my mother's father.

HIS NAME WAS Elmer Lamar Lowe and, like every one of my blood relatives on both sides of the family, he was raised in Louisiana. He was the son of a mule skinner and a rice farmer, and after the third grade he never went back to school. At age nine and ten he was working alongside his old man, tying thick rope to barge cleats, cinching it around the leather harnesses of mules who'd then pull the loaded barges alongside the banks of shallow muddy rivers and bayous. There'd be cottonmouths coiled in the trunks of cypresses and live oaks, Spanish moss hanging from their limbs my grandfather probably had to brush away from his young face. By age sixteen he was the foreman for a gang of gandy dancers, grown men laying miles of railroad tracks under the blistering Louisiana sun. By the time Elmer Lowe became the father of my mother and her older sister Jeannie, he'd established himself as a pipe fitter who helped build power plants that brought electricity throughout the South and Southwest.

But this was a man I barely knew. Not until my parents' marriage ended and our mother, Elmer's youngest daughter, began what turned into the next decade of raising us four kids alone along the Massachusetts-New Hampshire border. Many of these houses were in poor, tough parts of town, and with my small body, my glasses and long hair, I quickly became a target for cruel and angry boys, many of whom would grow into self-destructive men, just about all of whom are dead as I write this now; one to a stabbing, two to drug overdoses, another to cirrhosis of the liver, another to a car accident. That second summer after my parents' divorce, I spent a lot of time hiding inside our small, hot rented house, my younger brother and two sisters there, too, and all we did was watch hours and hours of whatever was on TV.

When our mother eloped with our father, Elmer told her, "If you get divorced, don't bother coming home. There's been no damn divorces in our family."

But that was ten years earlier and maybe that summer she called or wrote her parents. Maybe she told them her kids needed something to do or somewhere to go, or that she wanted her mother and father to know her kids, I don't know, but soon we were speeding down the highway in a black Trans Am, a repo car my mother was being paid to drive to New Orleans, where we hopped a bus north to Fishville and what would become for me the place I'd grow to call home.

It wasn't the camp itself, the outbuildings Elmer—we called him Pappy—had sided with riveted sheet metal. And it wasn't the ten acres of tall jack pine or our grandmother Fern's chicken, sausage, and okra gumbo, or Big Dean's creek, or Pappy's pickup we got to ride in the bed of up and down Highway 8. It was being in one place where people we were actually related to had lived for many years.

Since our parents' divorce in 1970, my sisters and brother and mother and I moved nearly once a year, sometimes more, from one cheap rented house or half-house to another. Just as we seemed to settle into one, we packed up and moved to another. Friends were hard to come by. Then, just as I was about to enter high school, our mother found a large house to rent in Haverhill, Massachusetts, a half-dead mill town, and we lived there for six years. I eventually became friends with a boy from a big Irish Catholic family, nearly all of whom had raised their families there. On his father's side alone, my friend had nine uncles and nine aunts and dozens of cousins. Up the Merrimack River in Lowell, he had about as many from his mother's side. On Sundays, my new friend spent the afternoons at a relative's house eating homemade dinners, throwing a football or baseball around with uncles and cousins, swimming in one of his aunt's backyard pools. For me and my siblings, Sunday was the day our father drove to our house to take us to a movie or out to eat, our mother home alone, the six of us the only family we knew, every one of our blood relatives two thousand miles away in Louisiana.

But every summer after that first trip in the repossessed Trans Am, our mother would drive us down during her two-week vacations. Some years we drove other repo cars—once a VW van, a Chrysler sedan with air-conditioning, a yellow Dodge Charger. But as we got older and could help with the driving, we drove our old red Toyota, and we took turns driving straight through so we could skip having to pay for rooms at a Howard Johnson's or Holiday Inn.

Then we four kids were all in our twenties with jobs of our own and summers were hard to take off. Pappy and Fern's fiftieth wedding anniversary fell in January, and we threw them a big party, and it was good being in Louisiana in the winter; the frost on the pine needles; the bare magnolia branches scraping the camp during a cold wind; the scrap fire we'd burn outside and stand around while Pappy smoked a brisket over hickory coals in his cast iron smoker. Somebody, probably my mother, suggested we start coming down every Christmas. To save money for travel, there came the No Presents rule: Too expensive. Too hard to carry. Let's just each draw a name. One name, one gift, and you can't buy it; you have to make it yourself.

One year I got a short blue candle poured in a mold for me by cousin Micky's seven-year-old son. The next year I got a case of mayhaw jelly from Micky himself. Another year, because he'd heard I'd started writing fiction, Micky's older brother Eddie, a carpenter, sanded a four-inch length of oak branch into which he drilled two holes to hold two pencils. One Christmas, I drew my sister Suzanne's name and baked her sour cream enchiladas I then froze and wrapped and tied with a bow. The following Christmas, I drew my cousin Micky's wife, Sue, and I bought wire and beads and bent her a pair of earrings. The year after that, I drew Pappy's name and didn't know what to make him so cheated and bought him some cologne and two Louis L'Amour novels.

Every year, at least one of us would cheat and go to a store and buy our one present we were supposed to make. That December night in 1986, I was tempted to do that for Jeannie, but I couldn't. I loved her too much. Whenever I saw her briefly during those summers or for a few days every Christmas, she seemed to *see* me, whoever the hell I was, even when she was going blind. She'd sit me down and ask me questions about my life: Are you in love? Are you taking care of yourself? Are you drinking too much? Do you know how you're going to make a living and be an artist?

Two years earlier I'd published my first short story in a magazine. She read it and called me on the phone. "Andre, I'm just so happy you're not squandering your youth."

I felt loved by this woman, my mother's big sister, and I wanted to show her that I loved *her* too.

Down below, just a few feet from my knitting girlfriend, TV men and women fought and made up or did other happy or melodramatic things I did not believe, but now I was looking closer at what was in my girlfriend's lap. It appeared to be a small blue blanket.

"What're you knitting?"

At first she didn't answer. I asked her again, and she reached for the remote and muted the TV. "A sweater."

"Who for?"

"My sister's new baby."

Her second or third, I knew that. But I hadn't seen the obvious, that my young, rich girlfriend was somebody's aunt, too. I may have told her that was nice of her. I hope I did, but maybe I didn't.

The previous Christmas, Jeannie had drawn my name. With her fading eyes she'd painted me a portrait of Pappy and his twin sister

Tootsie. It came from a black-and-white photograph taken in 1915 when they were ten years old. They're both on a log in the woods. She's leaning on it in a dress, a bow in her hair, and Pappy, in knickers, is squatting on it and whittling a stick with a knife. Jeannie had this painting framed under glass, and when I unwrapped it, sitting on the couch beside her down in Fishville, she said she could hardly see it anymore but she hoped I liked it. I hugged her and told her I did, though I more than liked it; somehow she knew how much having family meant to me; somehow she knew I needed tangible evidence of my own roots.

And what *Jeannie* needed was something she didn't need to see to appreciate. She needed something she could *touch*.

"You think you could teach me to do that?"

My girlfriend's needles stopped clicking against one another. She looked up at me, her expression cautious but hopeful. "If you really want to."

"I want to knit my aunt a scarf."

In seconds I was sitting on the couch beside my girlfriend choosing a roll of gray yarn to work with because that's what she had the most of. She put aside her nephew's sweater and handed me two knitting needles. "Number 10's," she said.

They were a little heavier than I'd imagined they'd be. I liked how smooth they were, but holding them I couldn't help feeling emasculated till I remembered Rosie Greer, that big football player, knitting on some TV talk show, and I felt better, but I also felt shallow and reactionary that I'd needed to feel better.

My girlfriend showed me how to "cast on," a process so complicated I gave up and asked if she could do that part, then hand it over to me once the actual knitting would begin. I watched as she rolled out the yarn and about two feet down tied a slipknot she cinched onto one of my needles. Then she took the other one, her thumb and index fingers working the yarn into loops and more knots. It was like watching a spider spin a web as naturally as breathing, and soon she was handing me both needles and telling me I should probably just knit Jeannie's scarf in a simple knit/purl pattern, whatever that meant. She placed both her hands lightly over mine. She showed me how to first make a knit stitch. These details are foggy now, but I remember pushing the point of my right needle into her slipknot and wrapping the yarn from the back to the front of the needle before pushing it back under another knot, which left the yarn somehow at the rear of my right needle, then I was pulling my yarn to the front, sticking my needle under a new knot I'd made, then doing it all over again, looping from the back, sticking in the needle, looping from the front and sticking, looping and sticking.

My girlfriend went back to her own knitting, and she left the TV muted and all I heard was the clicking of her needles and the much slower click and slide of my own, the snow blowing harder at our window, the street a muffled quiet.

Every night after dinner, the two of us would sit on our couch in front of whatever was on TV and we'd knit. After a few sittings, I had what was beginning to look like the first five or six inches of a real scarf, and while my girlfriend told me that this was a simple pattern, it looked wonderfully intricate to me, its raised ribs and soft valleys precisely one-quarter inch apart. It made me think of snakeskins and Native Americans and I felt joined to all the men and women across cultures down through the ages who'd done something useful with their hands, who'd made essential things from whatever was in front of them.

And I was looking forward to wrapping it and giving it Christmas morning to my Aunt Jeannie down in Fishville, Louisiana. But this feeling of joyful anticipation rarely came while I was actually knitting, for the act itself was too calming for that, the constant sticking and looping and light cinching and more sticking and looping, my fingers moving in a rhythm they'd never known before. It required me to focus and it allowed me to drift too, the way running a long distance required my feet and legs to do one thing while my mind could do another. I recall thinking a lot about my father, his new life to be lived in a wheelchair; I thought of the novel I was writing, of how most days I was convinced it just was not working because I was still too angry about the childhood I was trying to capture; I thought of my mother, how she'd raised us as best she could and now she was free of it all, living with her boyfriend on an island in the Caribbean delivering food and liquor to restaurants and hotels; I thought of my brother and two sisters, those years we huddled around the TV in our small, rented houses, how I was looking forward to seeing them again; I thought of Jeannie going blind, this woman who loved sculpture and paintings and books so much. I pictured her pulling this homemade scarf from its box, the way she'd squint her eyes at it, run her fingers over it, maybe smell it before I leaned over and kissed her; and I thought of my considerate, privileged girlfriend knitting beside me, how we probably wouldn't make it. We wouldn't. But that I loved her anyway. I also wished her and her family well, rich or not.

In the lamplight, her blond hair down around her shoulders, her eyes on the TV while her needles clicked away, she looked content and beautiful. She turned and smiled at me. Except for meals and sex and drinking in bars, there was very little we'd ever done together—but now she'd helped me to create something I couldn't have without her. Between us on that sofa her money had bought us, was something warm and palpable and vaguely parental. I felt shy in the face of it. I smiled back and returned to my knitting, to my looping and sticking and cinching in snugly before looping again, for this had become the conversation between us, the clicking of our needles, this soft woolen truce.

to knit a
knot, or not:
a beginner's yarn

by John Dufresne

*Mr. Maladroit, the subdextrous, has his knickers all in a knot. Knit,
he cannot. And yet he's brandishing his number 10 bamboo needles and
fondling a skein of acrylic yarn. He's reading his stitch guide and dreaming of a chullo hat with braided ties and a pompom. He can do this. He
casts on . . .*

I RECENTLY BOUGHT AN ILLUSTRATED KNITTING BOOK FOR
men, a knitting book for dummies, and a knitting book written in 1843 by authoress, as she's called, Miss Frances Lambert.
The *Pictorial Times* of London wrote of Miss Lambert's *My Knitting
Book*: "This is a pleasant book, a good book, and a book worthy to
be bought by mother and daughter, and studied, *con amore*, in quiet
parlors and snug nurseries." Promising, I thought. A "worthy" book;
my own quiet parlor. Success is in the offing. Then someone younger

told me that no one reads books to learn knitting or to learn anything else these days. There's YouTube for that and blogs (a Google search for knitting blogs turned up 38,300,000 results in .25 seconds!) and web pages and grandmothers.

So now I'm at Michael's at Oakwood Plaza buying yarn and needles as instructed by an exuberant young woman on a knitting-for-beginners *Vimeo*. I've chosen two number 10 bamboo needles, bamboo because I like the way they look, and I imagine their promise of a warm and natural touch, and because I figure that if this knitting enterprise fails, I can put the needles to some other decorative or practical use: drumsticks (Note to self: Buy *Drumming for Dummies*), marshmallow skewers, emergency chopsticks, or houseplant stakes.

I may be off to a bad start, I realize, because the square-jawed stud in the sumptuous sweater on the cover of my "hands-on guide to knitting for the modern man" is gripping a fistful of dangerous-looking *metal* needles in one hand and cradling two unsubtle red balls of yarn in the other. I've picked out a skein of Red Heart Super Saver 96 percent acrylic yarn, 260 yards of #505 Aruba Sea and #928 Earth & Sky. I'm not sure what those numerical designations signify because the shade itself is called Aran Fleck, which I like because it reminds me of J. M. Synge's *Riders to the Sea* and of my own visit, long ago, to Inisheer, a bleak and lovely island of sheep and stone walls, of biting winds and soothing Guinness, off the coast of Galway. The gentleman at the checkout counter wants to know what I'm knitting. I tell him I don't know yet and ask him if he needs a pair of mittens. He laughs. "We're in Florida, mon."

To KNIT IS TO tie with a knot, to form a close texture by the interlooping of successive series of loops of yarn or thread. The word comes to us from the Old English *cnyttan*: to tie with a knot or fasten. At one time, *knit* also meant "to geld a ram by tying the scrotum," as here described by Edward Topsell in his *Historie of Foure-footed Beastes*: "They use [*sic*] to knit them [the rams], and so in time their stones deprived of nourishment . . . by reason of knitting, do dry and consume away." The lexical usage, if not the shepherdly practice, is now obsolete. Elsewhere, the Reverend Topsell delightfully writes that "Goat's milk . . . gaggarized in the mouth, is very effectual against the pains and swelling of the Almonds," the almonds of the throat being the tonsils. And weasels, he wrote, give birth through their ears.

MY MOTHER KEPT HER yarn and needles in a green vinyl tube with a zippered top that, when open, looked like a bellboy's cap. We were living in a converted military barracks called Lincolnwood. Our roof leaked. The iceman delivered a block of ice every week for the icebox. My mother sat in the upholstered chair by the console radio and did her knitting. I sat in my Howdy Doody rocking chair and pretended to read the newspaper like my father did. I said, "What are you making?"

"Your father a sweater."

Beside her chair was an ashtray on a stand. When you pushed a button on the metal top, a little trapdoor opened, and the butts and ashes dropped to a bowl below. I loved making that mess disappear. Magic! My rocking chair had a metal music box on the right rocking slat that played Howdy's theme song; that is, it did until I decided to find out how it worked and disassembled the box.

I remember sitting on the floor holding a skein of yarn wrapped around my outstretched arms while my mother smoked a Pall Mall and rolled the yarn into balls. It occurs to me now that one can't knit and smoke at the same time and that knitting would be a wonderful cure for the addiction. So I just Googled "smoking and knitting" and found a site called *Knitting for Quitting*, featuring stories of people who did just that.

MISS LAMBERT'S BOOK, unfortunately, is not for novices. She begins with an explanation of knitting terms and then gets started on instructions for making Siberian cuffs, telling me I'll need to cast on ("the first interlacement of the cotton on the needle"), but how can I do that when I don't yet know how to hold the needles? And how do I achieve this interlacement exactly? And what on earth are Siberian cuffs? Shouldn't I be able to visualize the finished product? Maybe not. Maybe knitting is like writing a story—an act of discovery. But that seems unlikely, given the very precise directions I'm to follow: *Cast on sixty-four stitches with the darkest thread;—knit three plain rows* . . . and so on. I read the book anyway (a Catholic thing: finish what you begin) and learned, after consulting the OED, that muffatees are a kind of mitten worn at the wrist for warmth or to protect the cuffs; that a sontag is a knitted jacket or cape with long ends which are crossed in front of the body and tied behind, named for Henriette Sontag, a German opera singer, who, at eighteen, sang the solo for the first public performance of Beethoven's Symphony No. 9; that *gros de Naples* is corded Italian silk that looks much like Irish poplin. And I learned the elegant verb *assort*, meaning to distribute in groups, to classify. Siberian cuffs are wrist warmers.

. . .

I CAN KNIT MY brow. My fractured bone might knit itself. My stomach might be tied up in knots. I might forget to duck getting into the car, knock my head against the doorframe, and get a knot on my noggin. When upset, I may get my knickers in a knot. But knit? I cannot. Not yet. I've never tried until now, and have never been tempted to try. I've never been tempted to build a house either or to replace a faucet or install electrical service. I've inherited my father's blundering gene. I'm all thumbs. Subdextrous. Mr. Maladroit. But my friend Lynne Barrett promises she'll give me a lesson before she drives off to Maine for the summer.

Knots are my weakness. Knots of the interlooping kind. I remember the day I finally learned to tie my Buster Brown shoes, the answer to my exasperated mother's prayers. I was about to go off to school at Sacred Heart Academy. I was four, and shoe-tying was one of the two requirements for attendance; the other, of course, was being potty-trained. I didn't want to move my feet for fear the shoelaces would come undone. I had a right to be worried, it turned out. My laces never stayed knotted long. My custom, coming home on the school bus, was to ask one of the high school girls to retie my shoes. Usually I asked Cookie Pepper, on whom I had a delirious crush. I hoped that one day she might be my babysitter. We lived in a public housing project; a thousand other scruffy children also lived here, and every weary mother was in desperate need of a trustworthy sitter. I told my mother about Cookie. I dared to dream. Cookie seemed, however, to prefer my nemesis, David Marcoux, a feisty little berserker, who had a permanent squint in his right eye and had already sliced open my ear with a sharpened stick while we played pirates. I've recently consulted *Ian's Shoelace* website and have studied Ian's admirable standard shoelace knot, and although the graphics make little sense to me, I do think my technique is similar to his own. Ian's final knot, however, is more substantial and more symmetrical than my own. My shoes are often untied, and it drives my wife crazy.

MY MOTHER'S GREEN knitting case survived a tornado. When the tornado struck we were eating supper, and I felt, rather than heard, a rumbling and then saw out the living room window, a tree fly by our apartment. And then all the windows exploded. We huddled by a closet door. I watched lamps and furniture skate across the room. We lost most of our belongings, our car, and our home. My mother was seven months pregnant and was almost finished knitting the baby booties. We moved in with my grandparents and aunts. I slept in the dining room on an army cot we'd gotten from Catholic Charities.

When my father said it looked like we'd be moving into a house trailer, I was ecstatic at the thought of living in a house with wheels. We could go anywhere at the drop of a hat. We could go to Rhode Island and still be home. We could drive to Doodyville. We went back to the reconstructed housing project instead, but to a different apartment across the street. My mother now kept her knitting beside the foldout couch in the living room. We had an expansive coffee table upon which sat an oval tin of Cavalier cigarettes and a cigarette lighter shaped like Aladdin's lamp. My mother continued to knit but seemed more and more distracted by the soap operas on our new Crosley TV and never seemed to finish a project. "It's a scarf for your father," she said.

"You mean it *will be*," I said.

She shushed me. "I'm watching my story!"

. . .

MY FIRST VENTURE into handicrafts involved what we called gimp, the plastic-covered lacing that other people, I'm told, called lanyard or boondoggle. The word *boondoggle*, used in this sense, was coined by scoutmaster Robert H. Link of Rochester, New York, in 1929, when he and his clever little troop braided their leather lanyards as a way to hold their knives and whistles around their necks, thereby setting off a worldwide Scouting fad: boondoggle mania. The word's more common meaning is "a trivial, useless, or unnecessary undertaking," which is how I thought about gimp work.

Once every couple of weeks, the city's Parks and Recreation Department dispatched the gimp lady to Lake Park where about fifty of us kids played baseball every summer weekday from nine to three. This was the summer Marilyn Monroe died and the U.S. began using the defoliant Agent Orange in Vietnam. The gimp lady was typically a cheery high school girl who brought along her enthusiasm and a box of vividly colored gimp, which she handed out. Anything free was valuable to us. With this gimp, she promised, and a basic knowledge of knots and braiding, we would soon be making key chains, bracelets, zipper pulls, and other potential gifts for Mom. The gimp lady demonstrated the elementary box stitch, and we began our projects. But somewhere between the crossing of strands and the flip and the series of loops and the weave and the tug, my gimp came all undone. I was never a Boy Scout, as you've already surmised. If I had been, I would have already known the square knot, the clove hitch, the half-hitch, and the one where the rabbit goes through the hole.

I left the braiding up to Paul Bellino. Bella was a skinny little guy with buckteeth, a foul mouth, and a truckload of what we called *baditude,* who enjoyed intimidating bigger kids and talked trash constantly, but who, for some reason, liked me. He shook his head and took the gimp out of my hand. He made me a red and black key chain, standing there with his baseball glove between his knees. He didn't bother to explain the process, knowing a lost cause when he saw one. When I told Jimmy Wells later that Bella had made the key chain I was admiring, Jimmy said gimp was for girls. I said, You want me to tell Bella you said that? Bella was killed by a sniper's bullet seven years later at Hamburger Hill during the Tet Offensive.

I ABANDON THE knitting book for men when I decide to make the Aran laptop cover on page 52 with my Aran Fleck yarn, but learn that this is the wrong yarn, and I'm also going to need a circular needle, and what's this about gauge? I move on to the next project, a chullo hat that is the silliest-looking cap I've ever seen. It's made without the traditional earflaps, but with a drape over the neck. Even the suave metrosexual model looks like a woeful doofus in it. I look at the stitch guide and see all the letters and numbers strung out together—*P3 *K1 P5 K1 K1 P5 repeat from *, ending last repeat P3*—and I get the queasy feeling, which quickly turns to terror and paralysis, that I got in algebra class when I stared at quadratic equations. I flunked algebra twice in high school. I have mild dyscalculia. I transpose numbers without knowing it. That's not an excuse. I also had a sorry attitude and a flagrant indifference to mathematics in all its manifestations. And while I can quite happily follow directions, I can't or won't read them. Yet another character flaw.

The *Dummies* book begins with a spirited defense of knitting and an argument for taking up the needles:

1. *It's relaxing.* So is a martini. A dry martini and a good book: heaven.

2. *You get a feeling of accomplishment—you get to use your imagination, patience, and perseverance to create something from nothing.* Which is exactly what I already do all day when I'm writing stories.

3. *It keeps your hands and mind occupied.* Like writing stories.

4. *It's portable.* Ditto!

I put the books away, wonder how much they'll fetch on eBay. I'm going to heed the kids and go back to the Internet. Before I do that, my friend Lynne stops by and shows me how to cast on and gets me started on a row. She tells me some of the history of knitting, and we discuss Madame Defarge, naturally. "It would be easier for the weakest poltroon that lives, to erase himself from existence, than to erase one letter of his name or crimes from the knitted register of Madame Defarge." I get fifteen stiches done in one row, and when I say *I,* I mean Lynne mostly.

"WOMEN LIKE TO sit down with trouble—as if it were knitting," the novelist Ellen Glasgow wrote. That's what my mother, her mother, and my aunts were passionate about. Trouble in the neighborhood: gossip! Every Sunday afternoon during my childhood, we all met at my grandmother's flat for dinner. And after the meal—always a dependable pot roast, brown potatoes, and string beans—the men drifted to the front room to drink beer and watch sports on TV, and the women stayed in the kitchen, smoked their cigarettes, drank their coffees lightened and sweetened with condensed milk, and told stories about people we'd seen at Mass that morning. I stayed in the kitchen and listened. And that's where I learned to love stories: the knitting together of images, scenes, language, and plot. That turns out to be the fiction writer's job: to attend to the gossip and spread it as far as he can.

I HAVEN'T PRACTICED what Lynne taught me, and now I can't seem to replicate that looping. I find a how-to-knit website and learn that "finger knitting is a wonderful way to introduce children to knitting. It is also very safe because no needles are involved!" Sounds perfect. I put on John Dowland's "Forlorn Hope," a fantasy for lute, and begin. Looks easy enough, but I bollix the project and am left with what looks like a mating ball of acrylic garter snakes. On to a finger knitting video. I turn off the tranquil music. I follow the directions, and study the demonstration, stopping the action a dozen times, but I do not have what looks to be the desired "set of ladders" on the back of my hands. I note that my teacher is not wearing a wedding ring, and I wonder if my ring is somehow interfering with my own finger knitting. My cat Django is on my desk with his chin on the skein. And now he's licking the yarn. He's been quite taken with the skein since I brought it home.

MOM'S GREEN KNITTING CASE came with us on two more moves. We ended up, eventually, living in my father's parents' house when they moved to smaller quarters. My mother kept the now-neglected tube on the floor of her closet beside her rows of high heels and her bundle of pocketbooks. I called her and asked her why she started knitting.

"Because my friends were knitters. I think that's why."

"Did you ever make anything for me?"

"No, I didn't." She said she had to go. "Your father's making me crazy." My mother is eighty-six now, living with my father, her husband of sixty-five years, who increasingly spends his time living in his own past and speaking with the revenants who've come back to see him, and she's tired, and occasionally cranky, and she's embittered with regret, and she does not suffer fools like me gladly.

"You kept that knitting case for years after you stopped knitting."

"I always thought I would take it up again."

"Why didn't you?"

"I wanted to," she said. In the background my father was singing "In a Shanty in Old Shanty Town." "But then there were a lot of things I wanted to do."

"Like?"

"That I didn't do."

I PUT ON THE Marlins game and take out the yarn. I'm back to finger knitting. I can do this, right? Django stops batting his sister Molly in the head to come see what I'm up to on the couch. The mess I ended up with previously untangles quite nicely. By the fourth inning, the Marlins are down two to the Nationals, and I've aborted several shabby pieces of work. I head back to watch the video, figure out what I may be doing wrong, and shuffle back to the couch. How hard can this be? In 2004, eleven-year-old Gemma Pouls of Hamilton, New Zealand, finger knitted a 9,119-foot very thin scarf, all rolled up into an eleven-pound ball. Did that mean that for the year it took her to set the record, verified by the soothing *Guinness Book of World Records*, the yarn never left her fingers? So it would seem.

The Marlins tie the game, and I get into the rhythm of the weave, and something woolish grows down the back of my arm. When the yarn reaches my elbow, I cast off, moving the loops from pinkie to ring to middle to index finger, passing the tail through the remaining loop, and tying a simple unstable knot. I have crafted a very relaxed set of ladders here. And now I have to decide what it is I have made. I tie the ends together and have a tweedy-looking, but not very festive wreath. But it's not a wreath, I decide.

While I'm thinking, let me say a few words in praise of finger knitting and argue for putting down the needles, at least for an evening:

1. *It's even more relaxing.* You can drink your martini while finger knitting.
2. *It's so easy even a klutz can do it.* There are no extensive directions or stitch guides to follow.
3. *It's beyond portable.* No needles to schlep around. Airline says no to carrying on your dangerous metal needles? Fine, you can still knit at your seat.
4. *Who needs patience?* Stop whenever you want, and your project is finished, complete, done. You've got either a long potential scarf or a short one. We finger knitters, those of us who are not obsessed with setting records, are all about short-term gratification.

A scarf, then, or a network bandanna, for a cat. Django's on the coffee table watching the game. The Marlins are up by two in the eighth. I slip the handsome Celtic item over his shiny little head. He's not happy, I can tell. He doesn't move at first. He sulks but lets me take photos. Django's midnight black, and with this shawl on, he looks a little too much like a nun in her guimpe. He tries to back out of it, but fails. He looks depressed. Okay, so it's not a cat scarf. I lift it over Django's neck, and he bats it off the coffee table, and that's when it occurs to me that I've made a cat toy. Marvelous! I sprinkle it with a little fresh catnip, and Mr. Bad Example is in his heaven. He's lying with it between his paws and chewing on it. And now that he has a new best friend, maybe he'll leave his bedraggled sister alone. A scarf? What was I thinking? We're in Florida, mon.

home ec

by Hope Edelman

Summers spent knitting in Iowa connect the author's daughters with the grandmother they never knew.

THE CRAFTS STORE, APTLY NAMED HOME EC, SITS ON A leafy street in Iowa City across from everyone's beloved greasy spoon, The Hamburg Inn. My daughters and I stumbled upon the place in the summer of 2008, just a few months after it opened. Already the comfortable couches were crowded with women working on cardigans and baby blankets, looking for companionship and a cool place to escape an oppressive Midwestern July.

Inside, the store was pure eye candy, from the bright bolts of fabric lined up near the front window to the shiny coffee bar along one side. A workshop area in back sported rows of gleaming white sewing machines, and the shelves in the main room held neatly stacked skeins of colored wool. It looked as if a rainbow had exploded in the middle of the room, its shards landing in beautiful and orderly fashion along the walls. My daughters, then ten and six, loved the place. We ordered Italian sodas and sat down.

The draw that first day was Alisa and Codi, the pair of young women who owned the store. To me they were "young women," though in truth they were probably equidistant between my daughters' ages and mine, old enough to discuss the vicissitudes of local real estate but still young and hip enough, Codi with her funky eyeglass frames and Alisa with a delicate nose stud, to be older friends for the girls. They took an interest in each other immediately, my older daughter chattering away while Codi and Alisa listened with genuine interest.

I'd been hoping we'd meet some new people that summer. I'd attended graduate school at the University of Iowa in the early 1990s and now returned with my daughters to teach writing workshops every July. The other eleven months we lived in Los Angeles, with few family members on the West Coast. My parents were both gone, the rest of my family small and scattered; my husband's was large but lived overseas. There was no homestead to return to for holidays or vacations, something I'd once had in a suburban New York childhood full of great aunts and second cousins. So I was trying to turn Iowa City into a second home of sorts, a place where we could return every summer to familiar faces and slide back into a comfortable routine.

Most of my Iowa friends were writers and professors and former English students who were, like me, all forty-plus by now. The girls needed friends closer to their age. Alisa and Codi, though clearly adults themselves, seemed more like cool older cousins. They mixed Italian sodas and invited the girls to attend craft classes with other kids in town. We started dropping in to say hello whenever we walked by, which averaged once or twice a day.

And so began our summer love affair with knitting.

Or, I should say, my daughters' love affairs, since they became the real knitters that year. My older daughter already knew the basics from an after-school class she'd taken in kindergarten, while my younger daughter learned to knit that summer under Alisa's patient tutelage. Together, they cast on twelve stitches to start a scarf for her Webkinz dog. I sat at the other end of the red leather couch reading student papers, a grateful observer, thankful for an hour of quiet time.

One afternoon I watched as Alisa deftly undid a row of my younger daughter's work and handed back the needles. The little scarf looked as if the mistake had never occurred. To erase an imperfection so easily and leave no trace of it behind: this seemed like a tremendously useful skill to possess.

"Where did you learn how to do that?" I asked Alisa.

"From my grandmother," she explained. "When I wanted to learn in my twenties, I went to her."

That's usually the story, isn't it? Knitting as women's legacy, passed down through the ladder of generations. My mother learned to knit from my paternal grandmother, her mother-in-law, who we called Nana. Nana didn't fit anyone's stereotype of a knitting grandma, with her taste for stylish clothing and love of the dance floor, but she knew how to do complicated colorwork and whip up cable-knit sweaters for her grandchildren in record time. Without a daughter of her own to teach, she gladly answered my mother's call.

I imagine Nana learned the craft from her own mother, for whom knitting, crocheting, quilting, and cooking were the fabric of everyday life. Born on a Hungarian farm in 1887 where handiwork was necessity rather than hobby, my great-grandmother—we called her Mama—was legendary in the family for the standard of perfection in her crafts. I have a quilt she sewed by hand using tiny, flawless, even stitches. Hoping to repair a tear in it one day, I tried to replicate her work. I couldn't even come close.

Nana and Mama died months apart when I was nine, too young for me to recognize their skills or understand their worth. Eight years later, when I was in high school, my mother died, too. For the next fifteen years I mourned for what I no longer had as if her death were my loss alone. Then I became a mother myself, and discovered that my daughters had also lost a grandmother. Several times a year, this fact would come at me fast and painful, like a dropkick in the gut. They'd never have the chance to learn from my mother and, even worse, she had lost the chance to teach them. Or even to know them. She would have taught them how to knit, and despite Codi and Alisa's patience, watching my daughters learn to cast on from two women in a store filled me with a sadness I hadn't known to expect.

The obvious solution, I suppose, would have been for me to pass down my mother's knowledge and teach my daughters to knit myself. Thirty years ago, I knew how to knit. My mother taught me, more or less. I was the oldest of her three children, and she was eager to pass on what she knew. But I've never had—not then or now—the crafty, artsy aptitude so many other girls and women seem to naturally possess, the kind that requires unlimited patience and superior fine-motor skills. I'm sloppy by nature, and always searching for shortcuts. I can't strong-arm a sewing machine into submission no matter how many times I'm shown how, and I get no pleasure whatsoever from scrapbooking or anything that involves hot glue.

Nonetheless, in the summer of 2008, as my daughters sat on the Home Ec couch with their needles and yarn, I felt an unexpected tug of longing to join them. I felt . . . how do I say it? *Left out.*

For weeks I'd been admiring a sample scarf draped across the wall. Made from a bluish mulberry wool yarn, its tails were bunched up in an attractive manner that I didn't yet know—but soon would—meant that stitches had been decreased to create it.

I caressed a bumpy edge between my thumb and forefinger. "How hard is this for a beginner?" I asked Alisa. "Scale of one to ten?" She smiled. "About a three. I'll get the pattern."

I was such a novice, I didn't know what a beginner's pattern might look like. But when I looked at the card Alisa handed me, a memory came barreling back: my mother, stretched out on her bed with two pillows propped behind her, glancing at a well-thumbed knitting magazine splayed open at her side. It was 1977, maybe 1978. The lamp on her night table glowed beside her; *Three's Company* or *Alice* was on the TV. The pages of the knitting magazine were littered with cryptic notations like *K1, P1, K5, P2tog (p3, M1P)*, a complicated code only mothers seemed able to crack. A white plastic laundry basket on the floor next to the bed held her knitting supplies, year-round.

"I'll give it a try," I told Alisa.

I chose a yarn that shaded from purple to red to deep blue. Then Alisa helped me choose a pair of size 10 knitting needles from the display on a back wall.

Casting on was an elaborate geometry that took a while to get right. Alisa and I did a few practice rows together. I'd expected body memory from thirty years ago to kick in, but it turned out that knitting was nothing like riding a bike. Still, it was hardly astrophysics. After a half hour fifteen moderately neat rows hung from my needle and I hadn't dropped a single stitch.

"Good work," said Alisa, who then slid the whole thing off, ripped it apart, and wound the yarn back around the skein.

We cast on again, 72 stitches this time, and I learned how to knit two together per the instructions on the card. *K2tog.* It only looked difficult on paper. In practice, it wasn't that hard.

Then I tried it at home.

The problem with knitting a simple scarf with complicated ends is you have no choice but to start with the hardest part. The K2tog that seemed so straightforward at the store turned into a freaking mess on my own. It seemed to follow, logically, that if you start with 76 stitches and K2tog the result will be 38, except by some perverse form of math I wound up with 35. I didn't know how to undo rows, so I pulled the whole mess off the needle, ripped it apart, and cast on again.

The same thing happened again.

And again.

My ten-year-old looked up from the hat she was seed stitching. "Need some help?" she asked.

She cast me back on. With her assistance, the end of the scarf started to emerge in that attractive bunched-up fashion. Except . . . two-thirds of the loops on my needle now looked like normal stitches, while the other third looked weirdly pinched together.

I ripped the whole thing off and started again.

I ran to Codi for triage the next day, and worked with her until the end of the scarf looked as it should. The middle was a breeze compared to the beginning, and once I got a few rows in I started to relax. The repetitive back-and-forth, back-and-forth, and the tactile satisfaction of completing one row and starting another felt purely meditative. I started to get it, why people love to knit. In the evenings after dinner, the girls and I settled onto the living room couch for an hour before bedtime, where we knit and watched a half hour of *Hannah Montana* followed by an episode of *House Hunters International.* Somewhere between Miley Cyrus's impossible dilemmas and young couples shopping for first homes in Surrey and Croatia, a scarf that actually looked like a scarf began to emerge. Every few days I wrapped it around my neck to measure its progress.

My mother never worked from measurements. She used the human body as her guide. "C'mere," she'd say, swinging her legs over the side of the bedspread and motioning for me to stand beside her, while she wound a scarf around my neck or laid half a mitten against my hand. The winter I was fifteen she started knitting me a red ski sweater with a blue stripe across the chest. She designed it to align perfectly with the red stripe across the front of my blue ski jacket. I imagined strolling into a Vermont ski lodge with my friends after a day on icy trails and carelessly unzipping my jacket, everyone around me silently admiring the perfect calibration of my stripes.

Judging by how long the sweater was taking, it might have been the first one my mother ever knit. I'm not sure. As with so many other questions I'd like to ask her, I don't have the answer. I know it took her weeks to finish the front panel. Or maybe I was the one who slowed her down. Every few days she'd call me into her bedroom and hand over the needles. She believed in ownership, in the idea that investing personal effort in a project increased its perceived value. But I was fifteen and thought this thinking was ridiculous. I was invested in speed, and knew the sweater would get done faster if she did the work herself. And besides, I was in high school and I had, you know, a *lot* of other things to *do*. I'd rush through the rows just to make my mother happy and then try to get back to whatever else I wanted to do.

Haste is no friend to the knitter, I soon learned. My impatience led to sloppy mistakes which led to a mother's need to sigh loudly and fix them before handing the needles back, which doubled the time it would have taken to do the task slowly and properly the first time. An important lesson was to be learned from this, but I was too young to absorb it. Instead the rushing, the mistakes, the fixing, the redo, played out every time.

This scarf in Iowa inspired me to finally slow down and get it right. When it grew long enough to wrap around my neck twice and then some, Alisa taught me how to add stitches to create the other ruffled end, and then how to cast off. I finished the scarf that day.

The phrase "economy of scale" reappeared from a distant college macroeconomics class, its basic principle being that once you've invested the time and resources to make a single item it's cheaper and easier to produce it again (and again and again). With knitting, this turned out to be exactly true. I immediately started a second scarf from the same pattern. This one took half the time to complete, and since I already owned the pattern and the needles, it cost less, too.

By the end of July I'd produced three nearly identical scarves. One I mailed to my sister as a belated birthday present. One I gave to a friend in town. The third I packed up with my knitting materials and shipped home to Los Angeles, figuring I'd gift it to someone there.

My intention was to keep knitting that fall, but like all good intentions . . . well, you know how that sentence ends. In L.A. my days filled up quickly with writing and driving and teaching and driving, and the evenings were driving and dinner, followed by dishes, homework, showers, lunch boxes, and tying up all the other loose ends of a day. My daughters found time to knit during recess, at sleepovers, in the backseat as we drove to and from the dentist, but my leisurely hours with a ball of yarn and HGTV became a distant dream the moment I rolled my suitcase back through our front door.

How did my mother ever find time to knit with three kids? I wondered.

In truth, my mother knit only until March of my fifteenth year. A few weeks before ski season ended, and faster than I could have thought possible either then or now, what had been diagnosed as a "cyst" in her left breast turned out to be a "mass," which turned out to be a malignant tumor, which led to a mastectomy, which revealed a cancer that had already spread into all of her lymph nodes, which led to the kind of diagnosis no woman ever wants to hear. Breast cancer, stage 3.

It feels embarrassing now, and painfully narcissistic, to write about how the chemotherapy my mother endured for the next year stalled the progress of my ski sweater and how irritated this made me, but those really were my thoughts at the time. In October of that year, I lifted the unfinished sweater from the laundry basket and asked if she thought she'd finish it this year. I don't think I asked very nicely. I probably came down hard on *this*. It didn't matter. By then her bed had become a place to recover from chemo sessions. She wasn't knitting anymore.

Her cancer diagnosis sounded ominous but my God—I didn't know she was dying. Neither did she. Like every other illness we'd encountered in our family, we'd both naively believed this one could be cured by equal measures of medical attention and time. Plus, my mother's father had survived colon cancer and lived another twenty years. Surely, we thought, she'd get at least that much time.

She got sixteen months.

A few weeks after the funeral, my father asked me to pack up her side of the bedroom for donations to Goodwill. He couldn't do it himself, he said. My best friend sat with me one afternoon while I mechanically lifted stacks of clothing from my mother's bureau drawers and set them down in boxes, then pulled her clothing off their hangers in her walk-in closet. Residual scents of her Charlie perfume floated up from her blouses and scarves as I folded them with care. When I got to her night table, I wasn't sure what to do with the pens, playing cards, discarded paper clips and rubber bands in her night table. Behind them, I found the stack of letters my father had written when they were dating, along with every anniversary and Mother's Day card she'd received in twenty-one years. I left those there.

That's when I saw the laundry basket on the floor.

The unfinished ski sweater was just as my mother had left it, needles still attached. I picked it up and ran my fingertips along the careful stitches of the red stripe. Her stitches, my stitches, I couldn't tell the difference. I pressed the panel against my chest and lined it up with my shoulders. I'd grown some in the past year, and if my mother had finished the sweater on time it probably would have been too small.

I would have worn it anyway.

Under different circumstances, I might have taken the sweater and finished it myself one day. But already I was shifting into utilitarian mode, focusing on basic survival needs. What use was half a sweater? It was too small to be a blanket, too big for a place mat. Too square for a scarf. The first half of a sweater is exactly what it is: half of something, still in the process of becoming whole.

I didn't pick up a set of knitting needles for twenty-seven years, until that summer at Home Ec. The following July when my daughters and I arrived in Iowa City we headed straight to the knitting store. "Hey!" Alisa said, coming out from behind the register to give each of the girls a hug. She sat down to help my younger daughter learn to use the new spinning wheel. I chose a new pattern for the summer, this time a hat and scarf set made from chunky yarn. After gathering a pair of size 15 needles and a ball of thick vanilla wool I arranged myself on the red leather couch to cast on.

Except.

I couldn't remember a single thing. And I mean *not a single thing.* The string of yarn lay limp against my left hand. It might as well have been a length of electrical cord or a line of sailing rope for all it mattered. I wouldn't have known what to do with those, either.

Less than a year ago I was knitting every day. How was it possible for all memory of a repetitive action to evaporate so completely?

Meanwhile, Codi was getting my eleven-year-old daughter started on her first pair of socks.

"Need help getting started?" Alisa asked.

She retaught me how to cast on, how to K2tog, and I relearned how to cast off. Basically, I had to relearn everything. I made three hats that summer, two for my nieces and one for my younger daughter. Once again, at the end of July I brought my knitting supplies back to Los Angeles, where I found no time to knit, and when we returned to Home Ec the following July . . . well, you can pretty much guess how the story continued from there. Every July brought another memory crash, my internal hard drive wiped clean.

Why this happened is still a mystery to me. I can hold on to dozens of complicated facts and figures from year to year, I never forget a bill's amount or due date, and I pick up languages and musical instruments more quickly than you'd expect from someone middle-aged. Yet, every year, a set of simple knitting instructions in August wind up looking like an Armenian semiconductor manual by the following July.

I tell myself that maybe I just don't have the patience knitting requires. This could well be true. Or maybe it's my own private, latent adolescent refusal to become my mother. After all, a mother who can't start a sweater is a mother who can't die before it's done.

Or maybe I'm overthinking it. Maybe I just don't love knitting the way a knitter should, and only true passions stick. It could be that simple.

Or maybe the real reason is this: Maybe knitting is my way of letting my daughters know their grandmother on their own.

Everything they know about my mother comes from photos I've shown them and stories I tell. She's distant and mythic, an intangible presence in our home, coming to them only through my filter. But when my daughters knit they bypass me and forge a direct connection with her, doing an activity she loved and one she would have taught them, if she'd lived. She would have taught them. I know she would have.

Fourteen years of motherhood have taught me a great deal, but mostly they've taught me the value of getting out of the way. And so this past summer I didn't unpack my needles. My daughters are now old enough to go to Home Ec without me, and several times a week, they do.

I will never be a knitter. I understand that now. The torch passed over me the day I sat on the red Home Ec couch and remembered nothing at all. It just took me a while to accept it.

My older daughter is now in high school. Last summer she helped Codi teach a class at Home Ec. This summer, when she was packing for a university summer program in Chicago she included a set of knitting needles and two balls of yarn. Whatever gene makes someone good at crafts, she has it. I love that. All I know is that she didn't get it from me.

As I was packing my bags for Iowa this year, I reached up into my closet to pull down a summer purse. The scarf I'd knit that first summer at Home Ec, the one I never did give away, came tumbling down.

I wrapped it around my neck and rubbed my thumb against its ruffled edge. This was the first scarf I'd made, the one that gave me all the trouble. All that effort. All that time. And you know, it's a beautiful scarf. It really is. I gently folded it up and placed it back on the shelf.

My mother was right. I love it all the more because I made it myself.

"bingham" cabled head wrap

by Helen Bingham

A cabled head wrap created in the round is a wonderful last-minute gift to make for someone special in your life. Casey Bingham, my daughter, is one of the most thoughtful and kindest people I have the pleasure of knowing. She continues to teach me how to help others just for the pleasure of being nice. The pay-it-forward approach to life is her gift.

MATERIALS:

1 skein Merino Alpaca by ShiBui (50% baby alpaca/50% merino with 131 yards)
color: Ivory (1 skein will make 2 head wraps)

OR

1 skein Lark by Quince & Co. (100% American wool with 134 yards)
color: Frost
US 7, circular 16″ needle or size needed to obtain gauge

stitch markers

cable needle

SIZE: One size

FINISHED MEASUREMENTS: 18″ in circumference; 5″ in width
(not blocked or stretched measurements)

GAUGE: 20 sts = 4″ in stockinette stitch

PATTERN NOTES:

PM = place marker

SM = slip marker

C6B = slip 3 sts to cable needle and hold in back, knit 3 sts, knit
3 from cable needle

W&T = Wrap and Turn; bring yarn to front of work, slip the next
stitch, bring the yarn to back of work, slip the same stitch back
to the left hand needle (LHN), TURN, bring yarn to back of
work ready to knit the next stitch.

—When you get to the wrapped stitches, knit the wrap with the
stitch.

DIRECTIONS:

—Cast on 81 sts, place marker and join into the round, being careful not to twist stitches.

—Work the following foundation round:

Foundation Round: (P1, K1)10 times, PM, P2 (K6, P2)5 times, PM,
(K1, P1)9 times, K1

—Work the following rounds:

Rounds 1 & 2: (P1, K1)10 times, SM, P2 (K6, P2)5 times, SM, (K1, P1)9 times, K1

Round 3: (P1, K1)6 times, P1, K7, SM, P2 (K6, P2)5 times, SM, K7, (P1, K1)6 times

SHORT ROW SECTION

—Work the following rows (you are working back and forth in rows not all the way around the 81 sts).

—When you get to the wrapped stitches, knit the wrap with the stitch.

—Even-numbered rows are right-side rows/odd-numbered rows are wrong-side rows

Row 4: (P1, K1)6 times, P1, K7, SM, P2 (C6B, P2)5 times, SM, W&T

Row 5: SM, K2 (P6, K2)5 times, SM, W&T

Row 6: SM, P2 (K6, P2)5 times, SM, K1, W&T

Row 7: K1, SM, K2 (P6, K2)5 times, SM, K1, W&T

Row 8: K1, SM, P2 (K6, P2)5 times, SM, K2, W&T

Row 9: K2, SM, K2 (P6, K2)5 times, SM, K2, W&T

Row 10: K2, SM, P2 (C6B, P2)5 times, SM, K3, W&T

Row 11: K3, SM, K2 (P6, K2)5 times, SM, K3, W&T

Row 12: K3, SM, P2 (K6, P2)5 times, SM, K4, W&T

Row 13: K4, SM, K2 (P6, K2)5 times, SM, K4, W&T

Row 14: K4, SM, P2 (K6, P2)5 times, SM, K5, W&T

Row 15: K5, SM, K2 (P6, K2)5 times, SM, K5, W&T

Row 16: K5, SM, P2 (C6B, P2)5 times, SM, K4, W&T

Row 17: K4, SM, K2 (P6, K2)5 times, SM, K4, W&T

Row 18: K4, SM, P2 (K6, P2)5 times, SM, K3, W&T

Row 19: K3, SM, K2 (P6, K2)5 times, SM, K3, W&T

Row 20: K3, SM, P2 (K6, P2)5 times, SM, K2, W&T

Row 21: K2, SM, K2 (P6, K2)5 times, SM, K2, W&T

Row 22: K2, SM, P2 (C6B, P2)5 times, SM, K1, W&T

Row 23: K1, SM, K2 (P6, K2)5 times, SM, K1, W&T

Row 24: K1, SM, P2 (K6, P2)5 times, SM, W&T

Row 25: SM, K2 (P6, K2)5 times, SM, W&T

Row 26: SM, P2 (K6, P2)5 times, SM, K7 (remember to knit the wrap with the stitch when you come to it), (P1, K1)6 times

—Work in the round again as follows:

Round 27: (P1, K1)6 times, P1, K7, SM, P2 (K6, P2)5 times, SM, (K1, P1) repeat 9 times, K1

Round 28: (P1, K1)10 times, PM, P2 (C6B, P2)5 times, PM, (K1, P1)9 times, K1

Rounds 29 & 30: (P1, K1)10 times, SM, P2 (K6, P2)5 times, SM, (K1, P1)9 times, K1

—Cast off all stitches loosely.

—Weave in all ends and steam lightly.

For pictures of this pattern, go to www.helenbinghamdesigns.com.

soft, warm,
and fuzzy

by Janice Eidus

*A daughter's innocent question evokes a mother's memories of her own
childhood knitting.*

M Y NINE-YEAR-OLD DAUGHTER, SITTING ACROSS FROM
me at our dinner table, asks me out of the blue to teach
her how to knit. I find myself remembering the soft,
warm, and fuzzy feel of the yarn I used to knit with when I was
just a little older than she is now. At that time, knitting was all the
rage among the teenage girls in our Bronx housing project. Those
older girls struck me as the coolest, most rebellious people on the
planet, with their heavy black eye makeup, sleek hairdos, and tight
pants. They were always knitting something: mohair sweaters for
themselves, tightly wound scarves for their boyfriends.

My sister was a part of that teenage crowd, but she refused
to teach me, because she didn't like me. Many years later, before
her death from chondrosarcoma, a rare cancer, she told me she

had always viewed me as an "interloper in the family," the person who'd "stolen" my parents' love from her when I was born. When I objected, she silenced me. "I may not be rational, but this is how I feel," she told me.

My sister's friends wouldn't help me learn to knit, either. Their allegiance to her, their group's ringleader, was too strong. Like her, they perceived me at best as a pesky nuisance, and at worst, determined to ruin my sister's life.

There was a teenage girl, though, who wasn't a member of my sister's clique, and who I sometimes spotted around the projects, sitting on a bench and knitting. She was African-American, very pretty, with cat's-eye glasses and her hair pulled up in a tight, not-quite-fashionable beribboned bun. I knew her name was Retha, but beyond that I knew nothing about her. For a few days, I watched her surreptitiously as she sat quietly alone on the bench, moving her knitting needles seemingly effortlessly.

One day after school I gathered my courage and sat beside her on the bench. She nodded at me but didn't speak. After a few minutes, I pointed to what she was knitting. "That's very pretty," I said, even though I didn't like the bright yellow color.

"Thanks," she said. "It's a sweater for my sister."

Wow, I thought. A sister who loves her own sister enough to make a sweater for her.

The next few days I waited for Retha at the same bench, and she always came or was there already. The sweater was taking real shape. She knew my name by now, and always greeted me in a friendly way.

"If I buy needles and yarn, will you teach me how to knit?" I asked, feeling both brave and vulnerable.

She didn't answer right away. My heart hammered as I waited for her reply.

"Okay," she finally said. "Meet me here tomorrow."

I knew nothing about how to shop for yarn and needles, but the ones I bought with my allowance money at our local variety store earned her approval: thin, shiny needles and a tightly wound ball of soft red wool. With surprising patience, making me think she too was pleased by our relationship, she showed me how to cast on stitches and how to do the most basic knit and purl. I wasn't a natural but after a couple of lessons she said I was good enough to knit a scarf. "You don't need a pattern," she told me. "Just knit and I'll show you how to end it."

Retha and I didn't grow close, but she mentored me for a couple of weeks more, through the making of my first short scarf, and then she disappeared. She stopped coming to "our bench," as I'd come to think of it. I felt lost at first, and hoped she hadn't grown tired of me and that there was some other explanation—like maybe her family had moved away or she'd gotten a part-time job. Or maybe she just thought I didn't need her guidance any longer.

And so I knit on my own. I made long, thick scarves and short, lightweight ones, solid-colored scarves and scarves with luminous colors and interesting patterns. Sometimes I knit outdoors on the bench, and sometimes at home.

When I sat knitting in the living room, neither my angry sister, who was an excellent knitter by then, nor my chronically depressed mother, ever came over to compliment me or express interest. The only time my mother acknowledged what I was doing, she sighed loudly and spoke about herself: "I have too much to do around the house to do things like knit."

I began to fantasize about living as far away from them as possible—maybe in California or Paris—single and childless by choice, knitting away in my hotel room, making glamorous dresses and hats.

After another six months, however, I grew bored of knitting by myself day after day. I didn't have the patience to learn from a book how to move beyond scarves, and with Retha gone, I had no one to ask. I put aside the needles and yarn, and went on to other things—modeling with clay, watercolors, writing poetry and illustrating my poems—none of which my mother or sister ever asked about, either.

By high school, I imagined myself happily growing up to be a single, childless bohemian enjoying lots of love affairs and living in an artsy hotel, where someone else cooked and cleaned for me, and where I dedicated myself to my art and to opposing all things "status quo," including the kind of endless housewifery my mother performed.

By the time I graduated from college I made a commitment to myself that I would be a "real" writer. This entailed finding day jobs to support myself while I wrote short stories and poems in the evening. I worked in various offices in a few different capacities (receptionist; typist; file clerk) and eventually I began to teach creative writing to college students. I pretty much forgot about knitting. Although every now and then I'd see a movie or TV show or read a novel in which someone was knitting, and I would buy a set of needles and some yarn and attempt to begin anew.

Surely, I told myself, it's like riding a bike or swimming, and muscle memory would kick in. But it didn't, and once again I was too impatient to take a class or learn from a book, and I put aside the needles and yarn. After I got married and moved with my husband into a series of apartments in Manhattan (I never did become a single woman living in a bohemian hotel), I thought even less about knitting.

And then I became a mother, caring for an infant; knitting was the last thing I had time for. My life felt completely about diapers and bottles and burping. *My* mother, now a widow who never stopped grieving the death of her older daughter, became the best grandmother imaginable—happily hands-on and playful with my daughter in all ways, dancing and singing with her. "We're having *fun,*" she said frequently to my daughter, seeming as amazed as I was by this fact, since these were words she had never spoken to me. She was transformed into an entirely different person from the sad, remote woman who had raised me.

Now, at the dinner table, my daughter looks at me and asks again: "Mom, can you teach me how to knit?"

"Yes," I say without hesitation. I know she will be a wonderful knitter, quickly surpassing me. She loves clothes and clothing accessories of all sorts, and is graceful and gifted in all things spatial and visual. I promise myself that one day soon I will learn anew and get past my "wall," so that she and I will be able to sit side by side on the sofa near the windows of our apartment on the 24th floor with its achingly beautiful view (a view my mother would have loved, had she lived to see my family move into this Brooklyn high-rise), and together she and I will share the joys and rhythms of knit/purl, and the click/clack sound of the needles. I promise myself that together she and I will knit soft, warm, and fuzzy scarves, hats, sweaters, gloves, mittens—and more.

looped yarn

by Martha Frankel

When her best friend joined a cult, the writer found solace in knitting.

KAREN WAS MY BEST FRIEND, A TWIN, A TOE-WALKER, A tiny wisp of a thing who always seemed like she might just float off into the ether.

And then, one day, she did.

"You know how people talk about the tenth planet?" she asked plaintively, the day I realized she was no longer tethered to the earth. Tears were already forming in her eyes. She was shaking, and although it was frigid outside, I knew this had nothing to do with the weather.

"*Cast on loosely,*" Karen had instructed me a year before, sitting next to me on a towel on a deserted beach in Puerto Rico. "*Use needles two sizes bigger than you will be knitting with. It all flows from that.*"

"Yes," I said, and moved my hands in the universal language of "go ahead."

"Yes?" my husband Steve asked, incredulity on his face. "What tenth planet?"

I shot him a look and he backed off.

"Something bad is about to happen," Karen said, looking from one of us to the other, her eyes bouncing wildly, as if she were watching a tennis match right behind her eyelids. "Something *really* bad."

It was February 2002. Something really bad had already happened. But it turned out that Karen wasn't talking about planes flying into buildings, or people frightened by things they could barely name. No, she was specifically talking about that tenth planet.

"It's coming toward us," she said.

Steve let out a sound somewhere between a giggle and a groan.

I said nothing.

"Relax your hands. Let the yarn loop in a way that's soft and drapy. Put your pointer finger here, your pinkie there. Don't fight it."

"Where is it?" Steve asked, pointing out the window at the cloudless, cerulean blue sky.

"It's behind the sun. We can't see it yet. But it's out there and it's coming. Really fast."

"Start from the beginning," I said, because there had been something nagging at me for months. I had thought maybe she was still in shock from 9/11, that she and Sal were having problems, or that maybe she was mad at me. Or the worst possibility, that she wasn't feeling well. The word *cancer* had stuck in my throat a few times.

"I haven't wanted to tell you," Karen said finally. "But I have to now. We're going to Texas. We have to go be with our group."

She looked old and tired. Her gray hair hung limply down her back. I could see then how much weight she had lost. I thought that *cancer* sounded better than *group*.

"Your *group?*" Steve said.

"Yes. In Texas," she said. "We've been studying with them. She told us about the planet. It's coming in September."

"Who is *she?*" I asked.

"Our teacher." She told me her name.

"What does she believe in?"

"World peace," Karen said.

I started laughing. "Everyone believes in world peace," I said, "except maybe . . . Muammar Qaddafy." Karen didn't flinch.

"Your *group?*" Steve repeated. He walked right up to Karen, and put his hand over her heart. Then he tapped it, hard. "*We're* your fucking group."

You could hear all three of us panting.

"Then what?" I asked. "After the planet smashes into us, then what?" Something in me knew the end of this story had already been written for Karen, that in her mind she was gone gone gone.

"It will knock the earth off its axis. Water will rise. Over three billion people are going to die. We're going to have to start over from the beginning." Snot bubbles escaped her nose.

Relaxing my hands turned out to be near impossible. My stitches were so tight that I had to push the tip of the needle into the next stitch so hard that I often ripped the yarn. I tried a dozen different kinds of yarn, a dozen sized needles.

Karen and Sal, Steve and me—an odd foursome. Karen and Steve were artists; they took life drawing classes together. They were the real dog lovers, always on the floor throwing balls and teaching the dogs new tricks. Sal and I were sports fanatics; we watched baseball and football, played poker and golf. Karen and I spent hours and hours together, talking about family and bonds and the things that intrigued us both. Sal and I cooked elaborate meals, with recipes from Thailand and Morocco. Steve and Karen happily washed the dishes while they danced to *Big Chill*–like songs.

We lived a mile apart on a deserted road, had dinner together at our house three or four nights a week. We traveled together, to the Caribbean and New Mexico. We played knock rummy and the score was in the hundreds of thousands.

We played that game—if Sal and I died, what would Karen and Steve do? Adopt lots of dogs! Eat scrambled eggs every night (it was the only food either knew how to cook)! And if Karen and Steve died? Sal and I would watch sports at breakfast! Play poker every night of the week!

But Steve and Sal had nothing in common. Steve didn't like him, thought he was a pig, a slumlord, the kind of guy who would turn back his odometer before he traded his car in, who thought that kind of thing was okay. We argued about him sometimes, and although I took Sal's side, I knew what Steve said was true. Sal was a bit of a bully—well, more than a bit. He barked orders, was often short-tempered, and sometimes I was uncomfortable with how he treated Karen. When their dog was run over by the UPS truck, she called me and Steve, and we drove the mile up the road to her house and held her until we were all convinced that Duke was dead. When we called Sal at his poker game, he said he'd be home in a few hours and hung up.

And then one day, after dozens of bad samples, hundreds of missed stitches, thousands of sighs and moans, I finally relaxed my hands. The next stitches were—dare I say?—perfect. I was as excited as if I had learned to fly a plane.

"What does Sal think about all this?" I asked.

Sal was surely going to be my ace in the hole, a cynic who would never buy into this fantastical crap. "Let's ask him," Karen said defiantly, jutting out her chin like a teenager who's been caught with a bag of pot, taunting her Scotch-swilling parents to judge her.

When Sal walked in, it was as if I had never seen him before. He was scared. He was humbled. He actually talked about the planet as if he could see it.

In that first year I made dozens of scarves, then a baby blanket that only worked on a doll's bed. I made four hats, none of which could be worn by anyone with a head. But I kept learning, and whenever I felt uncomfortable I picked up those needles and things calmed down.

"Please don't tell anyone," Karen said as they left.

Steve and I were speechless anyway. I went on the Internet. I looked up their leader. Yup, world peace, but not much more. I looked up "rogue planet." Turned out the tenth-planet scam had been working for years. People got duped into believing it and gave away their money, their homes. Always to their leader.

I did what I do best—I researched. I printed out reams of paper. Every night I brought more evidence to Karen and Sal, but they just smiled and went back to sipping the Kool-Aid.

I shopped for yarn as if it were a new form of sex I had recently learned. I filled boxes with it, hid it under the bed and in the back of the closet. I rubbed it on my face. Yarn took over my dreams

I cried, I raged, I did not know what to do with myself. I decided that keeping quiet was the worst thing I could do for them, so I went to all of Karen and Sal's other friends. I told them about the rogue planet, but Karen and Sal had beat me to it; they spread the word that Steve and I were nuts, that we had made the whole story up, that they were moving to Texas because Karen's brother and his wife were moving there too (true, the brother was big in the rogue-planet cult), and that it was going to be a great opportunity for all of them.

In April Karen came to tell me that she was flying back to Texas for three weeks, that she was going to listen, to hear if God was talking to her. I didn't point out that hearing God was the first sign of all mental illness. I wished her luck.

And then it hit me, the thing I could do to change Karen's mind. I would knit. I would make five scarves; one for Karen, one for me, and one each for her three best friends. Each scarf would be a masterpiece. I would pour all my love into those scarves. If I did them right, Karen would stay.

I pick up a silk/wool blend. Gorgeous, soft, drapy. Different colors for each of the scarves. For the first one, I cast on 45 stitches on number 6 needles. I use the seed stitch. I knit from morning till night, hardly eating, obsessively worrying that every line is flawless. That first scarf takes eight days. At that rate I won't be finished and Karen will move away.

When I finish knitting for the day, I go to talk to Sal. I keep waiting to see what could possibly be in it for him, because by now I know what Steve has always said is true: he doesn't do anything unless there's an edge in his favor. But he's steadfast that he believes that a big honking planet is coming our way, and that he has to be in Texas when things go bad.

For the second scarf I cast on 40 stitches, and used size 8 needles. Knit one line, purl the next. I am halfway through when I notice a twisted stitch 7 inches below where I am. I spend hours debating, but what if that's the difference between whether she stays or goes? I rip it out. By the time I'm done with that scarf, thirteen days have passed.

I email their leader. I ask how she can live with herself, scaring innocent people, making them upend their lives because of some crap she made up. I don't hear back.

The third and forth scarves are thin, 30 stitches, number 10 needles.

They couldn't keep a mouse warm. But I don't care. The plan is to be done when Karen gets home, to deliver those scarves before she pulls into her driveway. This magical thinking is a full-time job.

When Karen comes back, we don't have to say a word. I hold out the scarf I have made for her—the blues and purples that she loves, the first cable I ever attempted. She leans forward and I place it around her neck. We hug and cry.

She leaves for Texas three months later. There's not a stitch I knit that I don't think, *Karen . . .*

teaching a
child to knit

by Sue Grafton

*"Teaching a Child to Knit" is about . . . hmm, how to say this . . . teaching
a child to knit. In this context, a "child" can be defined as anyone between
the ages of three and one hundred and three, give or take.*

> She had never married, never had children of her own. With me,
> she'd exercised her many odd notions about the formation of female
> character. Firing a handgun, she felt, would teach me to appreciate
> both safety and accuracy. It would also help me develop good hand-
> eye coordination, which she thought was useful. She'd taught me to
> knit and crochet so that I'd learn patience and an eye for detail.
>
> —from *D Is for Deadbeat*

THUS, HARD-BOILED FICTIONAL PRIVATE INVESTIGATOR
Kinsey Millhone describes her upbringing at the hands
of her eccentric Aunt Gin after the death of her parents
when she was five. It is worth noting (and I say this because I noted
it myself . . .) that even a wholly invented character like Kinsey Millhone recognizes the part knitting played in her wholly invented life.

While *D Is for Deadbeat* was published in 1987, I was knitting long before I embarked on the series and I've been knitting in the thirty-some-odd years since.

THE SUNDRY BENEFITS
OF KIDS KNITTING

T HERE ARE ANY NUMBER of reasons for teaching a child to knit. I may be preaching to the choir here, but I think it's worth reflecting on some of the tangible and intangible rewards for both the teacher and the pupil.

- Knitting encourages focus; an invaluable asset for children growing up in today's fast-paced world. Electronic entertainment (television programs, Game Boys, cell phone, touch screen tablets, and computers . . .), while superficially engaging, actually fosters a short attention span and promotes a tendency to flit from one activity to the next.
- Knitting teaches us to inhabit the moment, to savor the pleasure of sustained concentration. Knitting teaches patience, which is beneficial to children and adults alike.
- Knitting provides a unique form of companionship. What could be better (aside from eating chocolate chip cookies . . .) than Mom or Nana and a neophyte settling down together to knit?
- Knitting generates a common language that can link generations and cross cultural divides. Go into any knit shop in the world and the connection is evident.
- Knitting is easily portable; a worthy occupation for long drives, air travel, and waiting rooms. As an adult you can knit while sitting

on the sidelines at swimming pools, supervising playground activities, visiting other knitters, or watching those tedious televised sporting events with your significant other. For the child, knitting is the perfect antidote for claims that s/he's bored and has nothing to do.

- Knitting teaches children to take pride in a job well done. Knitting provides an opportunity to excel outside the classroom setting, where a child can accomplish goals independent of tests, grades, and report cards.
- Knitting stimulates a love of color and texture and an appreciation for design. Knitting can move from the practical to the abstract with countless stages in between.
- Knitting creates a context in which to teach a child the importance of finishing a task. Every job in life has its ups and downs. As a self-appointed knitting maven, you have an opportunity to introduce your young charge to the concept of beginning, middle, and end. Beginnings are always easy and reaching the ending generates a satisfaction of its own. But how do we get to the finish line? Children need to develop a tolerance for the pesky middle part of any project. When we feel discouraged, who can resist the urge to quit? Knitting teaches us to stay the course through that endless stretch that seems to start on Row 2 and continues to binding off. Children are not born with this ability. Most children have no stick-to-itiveness whatever. Someone, namely you, has to teach them the satisfaction of hard work. As a side note, it doesn't hurt to jump in and repair a few boo-boos and then add five or six rows after the junior knitter has gone to bed. It's a thrill for a child to return to a piece of knitting and find it looking so much longer and more "regular" than s/he remembers.

MY OWN EXPERIENCE

THE MYRIAD VIRTUES of knitting were brought home to me over the past two years when I decided to teach my two young granddaughters how to knit. Keep in mind that fine motor skills develop at different rates. I have a friend who taught her four-year-old granddaughter how to knit. My own two granddaughters were slower off the mark. Taylor and Addison were seven and five respectively when the three of us embarked on our knitting adventure. I was interested in how each would take to the task, given the contrasts in their personalities. Taylor is easygoing, thoughtful, and self-contained, with a sunny disposition and a naughty sense of humor. She excels in academics and I can usually find her curled up in a comfy chair, reading a book. Addie, two years younger, is the more energetic of the two. She's athletic, mercurial, empathetic, fearless, and adventuresome. In public, Addie is the one who approaches and befriends adults and children alike.

Since I see them at three- to four-month intervals, I introduced them to knitting more than once with varying degrees of success. Initially, the process was daunting and both girls, while interested, quickly lost heart. I thought Taylor would be the first to take to the job, but it was the ever-enterprising Addie who made the leap. On the third go-around, she proposed a knitting session, exhibiting a determination to conquer I hadn't seen in her before. She also announced when she was ready to move from the knit stitch to the purl. Taylor will soon realize, if she hasn't already, that knitting, like reading, is a form of meditation, offering a sense of privacy and soul-centeredness whether we're alone or with others in a social setting.

IN THE BEGINNING IS
THE BEGINNING

A WONDERFUL INTRODUCTION to knitting is embodied in that first ceremonial trip to a knitting shop. There is nothing more dazzling than a small retail space devoted to yarns, knitting books, patterns, knitting needles, crochet hooks, stitch holders, stitch markers, and other accessories. A large craft store might have knitting *supplies*, but that's hardly the point. A proper knit shop almost always has a coterie of knitters on hand . . . many of them mothers and grandmothers . . . whose encouragement and doting smiles reinforce and supplement your enthusiasm.

The purpose of a trip to a knit shop is to give a child the opportunity to acquire the necessary paraphernalia. Every knitter should have a large knitting bag in which to haul the ever-growing collection of tools and equipment. I gifted each of my granddaughters with a large canvas tote: red-and-white-polka-dot trim for Taylor and blue-and-white-polka-dot trim for Addison. I also selected five skeins of color-coordinated yarn for each of them . . . blue for Taylor, green for Addie . . . so they could easily distinguish their work. Were I to do it again, I'd take them with me to a knit shop and let them choose their own yarns and totes, though I'd probably still be standing there, glancing at my watch and tapping my foot, while they agonized. At the time, I chose a skein each of chunky weight yarn for their initial projects, thinking the work would go quickly and that the two would be heartened at the swift accumulation of knitted inches. This proved to be a problem because the dense yarn I selected was cumbersome to manipulate. The second time around, I found a lightweight cotton yarn that was easier for them to work with.

Even at a young age, a knitter-in-waiting will feel the pull of the choices on display. A novice knitter can't help but marvel at the array of yarns available; chunky and delicate, made of cotton, wool, and silk; in worsted, fingerling, and sock weight; hand-dyed lots from Uruguay and Ireland; yarns made from the sheared coats of sheep, llamas, and goats. Imagine the effect on a young child's imagination with such riches in reach, especially when Nana is paying the bill.

If you're averse to the pricey outlay, most chronic and incurable knitters have a stash of yarns tucked away; a perfect treasure trove for the apprentice knitter who probably won't require eight skeins of imported alpaca from the same dye lot to make a headband, a skinny scarf, or a bookmark.

TOOLS AND TERRORS

For TAYLOR AND ADDISON, I bought knitting needles of different sizes . . . both straight and circular . . . because I had no way to guess how adept they'd prove at using one type or the other or which they'd prefer. The handling of knitting needles is an alien act and I thought it wise to offer alternatives in case one proved especially unwieldy. Letting the inexperienced knitter weigh in on the needle size and type is also a means of providing *some* sense of control. To state the obvious, the advantage of circular needles is that the two ends are always attached, whereas one needle of a pair can easily slip out of the child's hands into that impossible crevice between the front seats of your car. I would assume that a trained knitting instructor has a clever trick or two up her sleeve for making the learning process both amusing and fun. I was forced to muddle through on my own.

THE CONTINENTAL VERSUS
THE ENGLISH METHOD

L ET'S FACE IT: on first acquaintance, there is something awkward and annoying about knitting needles; odd, unfamiliar "sticks" jutting out at all angles. Then there's the tangle of yarn, which you're expected to manipulate with a series of irksome moves that make no particular sense. I was taught to knit English-style, wherein the yarn is kept largely in the right hand and the loop is "thrown." This at least allows one to utilize that lilting rhyme, which serves as both guide and metaphor. "Under the fence, catch the Sheep, back you go, off you leap..."

With the Continental or German method, the yarn is held in the left hand and the loop is said to be "picked" instead of "thrown." By all reports, the Continental method is faster and more efficient, but I was taught the English style and since knitting, to my mind, is about the doing and not about the dashing through, I find myself happiest with the style I first learned. I do know a knitter who spent an entire weekend converting from the English to the Continental method and swears by it. I'm too lazy to bother.

SOURCE MATERIALS

W HEN IT COMES TO a working guide, there are numerous books available on the subject of teaching children to knit. In one quick visit to Amazon.com, I found the following:

- *Kid Knitting: Projects for Kids of All Ages*, by Melanie Falick
- *Kids Knit!: Simple Steps to Nifty Projects*, by Sarah Bradberry

- *Knitting (Kids Can Do It)*, by Judy Ann Sadler and Esperança Melo
- *Knitting for Children: 35 Simple Knits Kids Will Love to Make*, by Claire Montgomerie
- *A First Book of Knitting for Children*, by Bonnie Gosse
- *12 Easy Knitting Projects (Quick Starts for Kids)*, by Peg Blanchette and Terri Thibault

There is also the *Learn to Knit Set and Book* by Shure Products and highly touted DVD called *The Art of Knitting 4 Kids*, by Ryan Anderson.

With so many publications available, I find it helpful to scan readers' reviews before I decide which might best suit my purposes. Buying more than one such how-to manual is a smart idea because there are a variety of ways to teach any skill and your student might find one approach more appealing than another.

THE FIRST PROJECT

ONCE YOU'VE MADE a trip to the yarn shop (or you've given your proto-knitter access to your stash), it's time to get serious. If you've bought or borrowed a small collection of knitting books for kids, you should sit down with your novitiate and home in on a project, making sure you have on hand the recommended size needles and the suggested weight of yarn. There's some argument for casting on and practicing with throwaway yarn, but I leave that decision to you and your charge.

For the first undertaking, I like the garter-stitch washcloth, which can be made out of bright cotton yarn and allows the beginner to master the basic knit stitch. A washcloth is useful, it doesn't take six weeks to complete, and it's easy to hold. Your tenderfoot can cast on as many stitches as s/he likes and knit until the size and shape seems right. Learning a physical skill like knitting requires practice, which is best kept to short sessions over an extended period of time. Learning to knit is like learning a foreign language. The vocabulary of knitting has a subset of words and phrases . . . stitches and combinations . . . that build step by step, each added to the one before. My sole hesitation in suggesting the garter stitch is knowing the hellish consequences of dropping a stitch. Surely a small fortune can be made if someone will only invent a device that can easily retrieve a dropped garter stitch ten rows down. Having said that, I get dibs . . .

A FEW GENTLE ADMONITIONS
FOR THE KNITTING INSTRUCTOR

1. Be mindful of the fact that submitting to the will of another requires trust and humility. Learning places the student in a vulnerable one-down position and an instructor must always appreciate the power of her role and the delicacy of her ministrations.
2. The teacher and the student should sit side by side. This generates a sharing of body warmth and fosters a sense of the familiar. Close proximity is a comfort for those venturing into new and possibly dangerous territory.
3. No criticism whatever, please. A student embarking on a first knitting project already feels clumsy and out of sorts and doesn't need to have her feelings of confusion and inadequacy reinforced. Learning to knit stimulates long-suppressed

notions of weakness and stupidity, not pleasant under any circumstances. Your job as an instructor is to coax and encourage. We learn most easily when we feel most safe.

4. A steady stream of praise and reassurance will create the atmosphere of trust necessary to convert frustration into pleasure, hopelessness into determination, and failure into fulfillment. Keep in mind that *knowing* how to knit is a delight. *Learning* how to knit is a troublesome endeavor. Knitting is only a form of relaxation to those who've mastered the fundamentals. To the novice, the very act of knitting is a tense and exasperating struggle. The instructor's job is to cosset and protect.

5. Be enthusiastic and complimentary. To the knitting debutante, that lumpy and irregular construction is an object of pride. When my granddaughter knits, she can already imagine the amazement on her father's face when she bestows her handmade drink coaster. She can also anticipate the many occasions when her doll will need to go nighty-night on the blanket she knit, or the cat might curl up on a length of hand-knit bedding. As a tutor, you must never destroy the vision the elementary-level knitter holds in her mind's eye. The end game is what inspires the beginner to soldier on over rough terrain.

6. By the same token, make certain your praise isn't exaggerated or insincere. Your knitting recruit, while delusional, is not so easily taken in. Teaching a child to knit is process predicated on faith.

7. When teaching a child to knit, do not rush. We don't learn to knit by listening to lectures. We learn to knit by having someone demonstrate how a stitch is executed. Again and

again and again. Like so much in life, the joy of knitting isn't necessarily in the destination, but in the journey itself. A knitting instructor must remain serene. Even the faintest hint of irritation must be stripped from the interaction.

8. Like chess and bridge, knitting can be enjoyed at its most rudimentary level. At the same time, learning to knit carries the student into the realms of the exotic and the elegant. There is always something new to master. Knitting allows us to see beyond the immediate gain to future challenges.

9. Knitting teaches both child and adult a willingness to admit our mistakes and correct for them. There are two schools of thought on this point. Some knitters take a relaxed view, leaving egregious blunders in situ while toiling merrily on. Then there is the correct approach...that being mine... in which the object of the exercise is to complete a project without having to apologize. Clearly, I could take a lesson here myself. No one is perfect. We need to teach children what we ourselves must learn: that perfection isn't the goal, it's the occasional happy side effect.

10. Finally, remember that knitting can create an immutable bond between teacher and pupil; one that will resonate through a lifetime. Dearest reader, I'm begging you...don't screw it up.

knitting in kathmandu

by Jessi Hempel

When a boy teaches her to knit, the writer's sexual preference is suddenly called into question.

WHEN I WAS TWENTY-TWO, I FELL FOR A GUY I MET on a bus in Nepal. I was a first-order lesbian fresh out of college and backpacking through Asia with my best friend. Brian was a twenty-eight-year-old Floridian schoolteacher who kept trying to catch my eye when I glanced up from my novel. I doubt I would have noticed him but for the fact that he was working circular knitting needles to form the perfect mouth of a woolen sock. A boy who knit.

I didn't know very much about boys back then. I had never so much as kissed one. But I understood desire in many incarnations. I sat very still without looking up, and absorbed Brian's gaze. It burned into the exposed flesh of my legs. I stole a glance at the maroon yarn tangled around his left leg. He had a hairy leg, a boyish leg, the leg of someone who—like me—had spent twenty-one days climbing a mountain without a hot shower. I followed his leg to the edge of his natty shorts and up to a bristling brown goatee above which I found his eyes. He met my smile.

Our bus was headed for Kathmandu. We had just completed a twenty-one-day Himalayan trek that took us over an 18,000-foot mountain pass. Before this trip, I had never been hiking. My outdoorsy friend Heather had convinced me the trek would be a good idea, that it would somehow expand our perspective, and it had. The world looks different when you get that high. The skies are a clearer blue, unpierced by airplanes and electric lights. The white snowy mountain peaks that seem so imposing from the ground become companions, a feathery softness belying occasional rumbling avalanches. On the hike up, I had perched myself on a slab of rock and a large bird swept down over me, its wings spread wider than the full expanse of my arms. I had seen none of this before. I thought that if I could climb a mountain, surely I could talk to this guy. Next to me on the bus, Heather scribbled in her journal, occasionally flipping the tape in her plastic yellow Sony Walkman. Two rows behind me, Brian knit. He was traveling with his friend John, a dreadlocked pothead with round cheeks who was stretched out across a backseat, snoring. I weighed my options for a moment, then moved across the aisle to plop myself down in the seat next to him. "What are you knitting?" I asked him. We inched toward each other making small talk as the hair on his leg brushed against my own.

It wasn't hard to fall for Brian. He was a boy with heart. He told me he was the sixth of seven kids in an Irish family from Miami, and he rattled off their names—five brothers and a sister. He had been working abroad as a teacher for many years, first in Korea and then in Saudi Arabia, and he told me about the little Korean girl he taught to speak English. He had knit her a hat in the shape of a strawberry with a green yarn stem sprouting from the top.

The ride was long, and we stopped for a meal in a mountain town where farmers had recently shorn their herds of sheep that wandered the stepped fields. The wool had been spun into yarn and then dyed bright hues of purple and teal and red to become, eventually, those sweaters you buy in hippie stores in towns like Northampton and Asheville. In one of the only photographs I have of Brian from that time, he stands back in awe, his mouth open, gazing at the skeins. In my loopy adolescence handwriting, I've labeled it: *Brian looks longingly.*

I NEVER DIDN'T KNOW I was gay. As an overweight sixth grader with an unfortunate perm, I made my best friend a card that said *I love you* for Valentine's Day. She made a similar one for me. But she made her boyfriend a poster-size cardboard heart with glitter glue letters that spelled out *I ♥ you.* I wanted to be hearted.

As soon as I got to college, I came running out of the closet. At Brown University, I shaved my head, joined the ultimate Frisbee team, and sewed a rainbow flag patch on my backpack. I kissed some girls, and I fell in love for the first time—with a soft-spoken ultimate Frisbee player who didn't shave her legs. I watched movies like *Go Fish* and read the Alison Bechdel comic *Dykes to Watch Out For* and was thrilled to have stumbled into a culture where my poor fashion sense and bad haircuts weren't just ignored; they were rewarded. I was the BDOC—the big dyke on campus—and when I hosted a viewing party to watch Ellen DeGeneres come out on television, I had to borrow three television sets to accommodate the underclassmen who came from all over campus to watch.

As much as I understood and even commanded attention from gay girls, I had no clout in a straight world. Male friends talked to me as if I were one of the guys. Invariably, they crushed out on Heather, and she'd court their attention effortlessly. This intrigued me because I felt it eluded me. And though I had had sex by twenty-two, I felt myself to be inexperienced in the world—somehow still a virgin of a sort—because I had not slept with a man. This was a secret thought I did not say even to Heather; it was not politically correct.

In Asia, all of this changed. For one, three weeks of intense physical labor after months of traveling had thinned me out. My collarbone protruded and the skirts I'd begun to wear fell off my frame. My hair had grown in silky and blonder than I'd remembered, and I'd replaced my glasses with contacts so I could wear sunglasses all day. I noticed these differences from the outside in. Men on the street began to look at me. Fellow travelers hit on me. And when our bus finally pulled into Kathmandu for the evening, Brian asked if Heather and I would like to meet up with him and John for dinner. Hours later, after we'd finished off many slices of the cheese-cake Nepalese chefs learn to make for the tourists in international cooking school, we all repaired to the broad wooden deck of Brian's guesthouse for another round of beer. While John and Heather compared notes on the Bay Area, Brian offered to show me the strawberry cap he'd knitted. He pulled my elbow gently toward his room, and then knocked the door closed behind us with his foot. The brush of his heel on the door: that was how I knew what was coming. My stomach danced up and down. I leaned into him and before the hat ever materialized, we'd sunk onto his rickety twin bed.

At long last, my first boy kiss. It was clumsy and uncertain and then easy and then interesting. Brian was lumbering and gentle. We ventured awkwardly into the realm of sex. He pulled a condom from a drawer, and after a bit of fumbling we resumed position. Eventually, Brian fell asleep, but I did not. Instead, I turned the action over in my mind. I thought about the on-again, off-again girlfriend I'd left behind in the U.S. I remember there was a hole in the curtain above Brian's bed. I settled my head into the crook of his shoulder and watched a spider crawl back and forth through it a dozen times.

Sometime after the sun came up, I slipped out of bed and made my way down to the front desk. A sign advertised phone calls to the United States for $4 a minute, half the price of a night's lodging. I decided to call my girlfriend, who had moved to New York City when I left to travel. It would be dinnertime in Manhattan, where she worked at a charter school. I let the phone ring six times. When the answering machine picked up, I listened to her voice telling me she wasn't available. I don't remember if I left a message.

THAT DAY, HEATHER and I made our way to the Boudhanath stupa, a white circular temple that looms 118 feet in the air. Visitors—a few maroon-robed monks and a slew of Westerners—circle it clockwise, massaging strings of wooden beads to release prayers as they stroll. We walked in silence. I tried to clear my mind, to meditate, but it was scratchy full. My pelvis ached. No one had told me sex with men hurt. It was the physical reminder that something had changed about me.

My lonely middle-of-the-night thoughts had vanished; in their place, I began nursing fantasies of a life I could make with Brian. I could have a boyfriend! We could play house and make curried chicken together and knit cozies for all of our kitchen appliances. Maybe even have a kid someday. My fingers worked their way through the beads on my string, and with each rotation around the stupa, my fantasies billowed larger.

Later in the afternoon, Brian showed up at our guesthouse. Heather and I were preparing to leave Kathmandu. We would follow the typical backpacker's route south to the Indian border, check our passports to make sure our visas were up-to-date, and then head east. Our final destination was the tiny northern town of Rishikesh. (After the Beatles dropped by to visit an ashram there long ago, the city became known as the World Capital of Yoga.)

In a rash move, I invited Brian to join us. He and John had plans to go south, but he agreed that in a week he'd jump a train by himself for the seventeen-hour journey to Rishikesh. It was a thinly laid plan—there was a lot that could go wrong. This was 1998, a time before cell phones and email. We both agreed we'd aim for a guesthouse we'd read about in our Lonely Planet guidebook. I anticipated we'd have trouble finding each other. I didn't anticipate my coming ambivalence.

INDIA CAN MAKE YOU tired. It is an assault on the senses. By the time we got to Rishikesh, both Heather and I had contracted the infamous Delhi belly that results in permanent diarrhea. We'd spent hours shelved in sleeper train bunkbeds, clutching our backpacks to our chests so the porters wouldn't steal them while we slept. I'd been overwhelmed by the smell of a dog throwing up in a cobblestone Varanasi alley around the corner from the palm reader who told me I would marry at twenty-seven, make little money, and die at eighty. On one ominous bus ride, I'd felt a poking sensation on my bum and looked behind me to see a man's fingers wedged through the tiny crack in the upholstery.

Built along the green banks of the Ganges at the spot where it first emerges from the Himalayas, Rishikesh was to be our final destination before we headed back to the United States. By the time we reached the placid river pools, I had given up the idea of a love affair; I craved peanut butter sandwiches, Crest toothpaste, and the on-again, off-again girlfriend I'd left behind.

As it happened, we arrived a day before His Holiness the Dalai Lama was scheduled to hold an audience at the local ashram. The guesthouses were packed with sarong-clad Westerners amassing for the event, and pop-up gift shops sold copies of *The Art of Happiness* for 37 cents. Our agreed-upon guesthouse was full, but Heather and I settled nearby and hoped to run into Brian at the ashram. Early the next morning, we headed up the hill to join the growing crowd. It was far larger than I had imagined—a sea of white and brown faces wrapped in brightly colored cloth. After searching out Brian for some time, we gave up and settled in a sunny spot two-thirds of the way through the throngs and turned to our Buddhism primers to pass the time. I couldn't focus. I couldn't tell if the queasy feeling in my belly was relief or disappointment. As I pondered this, a ball of maroon yarn hit my knee and bounced sideways, beginning to unravel. I followed the string to its source: Brian sat two rows behind me, working his needles to fashion another sock. Catching my eyes, he picked up a second ball of yarn and lobbed it straight at my head.

I don't remember what the Dalai Lama talked about that afternoon, but I do remember that Brian smelled like Dr. Bronner's peppermint soap as he settled onto the blanket beside me. Even today, when I catch a whiff of it, I'm momentarily happy without thinking.

For the rest of our Rishikesh sojourn, Brian hung out with us. We did yoga and took hikes and read books in the sun. Sometimes,

I felt so attracted to him that I wanted to wrap myself up in him to see if I could make the lines between our bodies blur; but when he tried to make a move, I rebuffed him. I blamed—or credited—my newly discovered Buddhism and yoga.

Instead of having the crazy passionate affair I'd envisioned, Brian and I spent long hours knitting. He taught me how. Sure, I knew how to hold the needles, but Brian showed me the difference between using wooden and aluminum ones. He explained the purl stitch, and showed me how to use a round needle to make the mouth of a sock. And when I invariably messed up, adding stitches to my rows, he told me not to fake it. I unraveled most of what I knit, beginning again and again.

Privately, I wrestled with my own competing desires; I longed for a simple affair that wouldn't threaten my notions of my own sexuality, the bedrock of my identity. Instead, things felt complicated. I remember one particular afternoon. We'd just eaten our meal and been for a dip in the river, and we hiked into the woods to sit and enjoy the day. The pine needles felt itchy against the back of my bare legs as I settled against a tree. Brian was a few feet in front of me and Heather had stayed behind with another friend for an afternoon yoga session. My mind shot forward, and I tried to imagine Brian in New York. Could the life I left accommodate a knitting Floridian guy? And would this guy ever even consider coming along with me for the journey? Memory can be highly uncertain and undependable, but I remember this thought with a great deal of clarity because it catapulted me into the next chapter of my life. I wanted to go home then. I missed Ani DiFranco lyrics and the New York City subway and milky white deli coffee. I missed the girl I'd left.

Until this point, I had been purposefully vague with Brian about when Heather and I intended to leave. We discussed extending our trip, but I knew I didn't want to do this. I couldn't stay with him—and I didn't want to tell him I was leaving him. Not just leaving him in India, of course, but leaving him. So I didn't.

On the morning we left, I woke Heather early. We loaded our backpacks and walked lightly across the porch past the room where Brian slept, making our way to the train station. If Heather wondered about how I'd handle my love interest, she certainly didn't ask me. We boarded a bus that took us to a train that took us to the airport.

MY LIFE RETURNED to something I recognized after that. I joined Teach for America and moved to New York. It was a crappy year. I lived in an apartment that had no bedroom window. I had thirty-eight fourth graders in my Harlem classroom. And I broke up with my girlfriend for a final time.

Sometimes I thought about Brian. I wanted to apologize. I considered trying to find him, but Google and Facebook did not yet exist. I'd written his parents' mailing address down in my journal. But even if I were to write him a letter, what could I possibly say?

The following June, I decided to move to the Bay Area, where Heather had a great house share and seemed a good deal happier than me. My younger sister and I packed up my Honda Civic and we drove across the country together, taking two weeks to camp and hike and go whitewater rafting. We arrived in San Francisco on a Tuesday evening and found a parking spot with a provident amount of ease right in front of a taquería in the Haight. The air smelled fresh and crisp as we unfolded our tired bodies from the front seat of the car.

In San Francisco you can get a burrito for just $3.99 that will feed you for two meals—more if you're a light eater. I was explaining this to my sister as we walked into the joint and came face-to-face with the restaurant's only other patron, Brian.

For a third time, we locked eyes. There were long moments of silence. Then he spoke: "Where the hell did you go?" he asked me. I could tell he wanted to be mad at me, but that same gentleness that won me over on a bus in Nepal emanated from him. I was speechless.

Much later, I would apologize. He would invite me to dinner at the apartment where he settled after he returned to the States. It was just a few miles from the place where I would settle. I would explain everything I'd wanted to tell him about my sexuality and about how much I had liked him. After that, on Tuesdays, I'd come to his knitting circle and we'd get drunk on boxed Chardonnay while he showed the other members—all women—how to work the difficult part of the thumb on a mitten. But that evening, I waited for my first San Francisco burrito, and we sat down to dinner together.

ten things i learned from knitting

by Ann Hood

Who knew that by learning to knit, we also learn how to live?

I

CASTING ON

J EN SILVERMAN, the young woman who taught me to knit, handed me a pair of knitting needles and a skein of yarn, took a long hard look at me, and took them back. "I was going to teach you how to cast on," she said, somehow looping and pulling the yarn so that it magically appeared on one needle, "but you won't be able to do it. I can tell." Was it my trembling hands that gave me away? My sweaty palms? Or the look of terror on my face?

I was a forty-two-year-old woman who had come to Sakonnet Purls to learn to knit out of desperation. Grief was driving me crazy. I couldn't sleep at night. I couldn't read a book or write a simple paragraph. The loop in my life, unlike the ones that Jen expertly, easily used to cast on, was like a DVD stuck on play, the movie of the thirty-six hours I spent at my five-year-old daughter Grace's side as she lay dying in a hospital ICU. Whenever I closed my eyes, or found myself alone or still, the loop began. Friends had promised me that knitting would make it go away, at least while those needles were in my hands and I knit.

Jen gave me the needles again, now with fourteen stitches curled around one of them. "I'll keep casting on for you until you're ready to learn how to do it yourself," she said.

Casting on lays the foundation for knitting. It is the method by which stitches are formed. From there, you knit and purl your way to scarves and hats and all sorts of knitted wonders. I learned that long-ago autumn day, that sometimes, despite our desperation, our desire, we cannot cast on alone. It took many friends to lead me to Jen and learning to knit. It took me months of Jen carefully casting on my stitches for me. Then one day, she made a slipknot, and showed me how to begin on my own. I was ready to finally move on, to find my way back to wonder.

II

CABLE STITCH

ONE OF THE THINGS I loved about turning forty was that I could finally say no to all the things I didn't want to do. I was, I thought, a fully formed person who knew her likes and dislikes, her strengths and limitations. As a younger woman, when someone suggested climbing down a rocky cliff to a perfect beach below, I went along, even though my fear of heights inevitably left me clinging to the face of that cliff, waiting to get rescued. When a cheerful group of skiing friends headed for a black diamond, I went along, even though that same fear of heights combined with a real lack of interest in skiing at all left me stranded on a mogul until the ski patrol came to get me. I went on long hot bike rides, hating every minute. I endured camping out when all I really wanted was a nice air-conditioned hotel room with a TV and room service.

But then I turned forty and somehow that gave me the freedom to say no. No, I don't really like sushi that much. No, I don't want to learn to surf in those giant crushing waves. No, no, no.

Knitting, which seems to a novice to be a passive, easy way to spend your time, is actually filled with hidden dangers. These include things like knitting two socks simultaneously on something called a magic loop; lace knitting; knitting patterns, like ducks or moose, that require grids and graphs and complicated mathematics; knitting on needles the size of toothpicks; knitting on needles the size of a drum majorette's baton; decreasing stitches, increasing stitches, knitting behind and in front of stitches. Sometimes, knitting makes me dizzy.

For some reason that I don't remember, cable stitches seemed to me to be the hardest thing of all. I admire them, the way they wind around each other, the way they rise above the other stitches. "It's easy," knitters always say about difficult things. Like cables. One Thanksgiving my friend Matt arrived with an almost-finished oatmeal-colored scarf, neat cables running the length of it. Matt is a new knitter. A beginner. "How did you do that?" I asked him, shocked. "It's easy," he said. Of course. Then he offered to show me. It did look easy, the way he put stitches on a cute little stitch holder and knit around them.

The next day, a pattern for an Irish hiking scarf—cables!—in hand, soft pewter-colored yarn, and my very own cable stitch holder, I began. Everything Matt had shown me completely vanished from my brain. I tried. And I tried. And I tried again. In my knitting room are dozens of projects I abandoned because they were impossible. A sweater with no sleeves (sew the seams? huh?). A winter hat with crooked misshapen ducks crashing into each other across it. This Irish hiking scarf was about to join all those other lost causes.

But I really wanted to knit cable stitches. I thought of Matt's beautiful scarf, the cables snaking up it, intertwined. Determined, I went to YouTube and found a how-to video on knitting cables. I only had to watch it four times before I got it right. And although I still do not want to surf or scale cliffs or even eat sushi, I have found that on the evening I spent learning to knit cables, something in me changed. That is why I trekked into the Bwindi Impenetrable Forest to observe mountain gorillas, even though I was afraid. That is why I decided to write books for children, historical fiction, a television pilot. Because I'm not afraid to try, to learn, to knit the hardest thing.

III

SOME DAYS IT'S OKAY TO JUST KNIT DISHRAGS

ONE OF MY FAVORITE things to knit is dishrags. Although I have a complicated basket weave type pattern for them, and although those dishrags look really really beautiful, I prefer to knit simpler ones. I know the pattern by heart: Cast on 4 stitches. Knit those 4 stitches. Then knit 2, yarn over, knit to the end of the row until there are 44 stitches. At that point, you knit 2 stitches together, yarn over again, knit 2 more stitches together, and knit to the end of the row until you're back to 4 stitches. At that point, you have a dishrag. The yarn these require is cotton and sells at Walmart for about two dollars a skein. You get a couple of dishrags from that skein. I knit these so often that now I even make patterns, using up all my leftover bits to form stripes or zigzags or whatever. They are, after all, just dishrags. It's hard to make an ugly one.

I like to knit dishrags for hostesses, even though when I present them at dinner parties I'm often met with a really confused look. "It's a dishrag," I explain. "I knit it for you." "Um...thank you?" is a common response. I also like to knit them as thank-you gifts, or to give to people I really like. Some people love my dishrags. My friend Kimberley even asks for more of them. My friend Matthew held it to his face to soothe his aching jaw after he had his wisdom teeth out. I have friends who couldn't bear to use them as dishrags. Too special, they say. Too pretty.

My favorite dishrags I've knit are white ones that my cousin Gloria-Jean and I tie-dyed. Years ago, when we were about thirteen years old, we saw John Sebastian (he of the Lovin' Spoonful) perform solo at Brown University's Spring Weekend. We fell in love that night—with the song "Darling Be Home Soon," with any guy who plays a guitar, and with tie dye, which John Sebastian was decked out in from head to toe. That summer, we tie-dyed everything. We played "Darling Be Home Soon" and dreamed about boys and college and poetry as we tie-dyed in my hot backyard. This April, I had the opportunity to have dinner with John Sebastian and his wife. As soon as I learned about that dinner, I set to work knitting those two white dishrags. Then Gloria-Jean and I tie-dyed them and brought them to the dinner. The tie-dying was not so great; it had been forty years since we'd last done it. But I didn't care. John Sebastian is the owner of my dishrags.

You see, I'm an overachiever. As a kid, I fretted over grades. Even an A– was enough to send me into a fit of anxiety. I need to make cookbook-perfect dinners. I need to write beautiful sentences, wear foundation and blush even if I'm just running an errand, look good, be good, impress, do better than last time, and then better still. But when I knit dishrags, all that goes away. Sometimes, it's enough to just cast on 4 stitches, use cheap cotton yarn, and knit a really simple thing for someone.

IV

SOMETIMES I NEED TO
KNIT A BLANKET

THE SUMMER I DECIDED to knit my friend Hillary Day a blanket as a wedding gift, I thought I was doing it because I love Hillary and I wanted to give her the most special present I could. And I wanted to flex my knitting muscles a little since I'd only been doing it about six months and was kind of giddy about yarn. I ordered a pattern with yarn in shades of white, from pure white to eggshell and oyster and pale pink and even an apricot color. I spent hours on my sofa, the yarn tumbling onto my lap like waves washing over me.

When I knit, everything else vanishes. Sadness, anxiety, anger, confusion. It is just me and the yarn and the lovely sound of my needles clicking together. I didn't realize then, but probably the real reason I decided to embark on such a big and time-consuming project was to not think about Hillary's wedding. Hillary Day was the nanny for my kids, Sam and Grace, from two days before Grace was born until a few years later when Hillary graduated from RISD and moved away. We all adored her. She made us salads and hats and painted the walls in warm cheerful colors. After she left, Sam would call her and sing to her and Grace would send Hillary her drawings.

In 2002, Hillary had moved back to Portland, Oregon, and was working for Adidas. That April, Grace died, and Hillary came all the way across the country to be with us, clutching photographs of Grace as a baby to give us. The next summer, we were going to her wedding in Bend, and I began to knit that blanket. Looking back, I remember how I felt about that trip west, how being around strangers at that time made me panic; how Grace should have been there with us, dressed in pink and twirling with Sam on the dance floor; how time kept moving forward without Grace, and I couldn't stop it. So instead, I knit. For hours and hours, that wedding blanket eventually covering me.

A few weeks ago, sitting alone on a gray afternoon, I decided I wanted to knit a blanket. I found a pattern online and ordered the yarn. Every day, I impatiently checked the mail, wanting that alpaca to arrive, fast. When it finally did, I cast on those 144 stitches as soon as I took out the yarn. But this time, I understood my aching desire to take on a project as big as a blanket. In February, my beloved aunt, an intricate thread in the fabric of my family, was killed in an automobile accident. My mother, her best friend and daily companion for sixty years, had dropped into a depression. Sam, now nineteen, has gone off to college, and instead of spending the summer at home he is touring in Colorado with the Missoula Children's Theatre. Around me, friends have just learned they have cancer; friends are getting divorced. And this year marked ten years since Grace died. I still have not been able to stop time. And so, instead, I knit a blanket.

V

UNKNITTING

I N LIFE THERE ARE no do-overs. Or so I thought. Which isn't to say I didn't try. Too often, I let boyfriends back in, even though the relationships had failed. Not once. Or even twice. Sometimes more. I would think about all the potential it had, those dizzying kisses, the late nights telling each other everything. And do it again, always with the same disastrous results. I have even been known to obsess about what could have been, not just in love, but in life. Friends tolerate for a while, indulge me until they want to scream. *Let it go,* they say eventually. *Move on.* Still, I keep myself awake playing out different scenarios, better endings, better everything.

Add grief to this personality and the results are even worse. It is typical of a grieving person to question what has happened, almost as if they think that if they can make sense of the events, the death itself will make sense too. Like doing an impossible jigsaw puzzle, grieving people keep rearranging the pieces, hoping something will fit. It doesn't, of course. It can't. Still, we do it.

After Grace died, I replayed every piece of the puzzle of the last thirty-six hours of her life. Should we have gone to that birthday party? To ballet? Should I have called a doctor sooner? Called a different doctor? Insisted on IV antibiotics? Screamed louder? Somehow, if I could arrange the pieces differently, do it over and over, somehow the end would be different. By the time six months later that I learned to knit, I was weary from grief and from my constant reliving and questioning the events.

That first day, it took me a couple of hours to finally knit six or seven rows and be sent on my way to finish my scarf. As I got back in my car and glanced at the clock dashboard, I couldn't believe so much time had passed without me crying or falling into that agonizing What Could I Have Done Differently. Knitting, I realized then, was just what I needed to pass the hours in my heartbroken days. So satisfied was I that afternoon, I drove directly to my local grocery store, a place that had become a minefield since Grace died, full of Muzak playing her favorite songs, seasonal fruits she wasn't here to eat (blueberries in summer; seckel pears in fall), and well-meaning sympathetic acquaintances who approached me with such pity I often had to flee them.

But this day, a knitter now, already planning the sixteen scarves I would knit as presents by Christmas, I went into the Eastside Market and shopped. Until I looked up at an approaching well-wisher. Immediately, a panic attack set in. Short of breath and sweating, I fled to the safety of my car, where my knitting waited. I picked it up and knit like a crazy woman, not even really sure of what I was doing. In thirty minutes, I could no longer fit a needle into the next stitch, a sign I optimistically took as the scarf being completed.

The next morning, when Jen came to open the store, she found me waiting at the door. "I finished," I announced, holding out my lump of tangled yarn. "Finished?" she said, laughing. "Why, it's all wrong." And with that, she slid the stitches off the needle and gently pulled, sending all my hard work into the air, unraveling. I gasped. To me, a writer, that was like hitting the delete button without revising instead. But Jen just smiled at me. "Don't worry," she said. "I'm just going to fix it." "Fix it?" "In knitting," she said as she began to cast on again, "you can fix everything." Ah, the words I needed to hear most. At last, here was something I couldn't ruin. Something I could do over, and over, and over. In life, I know now, we can take that lover back or scream louder than anyone has ever screamed, but we can't rearrange the pieces. Not so in knitting. Which is why when I find myself trying to change the ending, I pick up my needles and yarn instead.

VI

BAD KNITTING

ONCE MY FRIEND Mary and I went to a knitting retreat at Ghost Ranch in Taos, New Mexico. Somewhere between the excitement of knitting together for an entire weekend, a visit with her first in Santa Fe, the gorgeous drive to Taos, and lots of margaritas, Mary and I missed that we weren't going to be working on our own projects. Instead, we were going to do lace knitting, a delicate, complicated, nearly impossible method. Lace knitting is characterized by stable "holes" in the pattern and is sometimes considered the pinnacle of knitting, because of its complexity and because woven fabrics cannot easily be made to have holes. In short, it's oxymoronic knitting. Add to this tiny needles, a pattern that required a grid similar to a Battleship game, about fifty women who knit ten or twelve hours a day for fun, and you pretty much have what our weekend held.

Friday night, I ended up taking out everything I'd done under the steely glare of a woman who asked me if I even knew how to knit at all. By Saturday afternoon, Mary and I cut class and went into town for dinner. We put wine in our coffee cups to help us get through that night's knitting. On Sunday, I gave up and worked on the fingerless gloves I'd brought with me.

What I knew going in to that retreat was that Mary is a good knitter. An excellent knitter really. She has fixed many of my knitting mistakes, picked up lots of dropped stitches for me. She knits sweaters without patterns, and she knits objects: Easter eggs and autumn pears and Christmas ornaments that look exactly like old-fashioned Christmas lights. What I realized leaving that retreat was just how bad a knitter I actually am. I did not like this realization. After all, I wrote a book called *The Knitting Circle*, which implies that I know my stuff. When I give talks, people often ask me knitting questions. I know my way around a knitting store. I have a stash of yarn and a container filled with needles of all sizes. And I knit, a lot. So the fact that, despite all of this, I am not a very good knitter came as a surprise, and a disappointment.

On the flight home, I thought about all of the truly bad knitting I had done. A raglan sweater so out of shape that it couldn't be blocked into something wearable. The sweater I knit for my daughter Annabelle that could only be rescued by turning it into a vest. All of the scarves and cowls I could not seed stitch correctly. The list grew as I headed east. Hats that didn't stay on heads. A pair of socks with one sock so large it could be hung on a mantel at Christmas. *I'm not a good knitter,* I repeated again and again. How could this possibly be?

But then I thought of all the beautiful things I'd knit. And I thought of all the things that turned out fine after months of working on them. I remembered how when I took ballet for the first time in my twenties, I never moved out of the beginner classes. I knew that I would never dance in *Swan Lake.* That I was taking ballet for fun, for the way it made me feel when the music swelled and I gracefully bent over the barre. What I was, was a very good beginner. So let it be with knitting, I decided.

Now, when I want to try something difficult, I sign up for a class. Often I'm the worst one there, but not always. I am usually the slowest, the one who asks the most questions. But unlike that weekend of lace knitting, when I make a mistake on these tough projects, I can laugh. After ten years, I am a very good beginning knitter. And that suits me just fine.

VII

THE KNITTING HOUR

"Do you still knit?" people always ask me. As if I learned to knit, wrote a book about it, and have discarded knitting altogether.

"All the time," I answer, which is mostly true.

For almost a year, I knit constantly, like it was a full-time job with lots of overtime. Grief-stricken, unable to read or write, I turned to knitting to fill the hours when Sam was in school, the hours of my insomnia, the long weekends that sometimes seemed to never end. Slowly, I began to reenter the world of words and the world of people. Some days, I read more than I knitted. Some days, I wrote more.

My knitting self seemed to know when a bad time was coming before my rational self did. Often I would realize that I had been knitting a lot because Grace's birthday was nearing, or the anniversary of her death. Even now, ten years later, when I find myself knitting more than anything else, I know grief has slapped me again.

But in general, although I carry my knitting everywhere with me, although I knit on airplanes and in airports waiting for airplanes, on long car rides or my weekly train trips into NYC, I don't knit as much as I did that sad year after Grace died, when nothing else soothed me.

Now, I like to knit for an hour at the end of an afternoon. I like, after a day of writing, to pick up Annabelle at school, help her with her homework, and then get dinner started. Maybe put on the water for pasta, chop tomatoes and basil and fresh mozzarella to toss with it when it's done. Open a bottle of wine and pour a glass, then take it into what we call the fancy living room. There, in my favorite chair, I pick up my knitting. Annabelle curls up beside me with a book or an art project. The sky turns from blue to lavender. We sit together, quiet, happy. I knit until I hear my husband's key in the lock. Then I put my knitting down, and the evening begins.

VIII

PLAYING WELL WITH OTHERS

I AM NOT A group person.

I was thrown out of Girl Scouts because I refused to do what the group wanted, which was to earn a Sewing merit badge by cutting a Clorox bottle in half and sewing a piece of fabric to it to make a curler bag. Me, I wanted the Reading merit badge, and had read double the amount of books needed to earn it. My troop leader, Mrs. D, said no, it was Sewing or nothing. I hung up my green uniform forever.

I tried book groups, writing groups, mommy groups, always with the same results. An enthusiastic beginning, an inability to behave myself, an abrupt departure.

But when I first stepped into a knitting circle, all of that changed. Unlike my character in my novel *The Knitting Circle* who found a perfect, magical one, I became a knitting circle addict. On the bulletin board in my kitchen, I kept a list of all the knitting circles within a fifty-mile radius. Like someone in AA, when the need came to knit, and knit in the company of others, I went to whichever one was meeting right then. There was the knitting circle in which everyone was older than me, by a lot. The one where everyone was younger and had tattoos. The one at the store with the bad yarn. The one led by a woman who yelled at us. The one that served wine. It didn't matter to me, I loved them all.

Unlike other groups, in a knitting circle you are really not required to say anything. It's polite to murmur approval if someone else shows what they've knitted. It's acceptable to ask for help if you get confused or make a mistake. But really, all you have to do is sit there and knit.

By now I have gone to many many knitting circles. And I realize that because of them, I actually do better in all kinds of groups. I have learned to listen, even to the person who can't stop talking about her knitting, her vacation, her husband. I have learned to respect people who are really different from me: younger or older; politically; socioeconomically; in every possible way. Because we can be together and knit and find a place for each other in this simple act. I have learned that I have a lot to learn, that the people in the knitting circle can show me shortcuts, patterns, new yarn. And I have learned that I don't always have something to say, or something to add to a group. That sometimes, I just want the company of other people. I just want to sit in a circle and knit. By doing this, maybe I am learning how to be a group person after all.

IX

THE THINGS YOU LOVE FIT IN
A ZIPLOCK BAG (OR SMALLER)

"ALL YOU HAVE to do," Stephanie told me, "is put it in a ziplock bag and then you can bring it everywhere with you."

Stephanie taught me how to knit socks on size 2 needles, maneuvering four of them at once like a puppeteer. I loved the sock yarn, how it revealed a pattern as I knit. I even loved those tiny needles, once I learned how to keep my stitches on them. I knit socks and gave them away—to my friend Barbara bedridden with cancer, to a friend off to Siberia on a grant. People are stunned into silence when you give them a pair of hand-knit socks. Pablo Neruda wrote: "What is good is doubly good / when it is a matter of two socks."

I took Stephanie's advice and placed my socks in progress on the tiny needles into a ziplock bag when I next traveled. On the plane, I took the bag out and happily knit to my destination. Ever since, I travel only with projects that fit in a ziplock bag. Which got me thinking one day as my plane to Florence took off and I removed my needles and yarn from their plastic bag. As I've gotten older, I travel alone a lot. This is funny to me, because when I was twenty-one, I became a TWA flight attendant and flew around the world, mostly alone. Back then, although I loved my freedom and independence, I often spent lonely hours roaming exotic cities, gazing at the Pyramids or navigating the steep route to the Acropolis, by myself. At night, I tossed in the strange hotel beds, missing my boyfriend or my parents or even my dog Maggie. I was a happy traveler, but I would wonder: Are they okay? What are they doing right now? I would convert the time zones, subtracting seven or five or nine to better picture exactly where they were in their lives.

Now, like my knitting, I have a way of holding the people I leave behind close. Maybe it's because I have lost so many of them and have had to learn the hard lesson that even so, they are still with me. Maybe it's because they can't come—my mother is aging, my husband is busy, my son is away at college, my daughter is too young.

Even so, I feel them all with me, tucked away. I take them out when I need to and hold them near me, always.

X

CASTING OFF

I T'S WHAT YOU DO when you finish knitting, you cast off the stitches. Some people call it binding off, but that sounds so final, so shut down. To me, you cast off. You send your knitted hat or mittens or socks away, onto your child's hands, your husband's head, your friend's feet. I keep almost nothing that I knit for myself. I used to. I kept that scarf in case I bought a coat it would match. I kept a stack of headbands that I would never wear. But then one day, someone—a knitter—gave *me* a scarf and hat she'd knit, gave it to me for no good reason except that she thought they matched my hair. "I feel good when I give my knitting away," she said. And ever since then, I give mine away. I cast it off into the world. Like good wishes, or love, I give it away.

"bowden"
coffee cozies

by Helen Bingham

Three unique patterns to fit to-go coffee cups. Using double-pointed needles and fingerling-weight yarn create a cabled, Fair Isle, or just a ribbed cozy. When I first learned how to knit, my go-to person was my mother-in-law, Jan Bowden. She always had the time and patience to answer my questions and fix my mistakes. In doing so she has taught me about perseverance and unconditional love. To this day she is always there for my family and myself.

MATERIALS:

1 skein Fingering in three colors by Claudia Hand Painted Yarns (100% extra fine merino wool with 175 yards)

Colors: Whirled Peas (#8129) for the ribbed version, Honey (#8037) for the cabled version, and CC for the Fair Isle version, Tranquility (#8096) MC for the Fair Isle version

OR

1 skein Sock in three colors by ShiBui (100% merino wool with 191 yards)

Colors: Ash, Ivory, Wasabi, Midnight, and Spectrum

US 3 double-pointed needles or size needed to obtain gauge

SIZE: one size fits most "to go" coffee cups

FINISHED SIZE: Average: 3.5" height × 9" circumference

The ribbed version finished, laid flat, measures 3½" long × 2¼" wide.

The cabled version finished, laid flat, measures 4½" long × 3" wide.

The Fair Isle version, finished, laid flat, measures 4" long × 3¼" wide.

GAUGE: 28 sts = 4" in 2×2 rib

PATTERN NOTES & ABBREVIATIONS:

C4B = slip next 2 sts to cable needle and hold in back of work, knit next 2 sts from left-hand needle, then knit sts from cable needle

C4F = slip next 2 sts to cable needle and hold in front of work, knit next 2 sts from left-hand needle, then knit sts from cable needle

MC = main color

CC = contrast color

DIRECTIONS:

DECAF (RIBBED VERSION):

—Using Whirled Peas (variegated yarn), cast on 56 sts, divide sts among needles as follows: 18 sts on first and third needle and 20 sts on second needle.

—Join into the round, being careful not to twist stitches using your tail as the start of the round marker.

—Work the following round:

Round 1: (Knit 2 sts, Purl 2 sts) repeat across round.

—Repeat this round till cozy is 3.5″ from cast on edge.

—Cast off in pattern stitch.

—Weave in all ends and lightly steam.

EXTRA- EXTRA (CABLED VERSION):

—Using Honey (solid colored) yarn, cast on 65 sts, divide sts among needles as follows: 21 sts on first needle, 24 sts on second needle, and 20 sts on third needle.

—Join into the round, being careful not to twist stitches using your tail as the start of the round marker.

—Work the following rounds:

Round 1: (P2, K8, P2, K1tbl)5 times

Round 2: (P2, K8, P2, K1tbl)5 times

Round 3: (P2, K8, P2, K1tbl)5 times

Round 4: (P2, C4B, C4F, P2, K1tbl)5 times

Round 5: (P2, K8, P2, K1tbl)5 times

Round 6: (P2, K8, P2, K1tbl)5 times

Round 7: (P2, K8, P2, K1tbl)5 times

Round 8: (P2, C4F, C4B, P2, K1tbl)5 times

Round 9: (P2, K8, P2, K1tbl)5 times

Round 10: (P2, K8, P2, K1tbl)5 times

Round 11: (P2, K8, P2, K1tbl)5 times

Round 12: (P2, C4F, C4B, P2, K1tbl)5 times

Round 13: (P2, K8, P2, K1tbl)5 times

Round 14: (P2, K8, P2, K1tbl)5 times

Round 15: (P2, K8, P2, K1tbl)5 times

Round 16: (P2, C4B, C4F, P2, K1tbl)5 times.

—Repeat Rounds 1 through 16 a total of 2 times.

—Work Rounds 1 through 13.

—Cast off all stitches in pattern.

—Weave in all ends and lightly steam.

REGULAR (FAIR ISLE VERSION):

—Using Tranquility (MC), cast on 60 sts, divide st among needles as follows: 20 sts on first needle, 20 sts on second needle and 20 sts on third needle.

—Join into the round, being careful not to twist stitches using your tail as the start of the round marker.

—Work the following round:

Round 1: (Knit 2 sts, Purl 2 sts) repeat across round

—Repeat this round a total of 5 times.

—Work the following rounds knitting every stitch but using the color as dictated:

Round 1: MC1, (CC1, MC3)14 times, CC1, MC2 (Honey is CC)

Round 2: (CC3, MC1)15 times

Round 3: (CC3, MC1)15 times

Round 4: MC1, (CC1, MC3)14 times, CC1, MC2

—Repeat these four rounds a total of 6 times ending with Round 4.

—Work the following round:

Round 1: Using MC: (Knit 2 sts, Purl 2 sts) repeat across round

—Repeat this round a total of 5 times.

—Cast off all stitches in pattern stitch.

—Weave in all ends and lightly steam.

For pictures of these patterns, go to www.helenbinghamdesigns.com.

judite

by Kaylie Jones

Her nanny Judite was the Queen of Crochet. Through her intricate, beautiful gifts she tried to communicate all the feelings she had no words to express in their daily life together. Unfortunately, it took the author her entire life to understand what Judite was trying to say.

J
UDITE CAME FROM ALPIARCA, A SMALL FARMING VILLAGE two hundred kilometers from Lisbon. I never could get her to tell me how old she was when she quit school, but there was tragedy and scandal in the family—her father had fled, leaving Judite's mother and three small children to fend for themselves. Judite had to go to work. When she was old enough, like many Portuguese girls of her generation, she went to Paris to become a nanny. That's where she found us. She was twenty-five when she came to work for my parents, and I was two months old. Her bedroom in our apartment was right next to mine, while my parents were all the way on the other end and down a flight of stairs. Judite had a single bed and a small rug over the blue linoleum floor. On the walls she hung small, bright prints in gold frames of biblical scenes—Jesus with his

hands spread out, feeding loaves and fishes to the masses; the Virgin Mary sitting demurely in her pale blue robes, holding the infant Jesus in her arms, yellow rays radiating from their halos. Above the bed she'd nailed a crucifix with a very lifelike Jesus who had wide, suffering eyes, and blood dripping from his wounds.

There was a small table with three chairs, covered by a tablecloth she'd fashioned out of plain white cotton fabric, along the edges of which she had embroidered a pattern of green leaves and pink roses. Sometimes, on Saturday evenings, other girls from Alpiarca would come by to gossip and have a glass of Porto. They thought I couldn't understand them, but by the age of four I knew enough Portuguese to absorb the gist of their conversations. Maria's *patron* kept two mistresses, and his wife had no idea! Laocadia's *Madame* took too many sleeping pills. Judite never volunteered much about my parents, only that they spent a fortune on liquor (she knew because she ordered it and did the household accounting) and that she worried they left me too often alone.

When I pointed out to my mother that I spent more time with Judite than with her, she said, quite indignantly, "One day you'll realize that Judite is only a maid, a servant. She's not your mother. I'm your mother."

In a corner of Judite's room was an old-fashioned thick black sewing machine that stood on its own narrow worktable, with a pedal underneath that made the needle stop and go. That thing terrified me and I wouldn't go near it. Judite also had a large, lidded wicker basket that contained her crochet work. Sewing, Judite did because she'd always had to, she told me, but her real love was crochet. I spent hours in her room watching the miracles of her handiwork take shape before my eyes. She'd learned as a little girl, at her mother's knee. In her crochet basket she kept books filled with patterns and sometimes Judite copied designs from photos she found in newspapers or magazines. She crocheted soft sweaters, and wool hats with multicolored, multilayered flowers on their brims; she made antimacassars out of the finest white cotton thread, complex patterns representing birds, flowers, stars, and all sorts of convoluted geometrical shapes. My mother loved cats and for Christmas one year Judite spent five months crocheting a set for our living room couches that had cats as the centerpiece. My mother did not know what to do with them. She murmured to me, when I asked her if she liked them, that she found them old-fashioned and perhaps a little low-class. She must have put them away somewhere, for I never saw them again.

Judite made doilies in the shapes of flowers for her girlfriends' weddings, which were happening more and more often now. Soon she was crocheting baby clothes. Every time she went to a wedding or a christening, she brought me back those candy-coated pink, yellow, and blue almonds with little silver candy beads sprinkled among them, in tiny white mesh purses with satin bows.

"When are you going to get married, Didi?" I'd ask her. I called her Didi. As a baby, I'd said Mama, Dada, and then Didi.

Bowed over her handiwork, she would giggle and blush and say, "Eh, perhaps one day."

When I was around six, I asked her to teach me to crochet. Immediately she handed me a crochet needle and a ball of fine red yarn. She made a little knot over her index finger and started me on a simple chain stitch. She painstakingly showed me, over and over, how to pull the yarn tight between my left index finger and pinkie, and hook the needle through the loop. I was able to crochet one fairly even row of simple chain stitches, but when it was time to go back the other way and build upon what I had created, I was overwhelmed. I was not a patient, easy child; concentrating was hard for me and I was easily bored. My report cards told my parents I was "*disippée*"—undisciplined—though, in my teachers' opinion, I was not lacking in intelligence. The truth was, I had insomnia and night terrors and was always exhausted. The only night of the week my parents stayed home was Sunday, and that was because it was Judite's night off. Every American in Paris knew it was open house on Sunday nights at the Joneses'. I started worrying around five in the afternoon that I would not be able to sleep, and when I'd awaken screaming in the middle of the night, Judite would not be there to placate me.

I persevered with my crocheting efforts, until I had managed to complete, with a good deal of help from Judite, a long, narrow scarf for my baby doll. I decided that no matter how much effort I put into learning, I would never be any good. I was riding a bicycle and Judite was piloting a rocket ship. And anyway, watching her strong, pale fingers working so swiftly and effortlessly, her fantastic designs materializing before my eyes, was much more fun than crocheting myself; so I went back to watching and offering her suggestions, which she received with alacrity and a warmhearted laugh.

TROLL DOLLS WERE all the rage in the States that next summer and I came back from our vacation with two large and three small Trolls—stark naked, the way they came in their packaging. They had hefty, androgynous plastic bodies, stout short legs and arms, and long hair in electric primary colors that looked like cotton candy and stood straight up from the crown of their heads. Their huge glass eyes came in different colors, but their upturned noses were all exactly the same. Judite found them to be the strangest dolls she had ever seen and they never failed to make her giggle. Nevertheless, I conscripted her into crocheting them outfits, which I imagined and described for her on the spur of the moment. She crocheted them halter dresses, swimsuits, sweaters, pantsuits, nightgowns, hats and scarves—all with little snaps and buttons since their arms and legs did not move, it was a bit like trying to dress a tree branch—but nothing was above her capabilities. I had the best and most elegantly dressed Trolls in Paris and was the envy of the other American Troll doll owners at the École Active Bilingue.

When I turned twelve and my breasts grew, almost overnight, I refused to go shopping for bras. There was just no way in the world I was going into a lingerie store to get measured by some stranger. However, the American girls in my school told me I couldn't go around "like that," just wearing undershirts anymore, so I went to Judite and asked her if she could make me a bra. She measured me, then set about crocheting the cups and straps out of a very fine, peach-colored stretchy yarn. She lined the cups with shiny satin, slightly darker than the yarn. Every day I asked her impatiently when my bra would be ready as I watched her crocheting, her fingers moving fast and swift as she worked. "Aïe!" she cried, and examined her finger. She had stabbed herself with the thin crochet needle and drawn blood.

It took her more than a week, for she had very little free time with all her other chores. Finally, the day arrived and I tried on my new bra in front of my closet mirror, having made Judite leave the room. The bra was indeed an original, with a pattern of tiny pale pink flowers, the darker satin peeping through the holes in the crochet, creating a bas-relief effect. Yet the bra, just like Judite, had an air of innocence and purity, which was not exactly the effect I'd been hoping for.

Boys had begun to call and often she would not give me their messages.

In school, in the locker room, when I changed for *gymnastique*, my new bra suffered ignominious teasing from the American girls in their plain white Playtex Cross Your Hearts. I went home and yelled at Judite and threw the bra in a drawer and never wore it again. She never said a word and I never apologized.

Judite, now nearing forty, told me she was saving her money to build herself and her mother a big house near the beach in Portugal. There would be rooms for herself and her future husband, and for her mother, and for her sister and brother and their spouses and children, and of course, for me, and my future family. She hoped I would have lots of children and we would always be welcome in her home. We could come during the summer, for no beaches were more beautiful than the ones in Portugal, she told me. Even the crazy pale English went there for their vacations and turned red as boiled lobsters in the sun.

MY FAMILY RETURNED to the States in 1974, and Judite stayed on in Paris. My parents did not ask her to come with us. I was growing up; they thought my attachment to her was unhealthy for a girl my age. Judite took a job as a housekeeper with a couple who had no children, and remained with them for the next twenty-five years. "No more children," she said to me over the phone when I called her, feeling lonely and misunderstood. *"C'est trop pénible."* It's too painful.

When I was sixteen, seven weeks short of my high school graduation, my father died of congestive heart failure, caused by malaria he'd caught in the Pacific during the war, and greatly exacerbated by drink; I fell apart.

After two difficult years of college, I returned to Paris for my junior year. Judite took care of me. Up under the eaves of the servants' quarters in her new *patron's* apartment building, she prepared my favorite meals, crocheted me a multicolored purse and a winter scarf and hat. She was afraid I was not eating enough, and that I would be cold. She did not know that I was drinking. She did not see how her crochet designs were for a much younger girl, hopelessly out of style for a nineteen-year-old college student. I never was able to tell her about the longing and the loneliness I had felt as a child and still felt now, as a young adult, or the fear that always stayed with me that seemed to involve some ominous presaging of my family's collapse. I was afraid of being alone. I *was* alone. All I had was Judite, and her crocheting and her comfort food, and it was not enough. I put the purse and scarf and hat away and did not bring them home with me to the States when my semester abroad came to an end.

FINALLY, AT SIXTY-FIVE, Judite retired and went home to Portugal. She told me in a letter that the house she'd built for herself and her mother was too big, too cold in winter, and far too lonely; her brother had moved to Brazil; and her sister, married to a British merchant marine, had no time to cross the Channel to visit. Then, Judite called to tell me that her mother had passed away.

She sold her dream house and moved into an apartment in the town of Caldas da Rainha. A few years later, at seventy-three, she married for the first time. Her groom, Virgilio, was seventy-nine, and a widower. He was a retired optometrist, she told me proudly over the phone, and had, in his youth, traveled to the U.S. to take an advanced course.

. . .

THIS YEAR, ON THE first warm day of spring, my fourteen-year-old daughter and I were shopping at a hipster store popular among Manhattan teens. I saw a crocheted tunic draped over a mannequin; it was mauve, fashioned in a loose diamond pattern, with little flowers at the corners of each diamond. I stopped to gaze at it, and finally my daughter persuaded me try it on. There were six of them, exactly the same, hanging from a metal rod. I took one and went into a changing room. Judite liked to crochet tight, it took more work but nothing ever unraveled. It was a beautiful tunic, and very expensive. I took it off and put it back on the hanger. On the way home I was glum and silent. My daughter asked me what was wrong. I did not know what to say. "My nanny Judite used to crochet," I told her, my voice hollow. "She made me the most beautiful things."

"Where are they?" my pragmatic child wanted to know.

How can you explain to a teen that by the time you realize the value of a thing, it's usually gone?

I THOUGHT ABOUT Judite over the next several weeks. On Mother's Day, I decided to call her. Judite and Virgilio had moved back to Alpiarca, Judite's hometown, after he suffered a severe stroke. I searched everywhere for their new phone number, which for some reason I never transferred to the address book on my computer. Finally, I found her mobile coordinates in an old leather-bound address book. My heart was racing as the phone rang. What if she'd gotten rid of that phone?

She must have recognized my number, because the moment she

picked up, she began a long, joyous litany in Portuguese. I started laughing and reminded her to speak French. Finally, she calmed down. She told me Virgilio was recovering some of his mobility, but the progress was slow.

I explained that it was Mother's Day here in the States and I had been thinking of her. "I never thanked you for all the beautiful clothes you crocheted for me," I said, my voice catching.

"It was nothing," she replied.

"No, it was everything," I said, "and I never said thank you."

She told me my call was a great gift on this joyous, important holiday in Portugal, Our Lady of Fatima Day. May 13, Judite explained, was the first day the Virgin appeared to the three shepherd children of Fatima in 1917.

"Is there anything I can do for you, anything you need?" I asked, feeling somewhat helpless.

"I have only one desire," she said, "and that is to see you again in this life."

where to begin

by Barbara Kingsolver

The writer looks at all the ways it begins . . .

IT ALL STARTS WITH THE WEATHER. COMES A DAY WHEN summer finally gives in to the faintest freshet of chill and a slim new light and just like that, you're gone. Wild in love with the autumn proviso. You can see that the standing trees are all busy lighting themselves up ember-orange around the hemline, starting their ritual drama of slow self-immolation, oh well, you see it all. The honkling chain-gang of boastful geese overhead that are fleeing warmward-ho, chuckling over their big escape. But not you. One more time, here for the duration you will stick it out. Through the famously appley wood-smoked season that opens all heart's doors into kitchen industry and soup on the stove, the signs wink at you from everywhere: sticks of kindling in the fire, long white brushstrokes of snow on the branches, this is the whole world calling you to take up your paired swords against the brace of the oncoming freeze. The two-plied strands of your chromosomes have been spun by all thin-skinned creatures for all of time, and now they offer you no more bottomless thrill than the point-nosed plow of preparedness. It begins on the morning you see your children's bare feet swinging under the table while they eat their cereal cold and you shudder from stem to stern like a dog hauling up from the lake, but you can't throw off the clammy pall of those little pink-palmy feet. You will swaddle your children in wool, in spite of themselves.

It starts with a craving to fill the long evening downslant. There will be whole wide days of watching winter drag her skirts across the mud-yard from east to west, going nowhere. You will want to nail down all these wadded handfuls of time, to stick-pin them to the blocking board, frame them on a 24-stitch gauge. Ten to the inch, ten rows to the hour, straggling trellises of days held fast in the acreage of a shawl. Time by this means will be domesticated and cannot run away. You pick up sticks because time is just asking for it, already lost before it arrives, scattering trails of leavings. The frightful movie your family has chosen for Friday night, just for instance. They insist it will be watched, and so with just the one lamp turned on at the end of the sofa you can be there too, keeping your hands busy and your eyeshades half drawn, yes people will be murdered, cars will be wrecked, and you will come through in one piece, plus a pair of mittens. It's all the same wherever you go, the river is rife with doldrums and eddies, the waiting room, the plane, the train, the learned lecture, the meeting. Oh, sweet mother of Christ, the meeting. The PTA the town council the school board the bored-board, the interminably haggled items of the agenda. Your feet want to run for their lives but your fingers know to dig in the bag and unsheathe their handy stays against impatience, the smooth paired oars, the sturdy lifeboat of yarn. This giant unwieldy meeting may bottom-drag and list on its keel, stranded in the Sargasso Sea of

Agenda, but you alone will sail away on your thrifty raft of unwasted time. You alone are swaddling the world in wool.

Strangely, it also begins with the opposite: a hankering to lose time and all sense of purpose. To banish all possibilities, the winter and the summer, the bare feet under the table, the shattered day undone and dregs of old regard and bitter unsettled tea leaves and the words forever jostling ahead of each other in line, queuing up to be written. Especially those. Words that drub, drub, drub at the skull's concave inner wall. Words that are birds in a linear flock, pelting themselves in ruined fury all night long against the window-pane. Nothing can stop the words so well as the mute alphabet of knit and purl. The curl of your cupped hand scoops up long drinks of calm. The rhythm you find is from down inside, rocking cradle, heartbeat, ocean. Waves on a rockless shore.

Sometimes it starts terribly. With the injury or the accident or the wrecked life flung down like a loud armload of broken chair legs on your doorstep. Here lies the recuperation, whose miles you can't even see across, let alone traverse. Devil chasm of woe uncrossable by any known bridge, here lies you. And in comes the friend bearing needles of blond bamboo—twin shafts of light!—and ombré skeins in graded shades that march through the stages of grief, burnt umber to ochre to gold to dandelion. She is not in a listening mood, the friend. Today she commands you to make something of all this. And to your broken heart's surprise, you do.

It begins with the circle of friends. There is always something beyond your beyond, the aged parents and teenager who crack up the family cars on the selfsame day, there is the bone-picked divorce, the winter of chemo, the gorgeous mistake, the long unraveling misery that needs company, reading glasses and glasses of wine and all the chairs pulled into the living room. Project bags bulge like sacks of oranges, ripe for beginning. Cast on, knit two together girlfriend-wise. Rip it, pick up the pieces where you can, along the headless yoke or scandalously loose button placket, pick up and knit. Always, you will have to keep two projects going: first, the no-brainer stockinette that can run on cruise-control when the talk is delicious. And the other one, the brainer, a maddening intarsia or fussy Fair Isle you'll save for the day when the chat gets less interesting, though really it never does. Knitting only makes the talk go softer, as long as it needs to be, fondly ribbed and yarned-over, loosely structured or not at all, with embellishment on every edge. Laughter makes dropped stitches.

It begins with a pattern. The arresting helical twist of a double cable, a gusset, a hexagon, a spiral, a fractal, an openwork ladder, an aran braid, a chevron and leaf, the eyes of the lynx, the traveling vines. The mimsy camisole you arguably could live without, the munificent cardigan you need. A mitten lost in childhood, returned to you in a dream. A pattern in a magazine, devised of course to tantalize. More embarrassing yet, the pattern hallooing from your neighbor's sweater while you're only trying for small talk, distracting you until finally you have to stop, apologize and ask permission to stare and memorize the lay of her sweater's land. And once it all starts, there's no stopping. The frame of your four double-points is a sturdy raised bed from which you cultivate the lively apical stem of sock-sleeve-stocking-cap. It's all in the growing. From the seed of pattern, the cotyledons of cast-on, everything rises: xylem and phloem of KP ribs, a trunk of body and branches of sleeves, the skirt that bells downward daffodilwise. You with your needles are god of this wild botany. It begins the first time you take the familiar map in hand, scowling it over with all best intentions, then throw it over your shoulder and head out to uncharted waters where there be monsters. Only there will you ever discover the promised land of garments heretofore undevised. Gloves for the extra long of hand, or short, or the firecracker nephew with one digit missing in action. Sweaters for the short-waisted, the broad-shouldered, the precise petite. Soon they are lining up, friends and family all covetous of the bespoke, because your best beloveds are human after all, and not off-the-rack. You can envelop each of them in the bliss of a perfect fit.

And a perfect color. It starts there too. Every eye has hungers all its own. The particular green-silver of leaves overturned by the oncoming storm. An alkaline desert's russet bronze, a mustard of Appalachian spring, some bright spectral intangible you find you long to possess. Colors are fertilized in vitro with the careful spoon and the potent powder weighed to the iota, and born by baptism in the big dye kettle hauled onto the stove. Flaccid beige hanks back-stroke listlessly in the boiling ink, waiting to be born-again, until some perfect storm of chemical zeal moves them suddenly to awaken and drink down all the dye molecules in a trice. Like a miracle, the dark liquid goes clear as water before your very eyes. Afterward the damp yarn sings its good news from dripping loops in the laundry room, waiting to meet the pattern the wish the cool weather the living room the days-long patient fortune.

It starts with a texture. There are nowhere near enough words for this, but fingers can sing whole arpeggios at a touch. Textures have their family trees: cloud and thistledown are cousin to catpelt and earlobe and infantscalp. Petal is also a texture, and lime peel and nickelback and nettle and five o'clock shadow and sandstone and ash and soap and slither. Drape is the child of loft and crimp; wool is a stalwart crone who remembers everything, while emptyhead white-haired cotton forgets. And in spite of their various natures, all these strings can be lured to sit down together and play a fiber concerto whole in the cloth. The virgin fleece of an April lamb can be blended and spun with the fleece of a fat blue hare or a twist of flax, anything, you name it, silkworm floss or twiny bamboo. Creatures never known to converse in nature can be introduced and then married right on the spot. The spindle is your altar, you are the matchmaker, steady on the treadle, fingers plying the helices of a beast and its unlikely kin, animal and vegetable, devising your new and surprisingly peaceable kingdoms. Fingers can coax and read and speak, they have their own secret libraries, and illicit affairs, and conventions. Twined into the wool of a hearty ewe on shearing day, hands can read the history of her winter: how many snows, how barren or sweet her mangers. For best results, stand in the pasture and throw your arms around her.

Because really, it does start there, in the barn on shearing day. The circle of friends again, assembled for shearing and skirting. One whole fleece, shorn all of a piece, is flung out on a table like a picnic blanket surrounded by women. All hands point toward the center like an excessive, introverted clock, the better for combing the white fleece with all those fingers, combing the black, fingers can see in the dark to pull out twigs and manure tags and cockleburs. White fleeces shaken free of second cuts, rolled and bundled and stacked, ready for spinning, look for all the world like loaves of bread on a bakery shelf, or sheaves of grain or any other money in the bank. The universal currency of a planet where people grow cold. On shearing day all ledgers will be balanced, the sheep lined up in the gates are woolly by morning and naked by night, as the barrows fill and the spindles make ready and warmth is bankrolled in futures. Six women can skirt a fleece in ten minutes, just enough time to run and collect the next one, so long as the shearer is handy. It starts early, this day, and goes long.

It starts in the barn on other days too, every morning of the year in fact. The sheep are both eager and wary at the sight of you, the bringer of hay, the reaper of wool, as you enter the barn for the daily accounts. You switch on the overhead bulb and inhale the florid scents of sweet-feed and hay and mineral urine and there they stand all eyeing you with horizontal pupils, reliably here for every occasion, the blizzard nights and early spring mornings of lambing. You hurry out at dawn to find dumbfounded mothers of twins licking their wispy trembling slips of children, exhorting them to look alive in the guttural chortle that only comes into the throat of a ewe when she's just given birth. The sloe-eyed flock mistrusts you fundamentally but still they will all come running when you shake the exquisite bucket of grain, the money that talks to yearlings and chary weth-ers alike, and loudest of all to the ravenous barrel-round pregnant ewes. They gallop home with their udders tolling like church bells. In all weather you take their measure and send them out again to the pasture. And oh, how willingly they return to their posts, with their gentle gear-grinding jaws and slowly thickening wool under winter's advance, beginning your sweater for you at the true starting gate.

Everything starts, of course, with the sheep and the grass. Beneath her greening scalp the earth frets and dreams, and knits herself wordless. Between her breasts, on all hillsides too steep for the plow, the sheep place little sharp feet on invisible paths and lead their curly-haired sons and daughters out onto the tart green blades of eternal breakfast. It starts on tumbled-up lambspring mornings when you slide open the heavy barn door and expel the pronking gambol of newborn wildhooray into daylight. And in summer haze when they scramble up onto boulders and scan the horizon with eyes made to fit it just-so, horizontal eyes, flattened to that shape by the legions of distant skulking predators avoided for all of time.

And in the gloaming, when the ewes high up on the pasture suddenly raise their heads at the sight of you, conceding to come down as a throng in their rockinghorse gait, surrendering under dog-press to the barn-tendered mercy of nightfall. It starts where everything starts, with the weather. The muffleblind snows, the dingle springs, the singular pursuit of cud, the fibrous alchemy of the herd spinning grass into wool. This is all your business. Hands plunged into a froth of yarn are as helpless as hands thrust into a lover's hair, for they are divining the grass-pelt life of everything: the world. The sunshine, heavenly photosynthetic host, sweet leaves of grass all singing the fingers electric that tingle to brace the coming winter, charged by the plied double helices of all creatures that have prepared and justly survived on the firmament of patience and swaddled children. It's all of a piece, knitting. All one thing.

the one-year marriage

by Jennifer Lauck

The writer knits her way through a brief, bad marriage.

"**L**ET'S GET SOMETHING STRAIGHT," MAXINE SAYS. "YOU'RE both equally screwed up."

We're getting a talking-to—Husband Number Three and me. It's tough-love marriage counseling.

We just arrived at Maxine's teeny tiny box of an office on the east side of Portland, Oregon. We aren't even through her narrow door. I still have my purse and a canvas bag that holds my knitting over my shoulder. Husband Number Three hasn't had time to shrug off his coat.

"Well go on then, sit down," Maxine says.

She waves us into her cubicle-sized space—three chairs, a collapsible Asian screen that cuts the view of her desk and a narrow shelf of books showcasing the relationship collection of Harville Hendrix: *Getting the Love You Want, Keeping the Love You Find, Giving the Love That*

Heals, Make Up, Don't Break Up, Wired for Love, Loving Your Companion Without Losing Your Self, The Couples Companion, and *Receiving Love.*

Hendrix is Maxine's guru. She teaches his technique called Imago.

"In my thirty years, I've never seen a couple who didn't have perfectly matched neuroses," Maxine continues. "We don't play the blame game here. If you spot it, you've got it."

Maxine perches on a black office chair. She is a large-breasted woman of medium height with a mushroom formation of red-brown hair that curls along the edge of her jaw. She wears high heels, bell-bottoms, and a tight Western shirt that snaps up the front in such a way her breasts snug together to create an impressive quantity of cleavage. Her lipstick is a deep shade of maroon.

Husband Number Three and I just attended her three-day intensive. Over the weekend I discovered I am the hailstorm in the relationship (high anxiety and hyper reactive). Husband Number Three is the turtle (depressed, passive, and withdrawn). Maxine says she has seen our dynamic a thousand times.

I don't like Maxine. She's loud, bossy, and she cut me off several times over the weekend when I had a question. But some of what she says makes sense. While Husband Number Three and his irksome nature grates on me the way it would grate to chew on tinfoil, I have plenty of faults too.

Husband Number Three is an extremely tall man with sandy-colored hair and a pasty Midwestern complexion made more so by our damp climate and lack of sun. He takes off his jacket and drops his lanky body into one of the two upholstered chairs, plush U formations with low seats and high armrests. Orangeish brown. Once down, he's all squished up like a toothpaste tube near its end. His knees splay wide and his shoulders lift near his ears.

I'm not as tall as Husband Number Three, not as wide in the shoulders. I fit in my chair just fine.

It's winter 2011. I've been with Husband Number Three about four years. We married last July with my best friend, Anne, as witness. As soon as the honeymoon ended, the therapy began.

"WE START WITH APPRECIATION," Maxine instructs. She points her angular chin toward Husband Number Three. "This is your time to tell Jennifer what you appreciate about her."

His watery blue eyes go blink, blink, blink behind the wire-framed glasses perched at the end of his narrow nose. While Maxine talks, it's *blink, blink, blink*. While he thinks, it's *blink, blink, blink*. While I wait to be appreciated, it's *blink, blink, blink*.

He is one of those mellow people you are just sure is on medication. Or at least smoking weed. He talks slow. He walks slow. He eats slow. He's a turtle.

"I appreciate you are here," Husband Number Three finally says. His voice modulated and even. *Blink, blink, blink.*

"Now, you mirror, Jennifer," Maxine says. "Word for word."

"So what I hear you say is that you appreciate I am here," I say.

Maxine nods with approval. "Now, you ask if there is more," she says.

"More?"

"Another appreciation."

"Do I need another appreciation?"

A small smile cracks over her serious face. Maroon lipstick smudges her front tooth.

"That's how it works," she says.

I eyeball my oversized purse wedged next to an orange plastic cube that acts as a side table. Next to it is my canvas knitting bag with a blue earth stenciled on the outside. The earth stencil has been modified to look like a woman's face. The man in the moon. The woman on the earth. Under the earth stencil, it reads: Listen to your mother.

I want to fish out my knitting and pick up where I left off. If I could just knit, I tell myself, I could calm down. If I could just knit, I'd be okay.

Maxine clears her throat to grab my attention.

"What's the question again?" I ask.

KNITTING BEGAN AS a productive way to express anxiety. I was unhappy with Husband Number Three but didn't understand why. He was, based on appearances (and his résumé), the perfect guy. I channeled inexplicable emotions—primarily a burning rage—into yarn and needles. And while I busied my hands, I tried to figure him out.

The truth was this: Husband Number Three set me on edge. Anne called him a spectator on the edge of life and it was true, he was a voyeur wherever he went. He didn't join conversations or have opinions. He was just there, detached and solitary. But that wasn't the reason I felt so much anxiety. There was something else that was "off" about him. He did these odd little things that bugged the shit out of me. If I asked him to keep his chickens (yes, he kept chickens) out of my roses he'd say "fine," but every single day, his girls were in the bushes. Peck, peck, peck. If I asked him to pick up his dog's doo, he'd say he did but then I'd find crap all over the yard. If I asked if he paid the mortgage, he would say, "yes, of course," but then we'd get a call from the bank—where was the check?

They were the kind of things that usually, in a relationship, are just part of life. He was the absentminded one and I was the A-type but I had a gut sense there was something more ominous at work. This guy seemed to exist in a realm outside the bounds of personal accountability, as if he could do whatever he wanted and there would be no consequence. Or worse, and more sinister, I worried he was a person who did these strange behaviors in order to rouse reaction. Was he like the bully who needled the smaller kid?

As I thought about all these possibilities, I transformed myself into a knitting machine. I watched YouTube and taught myself how to cast on, knit, purl, and cast off. I made trips to The Yarn Garden and got lost in all the textures and colors—cashmere, merino, woolen blends, red, purple, yellow, green. Those closest to me soon inherited knitted delights: a scarf, a hat, and fingerless gloves, which are so easy to make.

"I APPRECIATE YOUR WILLINGNESS to keep trying to work things out," Husband Number Three says.

Maxine hovers near our knees, close enough to touch. I can smell her breath—Tic Tac fresh. She nods that it's my turn to respond.

"So what I hear you say . . ." I begin.

WHEN I MET HUSBAND Number Three he was The Doctor, a highly recommended acupuncture specialist. He headed up a clinic and was a longtime professor at a local college.

"I'm here for what I think are trauma-related flashbacks," I told The Doctor at my first appointment.

I sat on a beige Naugahyde table in his examining room. It was covered with a white sheet of that waxy paper. When I moved, the paper made a horrible crinkle sound.

"Sexual abuse," I added. "Can you help with that kind of thing?"

The Doctor had his hands deep in the pockets of his white doctor jacket. *Blink, blink, blink.*

"Sexual abuse is my expertise," he said. "I have a personal interest in post-traumatic stress disorder."

"You think I have PTSD?"

"Flashbacks are part of PTSD," he said.

The Doctor put out his hand, palm up. An invitation. "I'll start with your pulses," he said.

"I APPRECIATE WHAT A good mother you are," Husband Number Three says, appreciation number three.

"Oh, that's a good one," Maxine coos. During our weekend workshop, Maxine shared the fact of her own motherhood. She has a daughter, I think, and a son.

I have a daughter and a son. Josephine, who is nine, and Spencer, who is thirteen. They are my children from a marriage that ended years ago, and Husband Number Two sees them every day. He lives up the street and despite our divorce we are pretty good friends.

In confidence, both kids confess Husband Number Three makes them feel odd.

"No one is *that* nice," Josephine says.

"He *never* gets mad," Spencer adds. "That's just not right."

·   ·   ·

"So what I hear you say is that you appreciate what a good mother I am," I say. "Is that right?"

"Right," Husband Number Three says.

"Is there more?" I ask.

He shakes his head. That's it.

According to the clock, we've eaten fifteen minutes of a ninety-minute appointment.

"Okay, Jennifer," Maxine says. "It's your turn."

When I came to see The Doctor, I was one of those people who had been through a lot. At three days old, I was adopted. When I was seven, my adoptive mother died of cancer. When I was nine, my adoptive father died of a heart attack. By ten, my adoptive brother and I were split up and raised in separate families—a little like foster care except that I was adopted a second time. When I was twenty, my adoptive brother killed himself.

I knew all about my personal tragedies, I had them all lined up and sorted out. I wrote books about my life, talked to therapists, and tried like hell to be a sane, normal person, a good citizen, a good mother, a good wife.

When I came to The Doctor, I was specifically trying to understand what happened at a summer camp in 1972. It had been the year after my mother died and the year before my father would be dead. Memories were in my senses, this series of flash-card snapshots I could hear, smell, and taste: Children's voices and laughter. The bittersweet smell of sweat and body odor and sex. The salted taste of blood in my sinuses and throat.

Over several weekly appointments with The Doctor, I unreeled the memory in bits. A camp counselor. He was eighteen? Or twenty? Being forced to take off my clothes. Crying and begging to be free. Not being let go. Trying to run. Him trapping me. Me giving in. I was eight years old.

As I talked, The Doctor listened, nodded, and scratched notes into my file. He also took my pulse, looked at my tongue, and put wire thin needles into my ankles at places he called "trauma points."

"I APPRECIATE THAT YOU have devoted your life to alternative medicine," I hear myself say.

Blink, blink, blink.

I am a reflection in his glasses. I see me talking to me.

OVER TIME, AFFECTION GREW. The Doctor was the keeper of my most protected, ugly secret. I told myself he was like this perfect guy. So calm. So Zen. Trust blossomed between us.

About month four of our sessions, he revealed his marriage was in trouble. He felt disillusioned with his practice and his choices in life.

Panic! What if I lost him? What if he stopped our appointments?

"Your wife must be a fool," I said.

My compliment perked him like water perks a parched daisy.

The Doctor said he looked forward to my appointments. To see my name on his schedule always made his day.

"SO WHAT I HEAR you say is that you appreciate I have devoted my life to alternative medicine," Husband Number Three says. "Is there more?"

I look at Maxine. "Can I just do the one?" I ask.

"You can think of another," she says. "Surely you can think of something?"

I press my fingers to my temples and rub between my eyes. Think, think, think.

ON WHAT SHOULD HAVE been our last day of treatment, seven months after my first appointment, The Doctor led me to an examination room. The halls of his clinic were narrow and the walls were bright white.

As we walked, I told The Doctor I was going to take a break. My flashbacks were gone. I felt good. I was ready to move on.

At the end of the hall, The Doctor opened a door to an exam room, and instead of washing his hands, which is something he usually did before we began, he sat down in a crumpled heap of khaki pants, a green button-up shirt, and his white doctor coat.

"I'm separated," he announced.

I eased myself into the chair, surprised. I thought the marriage was back on track.

"She finally left me," he said.

In that moment, I knew he was breaking a vital rule between a patient and healing professional. He was putting himself in the circle of trust meant for only me. He was violating the sacred code of his own profession. I knew it—in my gut—I could see it all happening to me but I couldn't raise my voice to stop it. The whole thing, just like the rape when I was eight, was out of my control. I infuriatingly catapulted back, back, back in time to be what I had been before. The victim.

. . .

"IT DOESN'T HAVE TO be a big thing, something small, from this morning or last night," Maxine prompts.

Husband Number Three waits, *blink, blink, blink.*

"I appreciate you took the garbage out today," I finally say.

"There you go," Maxine says. "Okay!"

Husband Number Three pulls on what I call his nice guy smile. It's a Mona Lisa smile on a man.

"So what I hear you say is that you appreciate I took out the trash," he says.

"Is there more?"

"No," I say. "I think that's about it."

IMAGO THERAPY DOESN'T go into the origins of a relationship. It's all about the attraction and how childhood conditioning is triggered by that attraction.

This means I will not get an opportunity to explore, at least with Maxine, how it took two weeks for The Doctor and I to find ourselves in a relationship. I won't be able to dissect how our roles flipped from him being a trusted caregiver to me becoming a rescuer who helped him limp through the complexities of his long and ugly divorce. I won't have a chance to really examine how a sexual relationship with the guy who helped me unearth sexual abuse was such a betrayal of my vulnerability that I would be reinjured all over again. And there will be no chance to reconcile that his actions went against the ethical code of doctors of acupuncture in our state.

When asked, Maxine will say our beginning didn't matter. She may not have agreed with his lack of professional boundaries but they were not relevant to the marriage or her work as our marriage therapist.

Any knitter knows that a project poorly begun is doomed to fail. You cannot cast on and forget a stitch or two and you cannot drop stitches and expect a well-crafted glove, scarf, sweater, or shawl. Structural mistakes lead to failure, something we accept without question when it comes to yarn. Yet I was not allowed to raise my voice and question the structural flaws that began our relationship—in therapy or even with Husband Number Three—who, like Maxine, said our beginnings were no big deal. Patients and therapists fell in love all the time, he said.

ONCE APPRECIATIONS ARE DONE, our task is to frame a concern into the form of an Imago dialogue while the partner listens, repeats, relates, shows empathy, and then summarizes.

I bring up the chickens, which seems to please Maxine.

"I am wondering why, when I ask you to keep the chickens out of the rosebushes, you say you will but then you don't and they ruin my bushes."

Maxine is quick to massage my concern into "I"-oriented language that focuses on my reaction and the concern is re-expressed: "I am frustrated by the fact that I ask you to keep the chickens out of my rosebushes, you say you will, but then you don't and they destroy my bushes. When this happens, I get angry and the story I tell myself is that I cannot count on you. When I feel I cannot count on you, I react with helplessness and rage. I feel helpless and angry because I am reminded of when I was a child, abandoned by my parents and victimized by people who hurt me."

Husband Number Three listens, mirrors, repeats, and then he stops short. When empathy is required, Maxine has to step in.

"Empathy is your way of relating to how Jennifer feels," Maxine prompts. "The story she tells herself is that she cannot count on you. Can you imagine how that must feel for her?"

Blink, blink, blink.

"She's lost her whole family," Maxine adds. "Jennifer's been alone most of her life and she needs someone she can count on. Can you see how she would feel that way?"

"She feels bad?" he tries.

It's Maxine's turn to blink a few times.

"Well, yes, but can you express empathy for how she feels?"

Blink, blink, blink.

"Um," he says.

LATER THAT SAME DAY, I'm at my office and on the phone with Anne. She is a tiny Greek woman with dark hair and eyes and I call her Saint Anne. She's the kind of friend who listens while I vent about Husband Number Three.

After my session with Maxine, I grab a cup of tea, a dark chocolate cookie, pull out my knitting, and call Anne to debrief.

"No empathy," I say. "None. Zip."

"I'm not surprised," she says.

"How can a person not have empathy?"

"He's a doctor," she says. "They turn it off to do their work."

"The thing is, he's not a doctor," I say. "He has a clinical doctorate. He didn't go to medical school."

"I keep forgetting," she says. "I always think of him as a doctor."

"He wants you to think of him that way," I say. "That's what throws people off. He's so nice and calm and seemingly accomplished and boom, next thing you know your rosebushes are pecked clean."

"I say send *him* to therapy," Anne says. "He's the one with the problem. No empathy? Come on."

I knit two, purl two, knit two, and purl two more.

"The thing is, I still can't stand her but at some level, Maxine got me today," I say. "She understood how I felt in the moment."

"And she's been your therapist for less than a week," Anne adds. "This Joker has been in your life for four years. There is a saying, 'When someone shows you who they are, believe them.'"

I know she's right but don't listen to my friend.

I'm stuck, have been stuck, in something bigger than me.

I come to the end of the row and stop. Instead of looking at the person he shows himself to be and more, at the person I am, I focus on the shawl I've taken on. I've knitted two balls in and have eighteen to go. I tell myself I'm making progress even though the truth is, everything is about to come undone.

"Well, I agreed to six months of couples work with Maxine," I say. "A deal is a deal."

"Get more rosebushes then," Anne sighs, "or maybe just stop planting for a while."

SIX MONTHS AND A couple weeks later, it's September 11, 2011, and I drive down a street in Portland called Couch. It's a one-way, east to west, and it has at least a dozen stoplights.

Anne is in the passenger seat and she wears a white cotton top, Capris and sandals. We're on our way to her house for dinner and to talk business but the truth is, I can't go home.

"We're calling it a legal separation agreement," I say.

"Will he help with the mortgage?" Anne asks. "Until you get a job?"

"For six months," I say. "At least that's what he promised. Who knows, he's such a flake."

Ahead of us, the sun is a magnificent orb of deep yellow and orange. The sky is bleached a dusty mix of gray and white. It's a hot night. 100 degrees hot.

"I just want him to leave," I say.

Six months of therapy went by, thousands of dollars, and we stayed pretty much the same. Husband Number Three continued to be a guy who let the chickens eat the roses, who failed to scoop dog doo, and who forgot to the pay the mortgage.

One thing did change over time and that was my own level of reactivity. In all of the dialogues—refereed by Maxine—hailstorm Jennifer downgraded to rainstorm Jennifer.

This shift in me created a shift in Husband Number Three and his efforts to get a reaction became more extreme. First he invented a story about my son, saying someone might have touched him in an inappropriate way while they were out shopping. The whole story had been a work of fiction. Husband Number Three had just been confused. Next he abandoned my daughter while he was supposed to watch her for a couple of hours. Confusion was his excuse again, plus a case of low blood sugar.

"It's like he wanted me to leave," I say. "Who would stay?"

"You did the right thing," Anne says. "He could have really hurt one of your kids."

The traffic signals are timed just so and I'm having perfect luck. Green, green, green.

"What gets me is that I stayed so long with a guy who is clearly a whack job," I say. "Maxine was right, I'm as screwed up as he is."

Saint Anne shifts in her seat, this tiny little woman who has all the answers. I think she is about to say what she always says, which is something like, "You're not as screwed up as he is, Jennifer, you trusted him, you thought he was a good guy, you got in over your head," but Anne doesn't speak. Instead she points and screams.

I glance over my shoulder and spot the gleam of an oncoming car. I steer hard to the right and put on the gas. Instinct, I guess.

The car tags my back end and the whole thing is maybe ten seconds of fast forward, car tilt, screaming metal, broken glass, and then a sharp hard stop over three freeway signs that rip out the axles from under my car.

The whole time, I hold the steering wheel as tight as I can, wrestle with my car like it's a wild horse, and I think, I can get out of this, I can get out of this, I can get out of this.

Once we stop, Anne looks at me and I look at her and then slam. Metal on metal. A car from out there somewhere crashes into her side and what the hell is going on? Is that a third car?

Between the seats are my purse and my knitting bag. *Listen to your mother.* I grab both, plus Anne's purse, and tug Anne out of the car through my door.

"Run," I yell.

At a safe distance from what used to be my car, I touch up and down my own body. I'm intact. Anne does the same and then she says she might throw up.

Up the road our accident is just two cars. Mine and the woman who ran a red light. She must have spun herself out and hit us a second time on Anne's side. The driver is okay and she's out of her car too.

Anne shakes and there are little cuts on her legs, probably from all that glass. She bleeds in thin ribbons that thread down her calves.

I ask her again if she's okay and she says she thinks so.

Crazy calm, I get into her purse, call her home phone, and talk to her husband. I tell him to come help because Anne has been in an accident, not to worry, she's fine but the car is totaled.

I hang up the phone and tell Anne her husband is on the way. Not to worry.

It's weird. I could have died but I'm one hundred percent calm.

There's something about this accident that is so honest. Cars hit each other, someone is usually to blame and in this case, it will be the other woman. There will be witnesses who saw her run the red light. The police will make a report and damages will be paid. The mess will be cleaned up.

Simple. Cause and effect. Action and reaction. Accountability.

Maybe that's why I'm not upset. Sure, I'm pissed my car has been trashed and I'm sad my friend has been hurt, but there's also something so perfect about being here on the sidewalk with my knitting bag. *Listen to your mother.*

With broken glass and twisted metal around us, it's a true death, a true ending to a process I've been stuck in. A four-year hell with a man who really hurt me and who I let hurt me—in a way—an extension of that first rape when I was eight, only now I am a grown-up and I finally got away.

The questions are these: Will I be able to back up, unravel the whole experience and start again? Yes, I have the raw material of a horrific childhood, a desire to heal, a bad marriage, moronic therapy processes (and some very good ones as well), friendships with patient people, and even a car wreck, but what will I do with all of it? Will I eventually knit myself, via these materials, into someone amazing? Will I learn? Will I grow?

Police cars, three of them, arrive at the scene. Lights flash and sirens wail and a lady cop in a bulletproof vest comes down the sidewalk. She has a notepad in her hand.

With Anne at my side and my knitting bag over my shoulder, I meet the cop halfway and tell the story of what happened.

knitting a family

by Anne D. LeClaire

A husband and wife form a couple; it takes the addition of a child to create a family. As the author waits for that baby to create her family, she turns to knitting.

ALL THE OTHER WOMEN IN THE OUTER OFFICE OF THE OB/GYN were expecting.

In various stages of pregnancy, they would chat among themselves, comparing experiences of morning sickness, backaches, swollen legs, varicose veins, baby names, and due dates. A number of them also knit while waiting to be called into examining rooms. They didn't look at their hands while they worked and I was amazed at the effortless way their knuckles looped yarn over and under slender-gauge needles as they created booties and carriage afghans and tiny sweaters in shades of pastel greens and pinks and blues and yellow. So many of them were busy with needlework that I joked with my husband that there must be a Knitting Hormone that is released when a woman becomes pregnant.

My own hands, like my womb, were empty; I was not expecting.

I was waiting. For several years we had been trying to conceive and more often than you might imagine we were asked when we were going to start a family. As time passed, some people even hinted that perhaps we didn't want to have children. We did. I did. I was drawn to children of all ages. Babies. Toddlers. Teenagers. I couldn't imagine a life without them. A husband and wife form a couple; it takes the addition of a child to create a family. I wanted a family and I yearned for a baby with a passion that was near hunger. My husband Hillary, too, shared this dream. Even before we were married, we had talked about a future that included children, a future I took for granted as easily as I did the morning sun. But, as with love or good health or any of the presumptive rights and privileges we too often take for granted, when I was visited by its loss, I was stunned and disbelieving.

I listened to the well-meaning advice of close friends. Relax, they counseled. Pray. Drink tea instead of coffee. Take vitamins. Try herbs. Have more sex. Have less. Eventually, we turned to fertility testing. Looking back, I see how completely unprepared we were, how naïve we were about the complicated and lengthy process on which we were embarking, one that would prove to be emotionally draining and, at times, physically painful. One aspect I would come to find particularly hurtful was sitting in the outer office of the OB/GYN with the pregnant, knitting women. Soon I learned to carry a book with me to occupy my hands and mind, an escape place for my eyes to focus on while I waited.

On my second appointment I carried in a small chart on which, as directed and for the duration of two months, I had recorded my temperature, taken every morning without fail before I rose or ate. When I looked at the chart, my hopes rose as sharply as did the mid-month peak on the graph, signaling that I did in fact ovulate.

The doctor confirmed this; we had cleared the first hurdle. We celebrated with lobster at our favorite restaurant.

The next month I appeared at my appointment accompanied by Hillary, who would also be tested. I was there for a cervical mucus test while he was dispatched to a bathroom with a small cup and a copy of *Playboy* to produce a specimen for semen analysis. "You always get the easy jobs," I told him. Later, when we were given the results, we celebrated with another night out, this time at Pate's, the place where we'd had our first date.

The following month, on a day determined by the spike in my ovulation chart, we were asked to arrive within a designated postcoital hour for a test to ensure that my husband's sperm could survive within my cervix. After my doctor had taken the swab, he slid the slide under the microscope and then shared the result with us. We viewed infinitesimal sperm, tiny tadpole-shaped entities swimming on the glass plate in search of the ovum they were programmed to fertilize. We cheered them on. That night we drank champagne to the little fellows.

Month after month, though, the fertility tests proved negative. I ovulated; my cervix was healthy with a lining thick enough to support conception; my blood work was textbook-perfect, my thyroid and hormone levels normal. The doctor said we were an incredibly healthy young couple and each month he would send us off with encouraging words.

As time passed, the tests became more complicated, more invasive. I underwent an endometrial biopsy and fainted when the doctor held up the specimen for me to see. Next was the formidable-sounding hysterosalpingogram in which dye was injected through my cervix into my uterus and fallopian tubes to check for a blockage. After I had dressed, the doctor asked me if I wanted to see the results. As I stared at the X-rays, I marveled at the tracing of my tubes, two minute lines no thicker than those drawn by a pencil. Was it possible that these threadlike rivers were the paths through which an egg could travel? I marveled, too, at the interior workings of my body and the many, many things that could go awry, preventing conception, and all the things that had to go exactly right. It seemed a miracle that anyone could conceive at all. And yet, women did. Easily. Tired women holding toddlers on their hips. Frightened girls of fourteen. Desperate or heartbroken women considering abortions. Malnourished, slip-thin women in Third World countries.

We remained positive. Hopeful. But when my periods arrived on schedule, I would weep in Hillary's arms with disappointment and a grief that felt isolating, even shame-based, my womanhood in question. I don't mean to give the impression that our lives were sorrowful, our days unendingly sad. We laughed and loved, played and worked. We packed picnic lunches and drove an old Willys jeep over the dunes of a Cape Cod beach where we drank cheap wine and bodysurfed. I wallpapered rooms, made curtains, experimented with recipes, planted an herb garden and grew to love the feeling of my hands in the earth. Hillary flew jets. I acted and wrote. But we no longer celebrated test results with champagne or nights out. I no longer brought up the subject of the fertility tests with friends. It became more difficult to sit in the waiting room with the knitting women, a sisterhood I was excluded from on two fronts. I could neither conceive nor did I knit.

In my childhood, my mother tried to teach me. I was used to seeing her with needlework in hand. She sewed our clothes. She knit. She crocheted a bedspread that covered a double bed, an ivory tablecloth in a lacy intricate pattern that draped our dining room table, round doilies with furled edges that adorned end tables and dressers throughout our house. My older sister already could crochet potholders and knit scarves. I would listen to her count. Knit one, purl two. Knit one, purl two. I thought she was saying pearl. My first lesson was the straightforward knit stitch. My mother reached in her basket and retrieved a small ball of yarn left over from a completed project. She cast a row of 20 stitches onto fat wooden needles that she then handed to me. With intense concentration, I followed her instructions. It sounded straightforward enough, easier than learning to tie my shoes, and yet within several rows, I had already created a mess. Fat loopy stitches in one row and tight, tense ones in the next. Gaps appeared where I had dropped stitches. Even more puzzling to me, several rows further on I had somehow managed to increase the stitches beyond the original count. When I showed her, she slipped the yarn off the needles, unraveled it, again cast on 20 stitches. My second and third attempts met with no greater success and eventually I gave up.

When I sat in the doctor's waiting room, the sight of the knitting women recalled for me this early failure.

Finally, we stopped the tests. We decided to adopt and so set out on another lengthy process fueled by a mixture of hope and anticipation and the dream of family. We filled out questionnaires, detailed our medical and familial histories, were interviewed separately and together, asked friends and clergy to write recommendations, attended group meetings with other couples. We were assigned a caseworker who scheduled a home visit to ensure our home was suitable. In preparation, I cleaned the house, baked cookies, all the while fighting resentment that we were to be judged as to whether we were worthy of being parents. At last we were accepted. And again we found ourselves waiting. This time for another woman to give birth to a child who would become ours.

We were told that a period as long as a year might pass before we heard anything.

Superstitiously, I refused to buy furniture or baby clothes. At this same time, my younger sister was pregnant and my mother was knitting her a baby blanket. The pattern was a lacy one called "Feather and Fan." One winter day on an impulse, I went to the local craft shop. I wandered the aisles and fingered the wools, seduced by the range of colors and textures. I settled on a skein of soft white wool and purchased two stainless steel needles. On my next visit to my parents' home, I asked my mother to show me how to knit a blanket like the one she was making for my sister. She offered to knit it for me but I told her this was something I wanted to do myself. She began by casting on 36 stitches, walked me through the basics, instructed me to knit four rows for the border and then follow this pattern, which she wrote down for me.

Row 1: Knit. Row 2: Purl. Row 3: Knit 4, then Yarn Over, Knit 1 (4 times) Knit 2 together three times, Knit 4. Repeat this pattern 4 times. Row 4: Knit. Repeat the 4-row pattern until the desired length is achieved and then knit 4 rows for the border that would complete the blanket.

I counted stitches carefully, attentively, fearful that this would become another failed project, but as I knitted it was as if the needles were held by hands other than mine. There were no dropped or miscounted stitches. No lapses in the pattern. Within days, I held the finished blanket in my hands. It was perfect.

One morning in early May, our caseworker called to tell us our daughter had been born. She was three weeks old and weighed five pounds six ounces.

Twenty-four hours later, I held her in my arms. She was wrapped in the white blanket; I was rapt in the sweet miracle of her: her fingers with minuscule nails, her almond-shaped eyes with lashes so thick and long they seemed too heavy for the burden of lifting blue-veined lids.

We filled out the paperwork. The caseworker asked if we had selected a name.

"Hope," we told her. "Hope D'Avril." We had settled on Hope in honor of Hillary's maternal grandmother and D'Avril because she had been born in April. Truly she was our hope of April. We had driven to Boston that morning a couple; we returned home that afternoon a family.

Objects are crafted from varied material. From wood and stone, glass, metal and fiber, they are carved, constructed and etched, molded and woven. Families and lives, too, are formed from disparate matter. We create from sinews and blood, muscles and bone, of course, but as well from a wellspring of hope and love and dreams and the annealing strength of disappointment, loss, and pain.

It was from these we knit our family.

knitting: epic fail

by Marianne Leone

Can a failed knitter still have knitting in her DNA?

I F MY FAMILY AND I LIVED IN A SOD HUT ON THE KANSAS plains in the mid-nineteenth century, we would all be freezing to death in badly thrown-together burlap sacks. I can picture myself churning butter and skinning rabbits with no problem, but knitting my family a scarf or socks to protect them from the subzero temperatures outside? "Sorry, I'm left-handed," I tell my blue-lipped, teeth-chattering frontier family as they huddle near the meager fire. "How about some rabbit stew? And here's a nice skin to drape around your neck. 'kay?"

It's not that I haven't tried to knit and purl; in my nightmares I can still see the looped expectant lines along the needle, the rows of dropped and mismatched stitches and my thirteen-year-old self realizing that like ballet, baseball, and sainthood, knitting would now be added to the growing category of epic failures already littering my young life. Come on, though, I'm left-handed! Everything was backwards, impossible. The world of handicrafts was a confusing fun-house mirror image that was anything but fun. I'm the one who leads when I dance with my husband. I can't dance backwards, either.

The left-handed excuse cut no ice with the nuns of Our Lady Help of Christians as I tried and failed to master the Palmer handwriting method. Every day I spent endless after-school hours trying to get my letters to curl nicely on the dotted line. Instead, they drooped and sagged below the lines like a chart predicting economic disaster into the next millennium. The sisters who taught me didn't smack me or tie my left hand down to make me use the preferred right one. They were too enlightened to say that the left hand was the hand of the devil, the sinister one, cockeyed, offbeat, wrong. They just clucked, disapproved, and kept me after school every day, even once it was clear that I could never do it right. I consoled myself by thinking that my left-handedness made me a *strega*, a witch, a person with as-yet-unexpressed supernatural powers. I knew the left hand was the one you used for magic, because that was the one my mother used when she did the spell to ward off the evil eye. But there was no magic in my left hand for knitting, or sewing, or crocheting.

There was also the problem of the language barrier. Not the *lingua segreta*, the secret language in Italian dialect my adult family used when they wanted to discuss something too racy or scary for their American children to overhear, but the language of knitting patterns. My Aunt Ellie knitted, and I saw the patterns she used. They looked like a language for Martians, or, worse, an algebraic formula, like the incomprehensible ones at school that were dragging my grades down and keeping me forever off the honor roll. I watched her eyes flick to the pattern—(n, o2, n) twice, k4, o, n, n, k1, o, n, k13—then her needles obediently clicking out the code into a sweater, or a cap, or a scarf. I knew I would never crack the code.

I wanted to blame my devilish left hand and the alien-looking patterns. But the real reason I was a failure at knitting was a basic unwillingness to try due to the unease I felt watching my mother, who reminded me of a modern-day Madame Defarge, smirking with satisfaction at the adulterers getting their comeuppance on the soaps she watched every afternoon. She crocheted wave after crashing wave of afghans in her zigzag pattern, delicate baby blankets in blue or pink threaded with ribbon and edged with silk, cunning little baby caps, oversized-looking booties. She plied her hooked needle night after night in front of the television, spewing designs in the same steely rhythm, silently, passively. I knew that the crocheting took her eventually beyond the onscreen melodrama, to a white-noise Zen place and no matter what show was on the television, in her head was the high-pitched hum that spun the universe, and nothing else.

But you couldn't crochet or knit and read at the same time, and reading was all I wanted to do. I couldn't produce an actual practical three-dimensional thing that could be used in the world. I could only spin out dreams from the books I read. And that, as far as my pragmatic, right-handed mother was concerned, made books time-wasting, mind-warping, female-deforming, dangerous drugs that were to be hated and shunned. In return, of course, it made me hate sewing, crocheting, knitting, and any housewifely crafts as incarcerating symbols of the "goin' to the chapel" early sixties culture of my girlhood, siren lures to lull me into early motherhood.

It was clear from the cartoons I watched, hens sitting on nests knitting impossibly with their wings while hatching their eggs. All the sitcom ladies clacked their needles together when they wanted us, the audience, to know that they were on the nest. When you knit something it meant you were expecting a baby. It meant you were content to sit at home in your nest and hear only the high-pitched hum in your head while you created a universe within. I wasn't deceived a bit by the groovy crocheted vests my mother made for me to wear over my minidresses. Or by the slippers with bright pink pompoms my Aunt Ellie knitted that turned into death skis on hardwood floors. Knitting wasn't cool. Knitting was terrifying, the gateway drug to love, marriage, and the baby carriage.

Once I escaped the oxygen deprivation of my warm and too-close neighborhood and the preordained early marriage to someone my Italian family knew from the same tiny medieval village back in the old country, I made my peace with housewifery. I had avoided the nest, and I could now, from the safe distance of a state university and in the first stages of feminist enlightenment, even appreciate knitting, quilting, tatting, and sewing as unique expressions of woman's art.

Even without learning to knit, I eventually wound my way to love, marriage, and the baby carriage. And loving tokens of my family's womanly arts receive pride of place in our home. There's an amazing quilt on the wall in the entryway to our house made by Mamoo, my husband's grandmother, from his grandfather's wildly patterned silk ties. Another of her quilts, with chunky Art Deco blue airplanes on a white background, covers a bed in the guest room. That quilt almost laughs out loud, personifying the storied wit of the woman who conceived and fashioned it. I snuggle in my comfiest chair under Aunt Ellie's zigzag afghan with the rescue dogs she would've loved. And I caress and sometimes sleep with the blue-ribbon-trimmed blanket my mother made for my son, on days when I miss them both too much, when I wish I could crochet like her and go there, where she was when she pushed her needle in and out again and again, to that white-noise Zen place vibrating only, I realize now, with the pure thought of giving, twining, and twisting the yarn like the DNA of mother love.

Today, knitting has had a resurgence of popularity and some of the women who might have marched alongside me in the late sixties chanting "Out of the kitchen and into the streets!" are meeting in knitting circles that provide the same communion and solidarity of those days, but without the speculums and vagina-peeking and rageful rants. I still can't picture myself in that circle. Or if I do imagine that meeting, it unfolds like this: everyone welcomes me, the newbie, enthusiastically at first. I am set up with my needles and basic, simple instructions to make something unchallenging, like a potholder or a scarf. I look around at the sumptuous yarn in the laps of my neighbors, the complicated, exquisite sweaters and hats other people are knitting in gorgeous colors. People pass delicious home-made goodies. I pick up a cookie and the crumbs fall into the holes that are forming around my dropped stitches. I am distracted, listening to the woman across from me describe an acrimonious divorce that involved the dognapping of a Labradoodle. I am hopelessly lost after only a few minutes. Now the yarn is my enemy, taunting me with another breach in the ranks where the straight lines of my potholder should be forming. I ask my young neighbor to the left for help. She obliges, all smiles. Her fierce nose ring and full-sleeve tats make her look like an avenging deity as she violently rips out all three rows of my stitches. I am back to square one. I start over, but become distracted again, and the same thing happens, the holes popping up magically, like a curse hurled by the right-handed goddess of knitting. I apologize to my neighbor, using my tried-and-true

"I'm left-handed" excuse. She tells me she's left-handed, too, excited, like we're now BFFs. My heart sinks, along with my stitches. By my third request for help—this time the needles are somehow crossed so tightly together they resemble scissors—my neighbor's smile is strained. On the fourth request, she pretends not to hear me. My grandmotherly neighbor to the right won't even make eye contact. The woman with the snatched Labradoodle stares with naked disgust at the mess in my lap. I don't stay until the end of the night. I pretend to get up for a bathroom break and slip out the door, leaving behind my hopelessly twisted would-be potholder. Everyone talks about me after they're sure I'm gone for good, shaking their collective heads with pity and the tiniest soupçon of smugness.

Like it or not, though, yarn is my true umbilical cord.

When my mother was barely out of her teens, she was a lonely immigrant living like an orphan on sufferance with a storybook too-stern aunt. The flinty aunt put my mother to work in her new business venture, a notions store that sold yarn and accessories for knitting and crocheting. It was a step up for my mother, who had worked until then in Boston's garment district sewing beside people from every country but her own, people who mispronounced her name, Merinda, in a way that made her feel even more a stranger. Her home in this country was a sofa where she slept at night, barely tolerated by the aunt's jealous son. The notions store was just a street away from my future Aunt Ellie's house. A bouncy teenager only a few years younger than my mother, Ellie was an avid knitter even then. She visited the store on her way home from school, giddy over the array of yarns and fabrics. Ellie spoke Italian as well as English; she released my mother from her mute and solitary prison into the barely remembered bliss of sharing laughter in her own language with a girl her age. The friendship between my mother and Ellie grew; she invited my mother to her house. My mother met Ellie's family, and understood for the first time that a home could harbor love and teasing and laughter, a galaxy away from her silent mountain farm, her grim-faced parents trapped in a loveless marriage. My mother, Merinda, met Ellie's two handsome brothers, Joe, a shy and gawky high school junior, and Jerry, a young widower still in his twenties. Merinda and Jerry married within the month. She unraveled the knots in his widower heart, and he introduced her to a new pattern, one she had never known before, layered with passion and joy.

And so, Knitting and Crocheting, even though you've been discovered by hipsters and are at long last cool, even though I may never love you enough to actually have the patience or talent to knit or crochet, I can still follow the skein that leads me to this truth: I have you to thank for my being here at all.

I bought this pattern book last spring

by Elinor Lipman

A poem about the knitter's stash and unfinished projects, and the hope that knitting brings.

It started with some stray pink wool
And from an early age I knew
That knit and purl were a duet;
The song they sang was Stockinette.

At five years old, my mom instructing,
But not a thing was I constructing.
A strip was all, just stitch by stitch
And still it scratched some untold itch.

And oh the projects I have started,
But then I find myself fainthearted.
I loved this cotton at the store,
But I don't like it anymore.

Closeouts, farm stands, wool online—
I hate the shanks I have to wind.
A ton of yarn I loved and bought,
But now it's looking not so hot.

That cashmere, yes it was on sale,
But in it I'd look deathly pale.
I started shrug for son's main squeeze,
But they broke up before the sleeves.

Will anything I ever knit
Earn the title "perfect fit"?
The "medium" is not quite right.
I must be knitting awfully tight.

To make a swatch takes discipline,
But I am eager to begin.
I start my gauge, but soon I'm bored.
Four rows seem all I can afford.

It's why I choose a baby sweater,
If way too big, moms like it better.
No doubt the best gift I could get 'er,
So where's the goddamn thank-you letter?

That poncho takes at least a year,
And cables are a new frontier.
And why is this four-needle mitten
Both difficult and so ill-fittin'?

Don't think that knitting saves you cash.
You're out of room to store your stash.
Will odds and ends from years ago
Become an afghan? Surely, no.

The project wilting in your bag
Could almost be a running gag.
If only each abandoned piece
Were not a sweater for your niece.

And once I've bound off final sleeve—
Ahead the task, the big pet peeve:
It's not the hobby of your dreams,
When next you have to sew up seams.

I bought this pattern book last spring,
And haven't made one stupid thing.
I meant to make that lacy shawl,
But months have passed and now it's fall.

Winter's near; it's getting cold
And I can knit a scarf blindfold.
I have two balls; that makes it free.
Of course I'll actually need three.

And who among this group has not
Cheated on the color lot?
You think you'll get away with fewer.
When you go back, the number's newer.

The clerk sends signal: *Told you so.*
But how's an amateur to know.
You didn't think you'd need it all.
Besides, it's twenty bucks a ball.

What thrill is there that can attract ya
Like going home with soft alpaca?
It's beautiful; it's red or rose.
A jewel to crown your drabber clothes.

Perhaps it won't work up so fine.
Perhaps I chose the wrong design.
Though never pleasing from the start,
My buttons are a work of art.

I started something new this week,
A cowl. It's soft. It's kind of chic.
For someone else, a birthday gift,
But now there's been a minor shift.

Luckily I didn't mention
My altruistic good intention.
This peach angora made from goat
Will look so nice with my brown coat.

I knit while watching bad TV,
It gives an air of busy bee.
I knit in bad times and in good.
It works for me like praying should.

I bought this pattern book last spring.
I never know what life will bring.
It features cardigans for men.
I might knit things like that again.

"ashworth" ruffled slipper socks

by Helen Bingham

These ruffled slipper socks will provide you with warmth and flair for your feet. They are knit in the round using sock-weight yarn at a slightly looser than average gauge usually used for socks. Mari Ashworth, my mom, gave me the greatest gift when she taught me how to knit. Not only did my mom give me my passion, she also taught me how to have inner strength. You are stronger than you think so just keep putting one foot in front of the other to get to where you need to be.

MATERIALS:

1 skein Unisono (100% merino wool with 330 yards)
Color: #1220 Red, #1220 Blue

OR

1 skein Crazy Zauberball by Schoppel Wolle (75% wool & 25% nylon with 459 yards)
Color: #1701
US 2, circular 40″ needle or size needed to obtain gauge

SIZE: one size will fit a women's shoe size US 6–10 (see Pattern Notes)

GAUGE: 28 sts = 4″ in stockinette stitch

PATTERN NOTES & ABBREVIATIONS:

—The ruffle is created first and the WS of the ruffle is facing you while the sock is being knit. When the sock is finished, fold the ruffle over so the RS is then facing when being worn.

—There is only one set of directions even though it is designed to fit a shoe size ranging from US 6 to US 10. The only difference per size is how long to knit the foot so it fits the length of your foot. When working on the foot of the sock, try it on and when it reaches the beginning of your toes begin the toe decreases.

—This pattern uses the magic loop method for sock knitting (You Tube has great videos explaining this technique).

Tbl = through back loop of stitch

Ssp = slip one stitch knitwise, now slip the next stitch knitwise, maintaining the stitch form slip the stitches back to the left-hand needle, put your right-hand needle into the front of the two slipped sts on the left-hand needle and purl them together

K2tog = knit two sts together

P2tog = purl two sts together

Ssk = slip a stitch as if to knit, slip the next stitch as if to knit, place left needle into the front of the two slipped stitches and knit them together

Psso = pass slipped stitch over

DIRECTIONS:

RUFFLED CUFF:

—Cast on 140 sts, join into the round (do not twist stitches).

Round 1: (P1 tbl, P11, P1,tbl, K7), repeat to end of round

Round 2: (SSP, P9, P2tog, K7), repeat to end of round

Round 3: (P1 tbl, P9, P1,tbl, K7), repeat to end of round

Round 4: (SSP, P7, P2tog, K7), repeat to end of round

Round 5: (P1 tbl, P7, P1,tbl, K7*, repeat to end of round

Round 6: (SSP, P5, P2tog, K7), repeat to end of round

Round 7: (P1 tbl, P5, P1,tbl, K7*, repeat to end of round

Round 8: (SSP, P3, P2tog, K7), repeat to end of round

Round 9: (P1 tbl, P3, P1,tbl, K7), repeat to end of round

Round 10: (SSP, P1, P2tog, K7), repeat to end of round

Round 11: (P1 tbl, P1, P1,tbl, K7), repeat to end of round

Round 12: (Slip 1 stitch purlwise, P2tog, PSSO, K7), repeat to end of round

Round 13: (P1, K7)*, repeat between *'s

Round 14: (P1, K7)*, repeat between *'s (there are now 56 sts)

Round 15: (P2, PK2), repeat to end of round

—Repeat Round 15 a total of 12 times.

HEEL FLAP:

—Work only on the first 28 stitches by doing the following rows:

Row 1: (Slip1, K1), repeat 14 times, **TURN**

Row 2: Slip 1, Purl 27 sts, **TURN**.

—Repeat the last two rows 14 times total (28 rows have been worked).

—Work Row 1 one more time.

HEEL TURNING:

—Continue to work on the 28 sts as follows:

Row 1: Slip 1, Purl 15, P2tog, P1 **TURN**

Row 2: Slip 1, Knit 5 sts, K2tog tbl, K1, **TURN**

Row 3: Slip 1, Purl to within 1 st away from gap, P2tog, P1, **TURN**

Row 4: Slip 1, Knit to within 1 st away from gap, K2tog tbl, K1, **TURN**.

—Repeat Rows 3 and 4 in this manner till all stitches are used up.

—End after working a RS row during this short-row process

—The last two rows worked will not have the K1 at the end of the row, you will end these two rows with P2tog tbl and K2tog respectively. There will be 16 remaining sts.

GUSSET:

—When picking up the stitches, pick up in the outside edge of the slipped stitch from the heel-flap rows.

—With the needle that holds the 16 heel sts and with RS facing, pick up 15 sts along the left side of heel. Continue to knit in the round by knitting across the 28 instep sts (these are the sts you ignored during the heel flap and heel turning). Using the needle that holds the instep sts, pull out a 3" loop, then pick up 15 sts up the right side of heel. Using the same needle, knit across the heel stitches and the picked up sts along the left side of heel, this is now the start of the round. Knit to the end of the needle (it is optional to knit through the back loop of the picked-up gusset stitches). The round now starts just before the instep stitches.

—There are 28 sts (instep stitches) on one needle and 48 sts (gusset and heel stitches) on the other needle. Work the following two rounds as follows:

—The first time you work Round 1, knit through the back loop of the picked up stitches to help close the hole that sometimes appears (this is optional).

Round 1: Knit across 28 instep stitches then work the heel stitches as follows: K1, SSK, knit till 3 sts remain, K2tog, K1.

Round 2: Knit every stitch.

—Repeat these two rounds till 28sts remain on each needle.

FOOT:

—Continue to knit every round till foot (start of heel to stitches on needle) reaches the beginning of your toes.

TOE SHAPING:

—With 28 sts on each needle work the following rounds:

Round 1: K1, SSK, K to last 3 sts, K2tog, K1, repeat for other needle.

Round 2: Knit all stitches

—Repeat these two rounds till 8 sts remain on each needle.

—Seam the stitches together using the kitchener stitch:

KITCHENER STITCH:

—Hold the two needles parallel, use a tapestry needle (TN), leaving about 15" of yarn.

STEP 1: On front needle: put TN through first stitch knitwise and take off needle, put TN through second stitch purlwise but leave on needle.

STEP 2: On back needle: put TN through first stitch purlwise and take off needle, put TN through second stitch knitwise but leave on needle.

—Continue these two steps till all stitches have been used. Pull yarn through last loop and weave in the ends.

CONGRATS! Start the next sock.

For pictures of this pattern, go to www.helenbinghamdesigns.com

the supernatural power of knitting

by Alison Lurie

The writer takes us on a personal, literary, and historical journey through the magic of knitting.

A S A CHILD, I THOUGHT OF KNITTING AS A KIND OF magic, in which a one-dimensional object became two-dimensional or even three-dimensional. While you watched, a very long piece of string somehow turned into a hat or a sock or a mitten, something with shape and weight, an inside and an outside. Appropriately, this transformation was accomplished with long shiny sticks, like the magic wands in fairy tales.

It wasn't only the materials that, for me, were transformed. The people who could perform this magic seemed, in everyday life, to be everyday humans. But when they picked up their wands they turned into sorceresses or fairy godmothers, mistresses of a secret art.

My mother, like most of her friends, could knit, but she much preferred sewing, and made charming clothes for my and my sister's dolls on her old treadle Singer. When I was seven she tried to teach me to knit, but without success. Under her reluctant instruction I managed about twelve inches of a hateful lumpy scarf in alternating wobbly stripes of brown and canary yellow garter stitch. Then I gave up, and for several years refused to try again.

My mother was of Scottish descent, and always reluctant to waste anything. After a while she took over the wool and created an afghan of alternating brown and canary yellow squares. It was one of the few knitting projects she ever completed, but it lasted for a long time. It was admired and even loved by my younger sister and eventually by both her children and mine when they were small. For one of them it temporarily became a "blankie," or as psychologists call it, a beloved and comforting "transitional object." Only I never liked the thing, no doubt because it reminded me of my wonky failed scarf.

Eventually, a friend of my mother's managed to teach me to knit in the rapid European method of knitting, in which the yarn is held in the left hand and there is less movement of the arms. My first project was also a scarf, but this time a more successful one, in a light, soft, blue wool.

ACCORDING TO HISTORIANS, knitting is probably very old. Few examples have survived, though socks from Egypt are believed to date from the eleventh century. Though archaeologists have found many more ancient woven textiles, it seems likely that knitting may predate weaving. Weaving demands a settled environment, and bulky equipment in the form of a loom. Knitting requires only a ball of yarn and needles, and it would therefore be well suited to nomadic people who followed the migrations of game or the seasonal ripening of fruits, vegetables, and nuts. Knitters can and still do carry their work with them: even today you will often see women knitting on long journeys, though they may travel by jet plane rather than in an oxcart or on foot.

By the late Middle Ages knitting was well established. A fourteenth-century painting by Bertram von Minden shows the Virgin Mary finishing up what looks like a loose pink short-sleeved top. Mary is clearly very skilled: she is knitting in the round on four double-pointed needles, which are much more difficult to manage than two single-pointed ones. The advantage of using four needles (or one circular needle) is that you need never switch from knit stitches to purl stitches in order to create a smooth surface, or sew separate pieces together. The resulting garment will be seamless, like the one Jesus wore at the Crucifixion, which was made by his mother—see John 19:23–27. Possibly the seamless garment in van Minden's painting is also intended for Mary's son, who lies on the grass beside her wearing a rather shabby-looking brown robe. He seems to be about six years old, but is evidently precocious, since he is reading a book.

WEAVERS AND SEAMSTRESSES typically work sitting down, but it is possible to knit while standing, or even while walking. It can also be done when it is too dark to sew, something that was especially important before the invention of electricity. Shepherds and shepherdesses traditionally knit as they watched their flocks, and there are many seventeenth-, eighteenth-, and early nineteenth-century paintings of women in peasant dress knitting, often while standing up. Back then, it wasn't just a hobby, as it often is today, but an essential household craft. Many women (and occasionally men) either created wool socks, scarves, and sweaters for themselves and their families, or went without.

Since it did not demand physical strength, knitting was something you could do at any age, and to judge by the art of the period, the very young and the very old were frequent knitters. Some not only supplied their families, they also made things for sale, including fine silk stockings for the rich. *Young Knitter Asleep*, a painting by the eighteenth-century French artist Jean-Baptiste Greuze (1725–1805), shows a little girl about seven years old who has dozed off over this monotonous task.

CROCHET, PATTERNS FOR WHICH first appeared in the early nineteenth century, was at first a very different kind of handcraft. It belonged to what was referred to often as "fancy work," which included tatting, tapestry, and embroidery. The important thing about fancy work was that it was both artistic and inessential. It was a characteristic leisure occupation of well-to-do women who did not need to create anything essential. Instead they demonstrated their taste and skill by making decorative objects: embroidered handkerchiefs and slippers, crocheted lace for edgings and trimmings, little net purses, doilies and runners for tables, and fancy antimacassars for sofas and chairs. Knitting was practical and plebian: fancy work was largely decorative, and prestigiously useless.

In nineteenth-century literature it seems sometimes to be true that good women knit and bad women crochet or do fancy work. In Jane Austen's *Emma* the long-suffering good girl, Jane Fairfax, is a dedicated knitter, as is her aunt, Miss Bates. (Emma herself does not knit.) Hester in Hawthorne's *The Scarlet Letter* is a self-supporting single mother who knits and sews for a living. On the other hand,

Thackeray's antiheroine Becky Sharp, in *Vanity Fair*, practices fine netting in order to show off her long white fingers and captivate Josiah Sedley.

In Tolstoy's *Anna Karenina*, Lenin's loyal and lovable wife Kitty knits while she is in labor with her first child. Anna herself crochets nervously and automatically as she confronts her lover, Count Vronsky, who has just returned from a party:

> "...You don't know what I have suffered waiting for you [Anna tells him]. I believe I'm not jealous. I'm not jealous: I believe you when you're here; but when you're away somewhere leading your life, so incomprehensible to me..."
>
> She turned away from him, pulled the hook at last out of the crochet work, and rapidly, with the help of her forefinger, began working loop after loop of the wool that was dazzling white in the lamplight, while the slender wrist moved swiftly, nervously in the embroidered cuff. (Part 4, Chapter 3)

The virtuousness of knitting was emphasized in wartime, when even well-to-do women were encouraged to knit for the troops. In Louisa May Alcott's *Little Women* both Jo and Beth do so during the Civil War, Beth happily and uncomplainingly and Jo with some irritation.

> "It's bad enough to be a girl, anyway, when I like boys' games and work and manners! I can't get over my disappointment in not being a boy. And it's worse than ever now, for I'm dying to go and fight with Papa. And I can only stay home and knit, like a poky old woman!" And Jo shook the blue army sock

till the needles rattled like castanets, and her ball bounded across the room. (Chapter 1)

The tradition of patriotic knitting for the military continued for years, both in fiction and in real life. During World War II, when I and my friends were in high school and college, we were recruited as knitters. I still remember the hanks of heavy, slightly oily, dark khaki yarn we were issued, and the blurred mimeographed patterns for scarves and socks. The more expert knitters among us were also able to produce thick gloves, and helmets that covered the whole head except for eye and mouth holes. Today we are used to this design in ski masks, but when I went into the Unitarian Church on my first day as a volunteer and was met by a figure wearing one of these death's-head helmets, I was terrified.

In fact, this apparition should have been no surprise: the association between knitting and death is a persistent dark side of the craft. Readers of Conrad's *Heart of Darkness* will remember the two women, one young and one old, who sit silently knitting black wool in the office of the company that is about to send Marlow to the Congo. As he looks at the older of the two, he tells us:

An eerie feeling came over me. She seemed uncanny and fateful. Often far away there I thought of these two, guarding the door of Darkness, knitting black wool as for a warm pall, one introducing, introducing continuously to the unknown, the other scrutinizing the cheery and foolish faces with unconcerned old eyes. *Ave!* Old knitter of black wool. *Morituri te salutant*. Not many of those she looked at ever saw her again—not half, by a long way. (Chapter 1)

The most famous and sinister knitter in literature is surely Madame Defarge from Dickens' *A Tale of Two Cities*, set at the time of the French Revolution. Madame Defarge, whose husband keeps a wine shop in Paris, is a tall, handsome black-haired woman in her forties. Her father, brother, and sister have died as the result of the cruelties of an aristocrat, and she seeks revenge on him and his family. As she waits, she knits the names of potential victims of the guillotine into her work. Dickens says that she does this "in her own stitches and her own symbols" (Book 2, Chapter 15) but not how. Possibly Madame Defarge spells out her code in a different color; perhaps, more subtly, she simply reverses her stiches from knit to purl or vice versa, creating raised letters. Later, she and her friends go to see the deaths she has forecast. Dickens did not invent this detail: many scholars have recorded that revolutionary women would often knit as they stood watching the public executions.

The best-known knitter in twentieth-century fiction is also closely associated with violent death, though as a benevolent rather than a malevolent sprit. This is Agatha Christie's Miss Marple, an elderly lady, constant knitter, and amateur detective who lives in a tiny English village where she solves one case after another. Anyone who has lived in such a village themselves, or cast even the most passing glance at crime statistics, cannot help but be surprised at the number of murders that take place in or near St. Mary Mead. Can it be that Miss Marple's hobby somehow draws them there? After all, there has always been a kind of uncanny aspect to knitting, sometimes good, as with my mother's afghan, and sometimes evil. A steel knitting needle can be a weapon, especially if its point has been quietly sharpened. There are several instances of murder by knitting needle in detective fiction; but as far as I know no one has ever been killed by a crochet hook.

.　　.　　.

EVEN IN REAL LIFE, knitters are aware of the supernatural side of their craft. What is widely known among us as the Sweater Curse is recognized as a superstition, but one which many personal accounts support. Essentially, it says that if you start knitting a sweater for any man in whom you have a serious romantic interest, he will break up with you before it is finished. A few knitters I know claim that the curse also works with scarves, but most deny this.

The rational explanation of the Sweater Curse is that a handmade sweater is typically thick, elastic, and clingy: it suggests that the woman who is making it wants to surround its recipient and enclose him. To be presented with such a garment is a signal to a man that its maker has serious plans for him in her life. If he is not ready for this, the gift will embarrass him and may frighten him away. (The same phenomenon, according to one of my informants, has been observed in relationships between two women.) It has been claimed that knitting a deliberate mistake into the sweater will break the curse, but according to one of my friends this doesn't usually work. Knitters would therefore be well advised to wait until after the wedding to start any such project—especially since it is also believed by some that a sweater made for a husband both warns off other women and keeps him safe at home.

straw into gold

by Joyce Maynard

When your mother can spin straw into gold, you expect her to also be able to live forever.

MY MOTHER TAUGHT ME HOW TO KNIT. AT LEAST A dozen times, she taught me—it just didn't take. Maybe because I knew I could always order up what I wanted, the need wasn't there to acquire the skill for myself. When a person has a mother like mine—all-powerful and endlessly competent—there's a danger that she'll feel no particular need to learn the things she's grown accustomed to her mother doing better than she ever could. Watching her whip up a casserole while advising a student on her college essay—chopping vegetables one-handed with the telephone pressed against her shoulder, flinging ingredients in the bowl, tossing out commentary on syntax—a mortal human could have gotten the feeling that she might as well give up right there. Nobody could hope to accomplish as much, as well, in a twenty-four-hour period, as my mother did. Though she taught me to try.

She was raised in the Depression—a fact as central to her

biography as her being Jewish, and very smart, and loving language, and having a laugh you could hear all the way down the street, if you were riding your bike home from school and she was out in the yard, telling some great story to a friend while planting tulip bulbs—and for all her days, even when her circumstances improved at the end of her life, and she was married to a wealthy man, she remained on the lookout for ways to cut costs, without ever scrimping on joy. She was a person who believed that something made by human hands—a meal, a garden, a pair of wool mittens—was invariably superior to the store-bought substitute. Truth was, we couldn't afford store-bought, or restaurant meals—but my mother taught my sister and me that what we got instead—home-baked cookies, home-sewn dresses, furniture salvaged from somebody's garage cleanout, and painted glossy red—all added up to what she called "gracious living."

(I don't think we bought this. We longed for dresses with labels on them. And a whole meal—not just an ice cream cone—at Howard Johnson's. I had the catalogue of official Barbie outfits memorized—down to the accessories. But my Barbies wore outfits stitched by my mother. And knitted by her.)

As capable as she was in what were called the Household Arts, my mother was not a classic 1950s housewife. Raised (in Canada) by immigrant Jewish parents who probably did not possess high school diplomas, she won a full scholarship to the University of Manitoba, and from there went on to earn her Ph.D.—summa cum laude—at Radcliffe. She had whole volumes of English literature committed to memory—romantic poetry, plays of Shakespeare, Chaucer's *Canterbury Tales*. She could whip up a poem on the spot, in iambic pentameter, or perform Macbeth's "Is this a dagger" speech without consulting the text. She knit me a pair of mittens one time—one a pig, the other a raccoon—that functioned like puppets, and another time, when I saw a picture of Twiggy wearing a particularly irresistible hot pink miniskirt I longed for, she crocheted one, based on nothing but that picture in the magazine.

She cooked wonderful meals. She baked the best pies. She sewed. She crocheted handmade borders on our nightgowns when they started to fray. And oh could she knit.

After earning her degree from Harvard, my mother married my father and moved with him to the small town in New Hampshire where he (with his lowly bachelor's degree) had gotten a job at the state university. But not her wit nor her bearing nor her Harvard degree could win her a job there. The problem: she was a woman. The university had a policy not to hire faculty wives.

And so my mother made her career in the home, and channeled those prodigious, inexhaustible energies of hers into finding interesting new uses for canned tuna and making curtains. The sewing machine was never put away at our house. She never sat still, without a pair of scissors in her hand to cut coupons out, or—in the garden—a cultivator for pulling up weeds. She never sat still period.

Maybe that is part of what knitting offers a person. (A woman, nine times out of ten. Ten times out of ten, back in those days.) Knitting provided a way of being productive, of demonstrating—as a woman was meant to do—love for her family, and care, even when seemingly at rest. *See, I am still tending to your needs,* the click of the needles signifies. *I am here to keep your hands warm, and your neck protected from the wind. Your toes wrapped in argyle.*

All through my growing up, I witnessed my mother's silent frustration—more than that, her grief, and rage—at what the world of men denied her. One year she tutored a student in our living room, in Latin (a language she hadn't known before, but swiftly taught herself for the purpose of earning that one-dollar-an-hour fee.) Another time, she got a job selling encyclopedias door to door, on commission. She taught night school—remedial English—to servicemen at a nearby airbase. She peddled poems and articles to magazines, about subjects like toilet training your baby, or inspiring your children's creativity, and eventually she started selling a few of these articles. Fifteen dollars here, twenty-five there. Barely enough to pay for the yarn for one sweater.

And I didn't want a hand-knit sweater anyway, back in those days. I wanted the kind they sold in Manchester—the big city closest to where we lived—at the Pandora Sweater Mill. I didn't want my mother's homemade pies. I wished I lived in a house where they kept Oreos in the cookie jar.

When I was in junior high, my mother got a regular writing job: as the ghostwriter for the popular psychologist Dr. Joyce Brothers—a woman roughly her age, who'd managed (thanks to her appearance on a TV game show) to parlay her own credentials into a lucrative career as a TV and radio advice-giver, with a monthly column in *Good Housekeeping.*

Dr. Joyce Brothers was too successful to actually write her own columns, so the person who did was my mother. Once a month a packet arrived in the mail for her, with that month's topic (sibling rivalry, jealousy, depression) along with a handful of clippings from other magazines, which constituted Dr. Joyce Brothers' research.

Spin straw into gold, my mother said, laughing, when she opened that month's packet. Transforming some cheap and commonplace material into something of value: what women did. What they knew best. Substituting their time and hard work (which seemed to hold so little value) for what they didn't possess: status or money.

She taught me how to lay out a pattern, and how to divide iris bulbs, and how to baste a turkey so it wouldn't dry out. Many times, over the years (because I kept forgetting), she taught me the basic stitches, knit and purl. We'd make a trip to the yarn store then, to pick out the yarn for my project (always a scarf, to begin with) and for a day or so I'd click away myself, but I never got past the first few inches. I had better things to do. Unlike my mother, whose life—though she was barely in her forties—seemed to have reached a dead end, I was going someplace.

These were the years—the middle sixties now, then the late sixties, then a whole new decade—when so much was changing for women. The all-boys' prep school a few miles from where we lived, where for as long as anyone could remember, all the smart boys of my class had been skimmed off in ninth grade—announced they'd be accepting female students for the first time in their two-hundred-year history, just in time for my senior year.

I got a scholarship and headed off to the world of men. No time for cooking, or sewing. There were more important things to do than sit around with a pair of knitting needles and a ball of yarn. No more baking cookies and planting tomatoes for me.

Groomed as I was, from early childhood, I was getting writing jobs of my own now—mostly for *Seventeen* magazine. My big moment came when the magazine asked me to fly to Washington, D.C., and interview the daughter of the president—a twenty-one-year-old Julie Nixon Eisenhower. My mother, learning of the assignment, sewed me a sailor dress from a *Vogue* pattern, in red, white, and blue (and never mind that we were Democrats. This was still the White House).

The next year—at college now, another formerly all-male bastion, Yale—I got invited to a debutante ball at the Plaza Hotel in New York City. Other girls might have headed off to Bloomingdale's with their mother's charge card in their pocket to find a dress. My mother found an old dress from her own youth, in our attic. The style was all wrong, and the dress was too big for me, but the fabric was wonderful—black silk taffeta, with multicolored stripes running through it—so she took the dress apart and reused it to make my ball gown. That night I wore the only black taffeta in a room of pink and mauve and peach. I didn't know yet that mine was the finest dress in the Plaza.

These were days that saw big change in the lives of women: the passage of *Roe v. Wade*, and Title 9, and Billie Jean King's defeat of Bobby Riggs, to an audience of millions who'd heard the boast, from Riggs, that no woman could beat even a broken-down tennis player, if that player was male.

Back in the house where I grew up, my mother—turning fifty now, the children who had formed her chief career grown and gone now—published a book about her growing-up years, and then another. Her marriage to my father ended, but her life didn't. If anything, she burst into bloom.

Here was a thing about those days—those early days of my feminist youth, when my girlfriends and I were so busy establishing ourselves as strong and independent women, with careers in front of us. All those old skills our mothers had mastered and turned into art—feeding families on a budget, baking cakes from scratch, growing gardens, sewing their own clothes, and their children's, knitting the most elaborate patterns—came to symbolize everything that was wrong (shameful, practically) with women's lives. If you were good at those household arts, it meant you had nothing better to do than sit around the house, rolling out dough or counting stitches. If you were really successful—and going somewhere—you'd be too busy for all that.

When she was in her late fifties—divorced from my father, living in a cosmopolitan city far from the little New Hampshire town where I grew up—my mother became a minor television personality in her own right, hosting a talk show in Canada where her own Ph.D. was attached to her name, as she dispensed advice on raising children, maintaining healthy relationships. But when I came to visit, with my own children now, it was her roast chicken we wanted, and her pies.

Sometimes, back then, I'd leave my daughter to spend a week on her own with her grandmother. When she did, they always took out the sewing machine, the crochet hook and the knitting needles, along with my mother's scrap bag, full of bits of interesting fabric and buttons rescued from discarded clothes. It was those increasingly rare and little-practiced household arts my child loved best, that I seldom had time for. Work created by one's own hand. The art of spinning straw into gold.

Later (I was in my thirties by this point, my forties even) it would become fashionable for an educated, intelligent woman—a career woman, a successful individual—to bake her own bread, or grow her own tomatoes for the sauce she simmered on her own stove. (Heirloom tomatoes, they call them now.) Later, yarn stores would crop up in trendy places alongside boutiques and day spas, and it didn't matter that knitting a sweater with the yarn you bought there might cost three times as much as what the store-bought version would.

I remember a time—in some business meeting in New York City—when I saw a very fashionable, powerful-looking woman with a pair of knitting needles sticking out of her briefcase. I thought about my mother, who didn't get a briefcase until she was close to sixty (though she was never without a pair of knitting needles, or crochet hook, or a seam ripper, used for taking some old dress apart, to transform into a new one).

We were in the nineties now. Women were far enough along by that point, maybe, that proficiency in the household arts no longer stood as a badge of inferiority. Name a woman with a more glorious success story than Martha Stewart. And she earned it through the superlative practice of the household arts.

My mother—if she'd lived to see this (she did not) would have smiled ruefully, coming as she did from a generation of women— many of them hardworking, talented, possibly even brilliant—whose accomplishments took the form of meals served, children clothed, gardens weeded. Back in her day, a woman didn't become the CEO of a multimillion-dollar company for baking great pies, or knowing how to throw a party, or to knit personalized Christmas stockings for every member of her family. They called those women housewives, and because the definition of working involved earning money for what one did, it was said that housewives—women like my mother—didn't work.

I am old enough to remember the time when to admit you liked to knit, or bake, or sew would call into question a woman's ability to have a serious professional career. Back in the newsroom where I worked as a young reporter, in the seventies, it was almost an act of treason for a woman to announce she'd decided to quit her job because she wanted to have a baby, and stay home to raise her child for a while.

I know this, because I did it. Groomed by my mother, to have the career she never got for herself, I am my mother's daughter in other ways she may not have consciously planned for, shaped not simply by the goal she set for me—to have the career she did not get—but also, to recognize the value in a piece of work—a meal, a garden, a scarf, a potholder—made with one's own hand. As little valued as that piece of work may be, out in the marketplace. But valued by someone, as I have come to value that pair of pig and raccoon mittens. Those pies.

My mother never got much time for her long-deferred career. She died of a brain tumor twenty-four years ago, at age sixty-six.

Sometimes—surprisingly often—I find myself wanting to explain, to some friend who didn't know her (as most of my friends now did not) what kind of a person my mother was: her curious brand of fierce and passionate devotion to her children, her resourcefulness and boundless energy, and the way it found expression. Born in another time—this one, for instance, or even the year I was born, 1953—I have no doubt my mother would have made a large and dazzling career for herself. She was a wonder, at the typewriter, and she was also queen of the kitchen, the garden, the sewing machine.

But when I want to conjure my mother up for somebody, the story I tell features her knitting. It is a very short story, but as well as any other I might offer up, I like to think it conveys what a woman can do when she is left to channel all her big, wild talents and burning ambitions through something as rudimentary as a pair of knitting needles. Something even less than a pair of knitting needles, as it happened.

So: I had this stuffed bear I loved. I wanted the bear to have a sweater. I wanted this sweater to be red. I had no doubt my mother could deliver this item, when the request was made. She could do anything.

This was not your average bear. This bear was approximately one inch tall—roughly the size of my thumb. Still, I wanted this bear to have a red sweater, and I told my mother this.

She was magic, of course. She could have been Martha Stewart, or The Barefoot Contessa, or Oprah. I can't think of too many realms beyond her reach, had she been able to pursue them.

As it was, three days later, I woke up to find the bear wearing the sweater. She had knitted it on toothpicks.

Why would I learn to knit, when I had a mother like that, to deliver what I ordered up, right down to the buttons? (Those were seed pearls. Three of them. With the buttonholes bound off, same as you'd do for a normal-sized sweater.)

My mother could spin straw into gold. The only thing my mother couldn't pull off, it turned out (and this came as a brutal shock) was living forever.

failing better

by Bernadette Murphy

Knitting teaches this perfectionist that what is truly precious in life is a radical acceptance of errors and an appreciation of our human capacity for resiliency.

I FIRST LEARNED TO KNIT WHILE LIVING IN DUBLIN, IRELAND, the fall after my mother died. I was twenty years old and felt profoundly alone in the world for the first time. Having suffered a dance-related injury to the point where I couldn't walk, and stuck living with my elderly Auntie Peggy and the few books she kept on hand, I was bored out of my mind. To pass the hours and to get to know each other, she suggested we knit. It sounded like a terrible idea to me—I have not the smallest bit of patience and was sure I'd fail miserably at the project. But stranded as I was in a foreign country with only two television stations and a raft of religious books to distract me, I became willing as only those who have no other options become willing.

Auntie Peggy, like both my parents, like just about everyone from their generation, seemed to believe in very clear-cut lines. There were the right things in life—Catholicism, married relations that produced children, men leading the way and women bringing up the rear. And then there were the wrong things in life—Protestantism, young people "living in sin," women working outside the home after children were born, single mothers. Not that they would have lacked compassion for those who found themselves inexplicably on the wrong side of this divide, but it was hoped that those who hewed to a properly focused path would be able to stay on the side of right.

I see now, nearly thirty years later, that it was with this same ethos that Auntie Peggy taught me to knit. There is a right way to knit (English/Irish style, throwing the yarn yet always keeping the right hand on the needle), and a wrong way (anything that deviates from the aforementioned right way). When I was learning, I made mistakes.

Mistakes, I quickly learned, were not allowed.

"Can't you see that side was meant for knit, not purl," she'd ask, derision thick in her voice. I was so afraid of her kindhearted but nonetheless scathing disapproval that I paid extra-close attention. Still, even with the most painstaking concentration I could muster, we ended up tearing out and redoing more patches of my messed-up knitting than I care to think about, Auntie Peggy grumbling the whole while about how avoidable my mistakes where.

It reminded me of doing writing exercises on that parchment-thin ale-colored paper in kindergarten with the big thick lines, the dotted line in the middle to rein in exuberant young fingers. Try as I like to make perfect letters, to spell out my infuriatingly long name in stately-looking letters, I could never do it. So I'd erase and start again. And then again. Until the paper eventually gave way beneath the assault of my erasures, leaving only holes and shredded bits of newsprint to show for my efforts.

That said, Auntie Peggy's teaching technique obviously worked. Before I moved home to Los Angeles from Dublin, I had completed three sweaters and was well on my way to discovering for myself the meditative, creative, and spiritual benefits of knitting.

In the years that followed, I taught countless people to knit—friends of friends, people who bid on knitting lessons at charity auctions, friends' kids, you name it. Every time I did, I suffered silently. To sit and watch another person make mistakes is downright painful. Usually, when things got bad enough, I'd have no choice but to rip the needles and yarn from the learner's hands so I could immediately correct the errors made; leaving a mistake in the work was unthinkable. It's little surprise, then, to reflect on those early efforts and realize that no one I taught back then continued to knit. I beat any possible joy out of the experience with my insistence that it be done right.

Thankfully, during this time I was raising my children and starting to learn a thing or two about the benefits of mistakes and failure. Watching my children learn to walk, I had to restrain myself from swooping in and picking them up before they fell. Part of learning to walk involves falling, followed by the important part—learning to get up and try again. In grade school, when they did their homework, I tried not to insist they do it perfectly; I tried to embrace the more Zen-like approach that learning is all about the journey not the destination. Still, it took everything inside me to allow them, once in a great while, to turn in a homework paper on which I knew an error existed. Most of the time I couldn't stand it. I'd point out the error and help them correct it, thinking I was doing a good deed. Surely, they were learning important lessons in accuracy.

Really, what they were learning was twofold: (1) That I didn't think they were smart enough or capable enough to learn from their errors; and (2) that my need to be seen as a perfect mother outweighed their need to learn.

A FRIEND, CATHY, contacted me to help her plan a baby shower for a friend of hers. Could I teach a group of women to knit all at once, getting them far enough along that each could produce a 4-by-4-inch knitted square, which Cathy would then piece together into a baby blanket?

"Instead of getting a party favor, the women who attend will not only get a knitting lesson but a skein of yarn and a pair of needles to keep them going," she enthused, certain this was a great idea.

I worried about how the event would unfold: teaching one person to knit meant I could snatch the yarn and needles from the learner's hands in time to prevent errors, but what do you do when there are a score of people learning all at once? To make sure I'd have an extra set of knowing hands that day, I first taught Cathy to knit. We sat in my living room, side by side on the couch, as I taught her the rhyme I'd learned at the Waldorf School where they teach second graders to knit as part of the curriculum.

In through the front door
run around the back
peeping through the window
off jumps jack.

Whenever Cathy wound the yarn in the wrong direction, or tried to peep through the window going the wrong way, I did what I'd always done: attempt to yank the yarn and needles from her to correct the error as quickly as possible. But Cathy, unlike the other

people I'd taught over the years, would not be cowed by my insistence. Rather than relinquishing the knitting implements to my desperate grasping, as everyone else had always done—as I had meekly
done with Aunt Peggy—she simply elbowed me away.

"I can see your challenge with this experience will be learning
how to let other people make their own mistakes," she said very
matter-of-factly, as if such a thing were not only possible but to be
encouraged.

Of course I shouldn't let people make their own mistakes, my
insides cried. What would be the point in that? If I can save them
from making an error, isn't that the wisest course?

"You won't be able to work with each of the baby shower guests
one-on-one," she pointed out. "You'll have to explain the process well
enough that if people make mistakes we can just let it be. Unless the
faults will ruin the blanket, we'll live with them."

Live with the mistakes? What a terrible idea! If I had to, I'd
reknit every one of the 4-by-4-inch squares myself. How would the
edges line up if they weren't done properly? How would this be a
nice-looking blanket by the time we were finished?

As directed by Cathy, I purchased twenty pairs of size 8 knitting needles and twenty skeins of forgiving yarn. To make the event
go as smoothly as possible, I cast on the 12 required stitches on all
twenty sets of needles. Everything was ready to be placed in the
guests' hands at the party.

The day arrived and, as I'd been dreaming for nights, the experience of teaching that many people to knit at the same time, especially when they were all feeling social and wanting to chat with each
other, was like herding cats. Some paid attention to my demonstration. Others were busy sharing pictures of their young children with
each other. I tried to stay calm, teaching them the little rhyme, but I

heard the shrillness creeping into my voice. If they didn't learn to do this properly, it would be my fault. All that money spent on needles and yarn, wasted. Eventually, the knitting started to happen. A few of the women already knew how and offered assistance to the others at their little tables. Cathy and I floated from table to table, helping, repeating the rhyme ("in through the front door, run around the back," and intervening when needed. "The stitch is still on the first needle. Remember 'off jumps Jack?' Jack's still stuck here. You have to help him jump off"). By the time the baby shower ended, I'd sweated through my silk dress and had lost my voice. We were left with a pile of what should have been 4-by-4-inch squares. They weren't quite that. There were some good-looking ones, but most looked like what you'd expect from people just learning: misshapen, dropped stitches, extra stitches, uneven stitches. I was certain the adventure was a big fat failure and that Cathy was sorry she'd ever signed me on for it.

Eventually, she was able to piece together those semi-squares and add a crochet border that made up for all the funny shapes. By the time the blanket was done, it looked like what it was: a homemade gift of love put together by twenty disparate women showing their support of a new mother. It didn't look like it belonged in the pages of Pottery Barn, which is what I would have wanted. More like the potholder my kids made for Mother's Day when they were in first grade—messy, full of mistakes and equally full of love.

Cathy's words, though, didn't leave me. "I can see your challenge with this experience will be learning how to let other people make their own mistakes. " I took this thought to heart. Up until that point, I had seen my children not so much as their own selves, but as reflections of me. If they did well in school, it made me look good. If they received praise for their intelligence or hard work or talent, I soaked up the reflected glory. But in how many ways was I cheating them from being fully themselves when I insisted they be "right" all the time so that I looked good?

Around this time I was working on my first book about knitting and interviewed a woman who made fine art sculptures of food— ham dinners, snack cakes, sushi—by knitting them. Only she wasn't a very good knitter, couldn't actually do the knit or purl stitch, kept conflating them with crochet stitches. Instead of getting mad at herself or tossing the needles and yarn aside in a huff, she embraced what she was doing. One day, while laid up in bed after having her wisdom teeth removed, she tried to knit mittens. She couldn't get the hand part of the mittens right to save her life but she totally nailed the thumbs. She had so much fun knitting little stand-alone thumbs that she simply kept making them. Under the effects of the painkillers, she looked at her growing pile of thumbs and saw something new. A thumb is just about the right size as the little bed of rice upon which sushi is constructed. She no longer had a pile of thumbs, she told herself, but little sushi beds in different colors. And voilà, her first knitted food sculpture began to take shape.

I was talking with a friend the other day about the idea of a mind-set and he told me of a theory he'd been reading about: the idea of a fixed mind-set vs. a growth mind-set. With a fixed mind-set, a person believes himself to be born with certain skills and abilities—like the cards a dealer gives out in poker. This is your hand; you'll have to make the best of it. In childhood, this person may have received praise for being smart or funny or good-looking or any other positive attribute that may have been innate. He will spend the rest of his life trying to play the same cards, hoping that they'll be enough to get him the joys he wants in life. The person with the growth mind-set, though, sees things differently. She may know she has certain natural abilities, but is aware she can learn many other things as well by sheer effort. (I remember my friend Nancy, who attended medical school as a single mother of four, telling me her definition of intelligence: not necessarily being smart, but being able to learn what you need to know.) The person with the growth mind-set, as a child, was mostly likely praised for her effort, for trying new things, for making attempts and failing, only learning to fail better the next time. This person learns to engage a challenge, doesn't rely solely on innate skills but wants to branch out and learn new things, gain new skills. This person is likely to grow up feeling that she can learn to be competent at pretty much anything she sets her mind to, so long as she's willing to put in the effort. This is the benefit of making mistakes: realizing you not only can recover from them, but you can thrive as a result of what you learn about yourself as you recover.

I'd like to say I learned this lesson early enough to have had a positive influence on my three children, that I let them make mistakes and praised them for their fearlessness, that I no longer looked to them to provide me with reflected glory. Alas, no. But I did learn enough about the nature of mistakes while they were growing that I think some of these ideas got through.

I look at my own career. As a writer, I have created countless failed efforts. I have had to do this over and over again in order to find the right way to tell the story. I recently finished a first novel, nearly twelve years after I began it. It's not that it took me twelve years to write the 280 pages that comprise the book. It's that I had to write the story every possible way over the course of what was probably 2,000 pages spread out over more than a decade, to discover the way that best expressed what I was trying to say. I was tempted to write the words "the wrong way" and "the right way" in that last sentence, so strong is this pattern of thought. I have to physically stop myself and remind myself of some simple truths: In everything I do in life, there's isn't a right way. There are choices and there are consequences. What appears to be "right" for someone else may not, in fact, be right for me.

This lesson has finally come through in my parenting. It's painful to sit back and watch my children, now nearly fully grown adults, make mistakes. I don't mean to suggest a moral tone with the word "mistake" or to imply that just because it's a choice I wouldn't make, I necessarily think their choices are therefore "mistakes." There is a difference, I realize, between making an error ($2 + 2 = 5$) and making a judgment on someone else's choice. But hoping my son will not go so fast while riding my motorcycle on a windy mountain highway as to crash it, I believe, is hoping he not make an error in judgment fueled, most likely, by his youth and gender. (Though the bike was totaled, my son, thank God, was fine.) But they have to learn their own path. How many times have I wanted to jump in and save them from the error of their ways? If I know better, don't I owe it to them to save them that heartache? But I can no more do that than my parents could save me from making my own mistakes.

When I look back on my younger years, it's often the mistakes and how I recovered from them that taught me the important lessons. Getting pregnant at sixteen in high school. Becoming an alcoholic/drug addict as a young adult. Later, making poor financial decisions that led to losing a house to foreclosure. These have been the touchstones in my life. Events I wouldn't wish on my fiercest enemies, and yet . . . Learning that I had a kind of resilience in me that I didn't know was there? That's the greatest gift possible, and what turned me into a person with a growth mind-set though everything in my history should have dictated a fixed one.

If I had one wish to impart on my children, I think it would be that: that they discover their own resilience, their own ability to recover from the mistakes they make directly, as well as from the messes that occur when life is cruel and unfair. That they have a growth mind-set. That their knitting, like learning to write their names, like learning to crawl and walk, and drive a car and attend college and get a job—that all of life becomes a place to learn, and that they embrace the fact that errors are not the end of the world.

Looking back on that baby shower experience, I see that sharing an afternoon of love with a group of women who were learning to knit and finding joy was more important than producing a Pottery Barn blanket. You can buy one of those for a small stack of bills. But it's in knowing that you can build a life that uniquely fits, that you can stumble, make uninformed choices, and still learn and grow from the experience that matters. The lessons I first learned from knitting keep showing me this truth: that a kind of radical acceptance of errors and an appreciation for our human capacity for resiliency—that's what's truly precious. And there's no mistake about it.

how knitting saved my life. twice.

by Ann Patchett

How one scarf holds together the people the writer has loved and lost in her life.

CAST ON

IN THE BEGINNING there was my grandmother, with her knitting and the stuff of her knitting: the flat faux leather folder of colored aluminum needles that zippered up the side, in which the needles were all numbered and stayed in their designated slots. There were the mystery needles, the loose ones, those with points on either ends, and others that were held together by thin plastic cables that called mitten strings to mind. There were the balls of brightly colored dime store yarn that lived in a yarn bowl (like a wooden salad bowl on a waist-high pedestal that my grandfather had made). There were stacks of tatty pattern books, the tiny plastic stitch markers in white and yellow and blue, a hand-cranked ball winder, a metal needle gauge, a stitch counter that was also good for keeping track of how many times we walked around the block. My grandmother sat in her chair in the evenings knitting sweaters, sporty doll dresses, slippers. The whole business was magic as far as I was concerned. Yarn into sweaters did not seem so far from straw into gold.

She waited for me to ask her for lessons, and then she taught me. When I was a child I cast on as a child, wrapping the yarn twice around my index finger and dipping the needle through. "This is the wrong way to do it," she said. "I'll show you the right way later." What she wouldn't let me do wrong even for a minute was to hold my yarn in a pinch between two fingers up by the needles. My Aunt Rae was a master knitter, by which I mean argyle socks and gloves with cables down the fingers, and she held her yarn like an unschooled six-year-old and refused to change. My grandmother saw this as a failure of her parenting. It was not a mistake she was likely to make again. She started me off knitting squares, which she referred to as "knitting knitting." Instead of squares, I knit octagons, then trapezoids, then rectangles. I dropped as many stitches as made it back onto the opposite needle, and my grandmother patiently picked them up again and handed me back my knitting.

PATTERN

T HE SUMMER I WAS nineteen I won a cash prize for a short story I'd written and used the money to go to Europe with my friend Marti. Knitting was something I had dabbled in over the years, and only in the presence of my grandmother. I had gone beyond the square but had never progressed past the scarf. In Denmark and Brussels and in the countryside of France, Marti and I watched the women knitting. They knit in the parks, in the cafés, on the trains. They made it seem like a task that was essential to adulthood. "I don't know how to knit," Marti said, looking over her shoulder at the women we passed. Marti was from a family of intellectuals. I said I would teach her.

I was qualified to teach her how to knit a square. We bought some needles and some yarn, and then boarded a ship to Ireland. We started hitchhiking. We wound up wherever people dropped us off, in towns that did not see many tourists but which saw an endless river of yarn. While Marti went in search of art or meaningful architecture (she was dreaming), I went to the yarn stores and sat on the floor and knit. I wanted to stay ahead of her. I learned how to read patterns, how to work with different colors, how to use the funny little double-pointed needles. When I dropped a stitch, I simply walked up to any female person who was older than I was and handed her my knitting. I did not limit myself to women in yarn shops. If there was a woman in the British Isles in the summer of 1982 who didn't know her way around a dropped stitch, I never met her. "I've made a mistake," I would say by way of explanation.

"Oh dear," the woman would say, and then she would fix it. If she was very patient, she would show me how to fix it myself.

Marti, who could jump a horse and speak French and had an excellent grasp of art history, struggled with the burden of knitting. She said this was because she was left-handed, but I never cut her any slack. One day we hitched a ride in an eighteen-wheeler heading north through Scotland. The wide windows and high seats gave a panoramic view of the countryside. Marti and I shared the single front seat. I was knitting an Icelandic sweater on circular needles. She was still struggling with her square. I gave her a hard time about it, I will admit. I was sticking my fingers through the gaping holes, the Swiss cheese of wool. Marti ignored her dropped stitches, thinking that in time they might heal themselves. When we came to a gas station, Marti went inside to get a Coke, and once she was gone, the rig driver, who wasn't much older than we were, began to scold me in a Scottish brogue so thick I had almost no idea what he was saying. I asked him to repeat himself several times.

"You can't pick at her," is what he was saying, or something close to that. "You shouldn't be cruel. She isn't right."

It took some more explanation but finally I figured it out—he was telling me my friend was mentally handicapped—the proof of which was that she was a woman who didn't know how to knit, and I was cruel to continually point out that which should have been gently overlooked.

That night, Marti and I rented a room in a house on the desolate north coast of Scotland where a woman sat and pulled apart the most beautiful sweater I had ever seen, winding the yarn back into balls. "I wanted a new sweater," she said, while we sat there aghast, unable to save it. "I've had this one for years."

CABLES

THE SUMMER WE WERE in Europe, I taught Marti how to knit and she taught me how to smoke. After college, she became a runner, stopped smoking, married, and had two children for whom she knit tiny sweaters. My life took a different path. Try to knit a sweater and write a novel at the same time. It doesn't work. No one pushes back from her desk to knit a few rows and contemplate the sentence on the page, but a cigarette, with its two-minute burn, is the perfect vehicle for reflection. It's not as if I made a conscious choice to smoke instead of knit, but when I came to realize that the smoking had to stop, I did in fact make the choice to knit rather than smoke.

This had to do in part with the woman I had watched unraveling that sweater in Scotland. When she started to knit it up again, she did so with a cigarette clamped in the far right corner of her mouth, her right cheek raised, her right eye closed tight against the wafting smoke. She wasn't just holding the cigarette there while she knit, she was actually smoking it with an aggressive puffing that did not require that the cigarette ever be removed from her mouth. It created a picture so starkly unattractive that I knew I would never knit and smoke at the same time, even if I were alone with the doors locked and blankets thrown over every mirror and window. Knitting and smoking must never coexist. Knitting occupied my hands. My hands were needed to smoke. Every time I craved a cigarette I reached for my needles instead. I promised myself I only had to hold on for five more rows, after which the impulse had usually passed. Still, I found the desire for cigarettes could not be thwarted by simple Icelandics on circular needles. I needed something complicated. I started knitting cables. I counted stitches and adhered to rigorous patterns. I couldn't put my knitting down because there were too many needles involved for me to easily pick it up again.

It took me more than a single try to quit. I would finish a sweater, go to a party, and someone would offer me a cigarette. The next thing I knew I was smoking again. The next thing I knew I was knitting again. It's not as if I ever stubbed out a cigarette and someone pressed a ball of yarn into my hand, but the two things became so intertwined I could hardly keep them straight in my mind. I wanted to smoke. I wanted to knit. I quit smoking for good. I couldn't stop knitting.

Knitting, we may remember, did nothing for my writing. Smoking did nothing for my health. In the end I quit them both.

CAST OFF

O R I DID UNTIL Lucy died. Lucy was a terrible knitter. She'd start things every now and then, but she would always leave her knitting on the subway a dozen rows in. She had been my best friend for seventeen years. When she died we were both thirty-nine. I got into bed, not having any idea what I would do with the day or the next day or all the weeks and months and years that would follow. I got a pack of cigarettes. I smoked in bed. That was when my friend Erica sent me a box of yarn, skeins and skeins and skeins of thick pink wool, not a loud pink, not a girlish pink, but a pink that called to mind a winter sunset, dusky and tinged with blue. It was late December and cold. She sent me thick wooden needles and cursory directions—*knit two, purl two.* Forever. I put the skeins on my feet and rolled them into balls. It was the kind of yarn and needles children start with so that they can see fast progress. It was also a good yarn for the grieving because even on the days I did nothing, I could point to my knitting and say to myself, Look at all I've done. Several times I ripped it back and started again. I cast on. I wanted something wider, a little looser. I got out my grandmother's needles, which I had inherited, and experimented with the gauge. Like Penelope, I knew I never wanted to finish that scarf, and so I made it last a long, long time.

Erica is the best knitter I've ever known. She can make a cardigan with elegant buttonholes that lie flat. She's made me fingerless gloves to write in and lacy shawls to throw over my shoulders. And when I was at the bottom of the well, she threw down a length of yarn and told me to knit myself up. She didn't care how long it took. She would be waiting there at the top, holding on to her end.

Ten years later I am still wearing that scarf, though only on very cold days. It's enormous, like high Japanese fashion, an entire sheep's worth of wool. Sometimes I think that I'll take it apart and make something more practical, two smaller scarves, but then I think about all the people this scarf has to hold—my grandmother, who taught me to knit, and Marti, who I taught how to knit, and Lucy and all the things she didn't get to finish, and Erica, who made sure I got it done, and all of our collective love and hope and disappointment. When I think about it that way, I'm amazed I was able to knit it all in.

the clothes
make the dog

by Taylor M. Polites

In which the author learns to knit elaborately cabled sweaters for his very small dog, and in so doing discovers truths about himself.

MY DOG LOVES CLOTHES. THIS SOUNDS LIKE PARENTAL projection, I know, like a mother who insists her toddler loves to be in pageants. I do love putting clothes on Clovis. But the level of enthusiasm Clovis shows for raiment cannot solely be explained by my own myopic insistence that he wear things. He truly loves clothes.

During a visit to Palm Springs a few years ago, I found a man selling dog coats at a street fair. A faux fur coat in two tones caught my eye: earthy gray with a blond fur collar. It looked like a chinchilla peacoat Kanye West might wear. And with Velcro tabs for easy on and off. Very Clovis.

The cross-country drive had been long. Clovis was moody. He lay on the sofa at our rental, his head on his paws, sighing and distracted.

I said, "Do you want to see your present?" His ears perked up. I pulled the coat out of the paper sack and he jumped to his feet, bouncing and swiveling all at once. He panted. I put the coat on him. He looked like a marvel and he knew it. He pranced around the room like a Lipizzaner stallion. This dog loves clothes.

Clovis is about as small as a dog can get. He is a Chihuahua, weighing in at about four pounds (although he weighs more than he looks, like his father). He is too small to jump up on the couch or the bed, or down from them either. He can curl up into a ball to sleep on my shoulder and often does. He is like some magic sprite that inhabits my apartment. He has the Chihuahua swagger and their incredible capacity for devotion. He is an animal of calculated prudence, even timidity, yet he can be aggressive with large dogs and children. He trusts neither, and his instinct is to make as much noise as possible, which sometimes creates a situation. This means that I, too, must be watchful and prudent for Clovis. He talks, grunting out contentment or disapproval or voicing his concern about the course of a conversation. His prime directive is to be in physical contact with humans—with me in particular. I would not have it any other way.

How could you not want to bring pleasure to this strange creature that is in large part a dog, but many other mysterious things besides? To me, in case it is not already clear, he is more than a pet. He is a living being with a consciousness, preferences, desires, fears, and joys. I find myself comforted in the ways that I can comfort him and predict his needs. If he has a passion for fashion, I am happy to indulge it. Knitting is a skill I have picked up for Clovis. I laugh at the image it conjures: a forty-something single man sitting at home knitting sweaters for his small dog. It is both funny and discomfiting. I look at Clovis and it occurs to me that he doesn't give appearances a thought.

.   .   .

WHEN I LEFT New York City with the harebrained scheme of becoming a writer, I moved to Provincetown, Massachusetts, a resort town popular with gay and lesbian tourists at the furthest fingertip end of Cape Cod. In the summer, the little New England fishing village turns into a bacchanal of epic proportions. In the winter, as if to compensate for one season's excess of living, the town contracts to a modest estimate of two thousand or so people, something like a large high school or a small private college. One with miserable weather and sullen students who spend the bulk of their time hibernating or mood-altering. But like any normal high school, people always notice the new kids. I moved there in mid-winter. I knew two people.

New Englanders surround themselves with a wall of reserve. Coming from the South, even after many years in New York, I was struck by the cultural difference. I have heard the terms "salty" or "crusty" used to describe Cape Codders. The intensity of the tourist season heightens that suspicion and reserve, and Cape Codders relish the exercise of their saltiness. I once called a store to see if they were open. The man on the other end of the line said, "Well, the door's open and I'm here." Breaking through the reserve and making friends are not easy. Moving there in winter, away from the nonstop activity of New York, was even more of a challenge. I spent a lot of time alone and much of that inside my head. For a writer, this is crucial, although you risk landing yourself in a mental institution. One of my two P-town friends said P-town is the world's largest open-air asylum. The other really is in an institution.

Perhaps that is why I got it into my head that I needed a dog. Companionship. I had wanted a dog for years, but New York City does not lend itself to dog ownership. The work hours and commutes are long, not a good life for animals that crave companionship. By leaving my job to have a go at novel writing, I found I had space for a dog. But what dog? I considered every breed, from Great Danes to Vizslas to Weimaraners to Corgis.

In Provincetown, as spring arrived and the townspeople emerged from hibernation, I noticed a few Chihuahuas on the street. Their owners, heavily muscled, tattooed tough guys, all gay, were perhaps what I noticed first, but eventually my eyes were drawn below their beltlines to their Chihuahuas. Buster was black and white, about eight pounds, and so sweet and shy. Harley was bigger, over ten pounds, stocky and matter-of-fact. I loved these dogs. They had the personalities of big dogs, but were portable and easy to care for. They were devoted to their owners. Chihuahuas as a breed have the reputation of bonding with one person to whom they will be attached for life. The ancient Aztecs believed that after death (or more gruesomely, sacrifice), these spiritual little dogs would wait on the banks of the river of Death until their owners met them there, and then they would serve as their guides into the afterlife. Who would be fool enough to refuse a little postmortem assistance?

These P-town Chihuahuas were kin, too. I not only got to know the breed, but the breeder through her dogs. I spoke with her to understand her breeding philosophy. I checked in with her regularly to see if she had a puppy. Finally, after months of waiting, she said she had a little boy puppy that was perfect for me. I replied, "His name will be Clovis."

When I picked him up, he was eleven weeks old, but still so small he could stand comfortably on my hand on all four legs. His head was too big for his little fawn body. He looked like a bobblehead doll. I was terrified I would crush him. I thought that I had made a terrible,

terrible mistake. But we learned how to sleep with one another. I found myself waking up prior to rolling over. He would sleep curled up next to me until I fell asleep, then move to the furthest possible corner of the bed. He still does. We made room for each other, like the way he curls up so perfectly in my lap, almost becoming a physical part of me. I found companionship and a remarkable little personality.

Clovis's size always draws remarks. He gets the Chihuahua look and I get the big guy with the little dog look. In the Blue Ridge Mountains of North Carolina, we were walking along a lookout point. A group of bikers pulled up, all leather, tattoos, and outrageous facial hair. They would have fit in perfectly on Commercial Street in Provincetown, heavy on the masculine bravado. One gruff tough looked at Clovis, then at me, and said, "Your wife got a little dog and now you have to walk him?"

His friends laughed. I smiled.

Not exactly.

A FRIEND CAME OVER for coffee one winter afternoon and told me he was working on a pair of socks. Knitting them, he said. The sun was setting behind a low scrim of gray clouds. The fire in the fireplace crackled. Quiet, beautiful Provincetown winter.

Knitting socks? I thought to myself. That is an intriguing idea. I looked at Clovis, curled up beside me on the couch. Knitting, I thought. There were quite a few people in town who were knitters. One guy brought his knitting work to social events. There was a small group of men and women who gathered to knit and quilt and crochet. Why do gay men knit? Isn't knitting considered a woman's craft? My chauvinism was showing.

The behavioral spectrum of gay men is just as diverse as society itself. Some have hang-ups about gender roles that any straight man might. And there are, of course and obviously, gay men who are not concerned about inhabiting gender stereotypes. Most, however, dwell in between these, aware of and protective of their sense of masculinity, but also curious enough to give things that might be deemed "feminine" a try. If it contravenes established thought regarding gender norms, it becomes somehow more enticing. P-town is a world where those conventions are flouted, twisted, subverted, and challenged in so many ways. Your sense of identity and your willingness to experiment is broadened. You lose a lot of hang-ups. And why not? Living according to imaginary rules can be claustrophobic. Do we even realize their limitations? In Provincetown, the work of abandoning those rules, of rewriting them on a daily basis, is all part of the experience.

When I was in my "gay rage" phase, I read a book that introduced me to the term "genderfuck." Without knowing it, I had been engaged in genderfuck since I begged my parents for a play kitchen at the age of four. My parents were indulgent. Perhaps they thought later they had gone too far.

We all learn proper gender behavior in one way or another until we don't even realize what we have been taught. In Provincetown, there is every type of gender bender, real or imagined, from post-operative transsexuals of all persuasions to drag queens, heterosexual cross-dressers and fantasy freaks to party bears and old-school leather daddies with antiques shops who sing Judy Garland songs at the top of their lungs. And let's not forget the hetero-normative homosexual men with children acquired through adoption, surrogacy, or the ever-popular turkey baster. A man knitting is quaint by comparison. And that is the wonder of Provincetown. The element of play, not surprising in a resort town, is strong year-round. Dress-up and costume parties, like in the art-colony days, were a part of the summer season long before the gays arrived. But we have given it a new zest. Hell, I've put on a dress a few times.

Then I looked down at Clovis. Four pounds of fawn-colored fuzz. He makes little snoring sounds sometimes when he sleeps. I wanted to knit sweaters for him. What was Provincetown doing to me? Wigs, dresses, and knitting? Was I a stereotype?

I did love to go antiquing, poring over piles and piles of forget-table junk looking for that one fascinating treasure that only costs a dollar or two. I had learned to play bridge the prior winter from my eighty-year-old friend Peggy. I was in a writers' group with two women in their eighties, Claire and Helen. Not only had I assumed some sort of gender-subversive behavior, it was age-subversive as well. I was acting like an eighty-year-old woman. I thought of the dress I kept in the closet for those Provincetown moments when you absolutely have to wear a dress. It was sapphire blue and very forgiving in the waist, made of gathered cascades of shiny rayon so that with my arms out, it looked like some insane polyester star-burst. It was something Blanche Devereaux from *The Golden Girls* would wear. My God. Well, from that point of view, knitting made perfect sense. I thought of my great-aunt Vivian Morse. "Bibby," she was called. She died in 1992, but I got to know her when I went to college. She was an original. Sister to my grandmother Betty Jo. Also a true original. Maybe that's where I got my penchant for old lady manners? Bibby had never had children. She lived alone in a very nice brick duplex filled with mid-century remakes of eighteenth-century French furniture, embossed leather side tables, damask upholstery, and lamps with crystal pendants and fringe. She had a small Yorkie, Joey. She yelled after him constantly, "Joe! Joe! Joe! Joe!" The poor dog was traumatized, a constantly trembling, nervous wreck. And completely untrained. He knew enough at least to hide his misbehavior. There were small Tootsie Roll–sized poops behind the end tables and sofa. Bibby played bridge. So did Betty. Bridge, canasta, poker, rum, anything with cards. Betty ran a bingo bus to Milwaukee and Oklahoma over the weekends. They both smoked like chimneys, swore like sailors, spied on each other, were in a constant state of battle-ready alert, and were two of the most fantastic people I have ever known. Maybe that was it? My grandmother could crochet to beat the band. Afghans came streaming off her fingers when she found her stride. She could win at canasta while zooming along on a multicolored throw, a cigarette trembling at the edge of her lip. "Goddammit!" she would scream if she made a bad play.

I HEARD A KNITTING group was starting for the winter. My friend Katie was one of the ringleaders. Katie is like the Earth in Provincetown. She connects with people and helps them connect to each other.

The first meeting was in November. The season was long over. The banners and streamers had been taken down. The summer people had gone to their winter jobs in Fort Lauderdale and Palm Springs. The businesses were closed up, some with plywood nailed over the windows. The hard core of Provincetown residents was beginning to show like bone. These were the people who truly lived here.

The knitting group met in a recently renovated bar that sat on piers at the edge of the harbor. The tide came up underneath the floor. The walls were glass and the floodlights from the few fishing boats on MacMillan Wharf served as a backdrop.

I went on my own, not sure what to expect. Katie was there, ready to take care of anyone who wandered in. She and her cosponsor brought large baskets of yarn and a mix of needles. All you needed was a pair of empty hands and Katie would fill it. She taught me the knit stitch and purling with calm patience. She was my North Star into this new world. On those dark nights when the sun seemed to set just after it rose, I looked forward to the knitting get-togethers. I learned how to make a ball of yarn that you pulled from the inside. I learned German stitches and French stitches. I learned increasing and decreasing, how to fix a dropped stitch, and my holy grail, cabling, the technique of twisting stitches to create textured patterns.

Every week, there was a mix. Men and women, young and old. There were pretty young wives from Wellfleet. Portuguese women who brought Crock-Pots full of chili or sausage and peppers. Gay men who brought drag gowns for bedazzling. One night a local character wore a pair of large red plastic lips the entire night without giving the slightest indication that anything was out of the ordinary. A selectwoman came with her knitting work; she was also a bridge partner of mine. Local DJs and business owners, bartenders and yoga teachers, mothers-to-be and the hot-to-trot. As contradictory a group of people as you could find, all brought together for knitting and company. We were making things—for ourselves, for other people, for our animals.

I started with a scarf for Clovis. It was really only meant to be practice, but as it grew, I thought, Well, this is about the right size for a scarf. Why not? As I continued to knit, the stitches had the annoying habit of disappearing, so I kept increasing the rows. This gave one side of it an uneven, scalloped quality. A hole opened up at one end of the scarf as I was casting off. Should I throw it away?

Start over? I hated to waste my first effort. I put fringe on each end and sewed on a button that had popped off my pants. The accidental hole was converted to a buttonhole.

I showed the scarf to Clovis. His eyes got bigger. He shivered a little, keeping his tail low but wagging. He was unsure. Was it a gift for him? I wrapped the scarf around his neck and buttoned it to keep it in place. He looked regal. He knew it. He strutted around the living room, proud of his latest accessory.

I began experimenting with patterns for sweaters, finally arriving at a hybrid that seemed to work. As soon as the work started coming off the needles, Clovis realized what was going on. As with the scarf, that soft clicking was for him. That ball of yarn he grabbed with his fangs and shook like a dead mouse was being knotted and turned for him. Dark green tweed. Fire engine red. An experiment with sleeves. Finally cable-knit. A staghorn in hunter green with small round sleeves. Ribbed waist and collar. The pattern was beautiful. It is still my favorite sweater for Clovis. The pattern, the color, the fit. He wears it sleeping in my lap when I type. When he wakes up in the morning, yawning with sleepy eyes, stretching, I hold up a sweater. This one? He sits, his tail wagging, waiting for me to slip it over his head. He lifts each paw so that they slip through the sleeves. He is dressed and ready for the day.

I MOVED TO PROVIDENCE, Rhode Island, about a year ago. It's two hours from Provincetown, so I do not feel disconnected from that community where Clovis and I both sank true and permanent roots. I go back often and miss the culture and community, the gossip and get-togethers. But Providence is an incredible city in its own right, filled with people who are passionate about art, writing, architecture, and history. There are locavores and hipsters, artists and deadbeats. Like Provincetown, it has a strong sense of identity and community. Like Provincetown, Providence embraces expression.

My first day here, it was misty and cold. February again. In the middle of the park across from my apartment, there is a dog run. There were no dogs around to bother Clovis on that first morning, so we walked over. Clovis sniffed around the edges of the small enclosure. The bars were spaced wide enough for him to easily step through, but his prudent timidity kept him from doing something so daring.

A woman walked up with a giant, slow-moving St. Bernard. Annie, the dog's name is. She is sweet and mild, but Clovis had his barking fit. When he finally relaxed, my new neighbor and I had a chance to introduce ourselves.

She said Clovis was cute.

I said, "Thank you."

She said, "I like that sweater, too."

I said, "Thank you. I made it."

She looked at me and said, "You knit that?"

I said, "Yes," quite proud of myself.

"Oh," she said, digesting the fact. *"Ohhhhhhhh."*

Loaded with meaning. I suppressed a laugh. Yes, everything that this dog and this sweater imply is true.

Is that what I have become? I smile when I think of it and look at Clovis. Funny how we pick up things along the way, the elements of our outside selves that serve to define us. And how sometimes, too, those things pick us. Be it fate or some universal magnetic attraction, things coming together through affinity or a great and incomprehensible master plan. Either way, I get to knit elaborately cabled sweaters for my feisty, wry, and loving little four-pound Chihuahua. Getting hung up on labels is like looking a gift horse in the mouth. And what a gift he is.

I am a somewhat self-obsessed novelist with a small Chihuahua for whom I knit sweaters. I have put on a dress and wig a few times and had a good time doing it. I play bridge and like to antique. I love history and nineteenth-century novels. I am those things and many others that I know of and do not yet know. I am many things I have left behind and many things I have yet to pick up. I love my dog and the relationship we have. I am awed by the humanness in him. No, not humanness, but rather a fact of all warm-blooded mammals. We experience pleasure and pain, love and sadness. We crave community. We love to make ourselves known in different ways, through display, affinity, and connection. Clovis loves his clothes, and I love Clovis and the warmth he brings me. I admit, sometimes I wear him like my most important accessory. My love for him has bound him up in my identity and me in his. These paths we've taken to get to each other may be random, but what a gift that randomness is. Is it too much to suggest that a small Chihuahua has a life path of his own? I am no Saint Francis, but surely Clovis has taught me to love more broadly, to see a little of him in other animals, even people. What a minor miracle of life that I wanted a dog, but got this beautiful and devoted individual. And maybe Clovis feels that same sense of wonder and gratitude at the world. I would not be surprised if he did.

clovis's perfect-fit sweater

by Taylor M. Polites

The specifications here can be altered to suit the size of the animal for whom you are knitting. I use medium-weight wool like Cascade 220 from Cascade Yarns. I use size 6 (4mm or British 8) double-pointed needles, although the instructions can be modified for use with a magic loop. The trims and back pattern can be modified as well for various cabling and ribbing patterns. For the belt and collar, I have used garter stitch, moss stitch, one- and two-stitch ribs. On the back (the middle needle carrying 24 stitches), I have used a variety of cables. My first and favorite is the staghorn, which is included below.

Cut a few yards of yarn from the ball before beginning the pattern. This will be for the gap in the breast left when you make the sleeve holes.

Cast on 64 stitches and split between three needles 20-24-20. When knitting, I look at the inside of the sweater, so use "wrong side" instructions.

For the first 8 rows, purl 2 and knit 2 for a belt in the rib pattern.

The next row, purl all the way around.

Start the pattern, the staghorn on the following row, Row 1. You are dealing with a total of 64 stitches. The instructions reflect that.

Row 1: P17, K1, P1, K1, P1, K1, P1, K1, P4, S12, hold at front, P2, P2 from cable, S12, hold at back, P2, P2 from cable, P4, K1, P1, K1, P1, K1, P1, K1, P17

Row 2: p64

Row 3: P17, K1, P1, K1, P1, K1, P1, K1, P2, S12, hold at front, P2, P2 from cable, P4, S12, hold at back, P2, P2 from cable, P2, K1, P1, K1, P1, K1, P1, K1, P17

Row 4: p64

Row 5: P17, K1, P1, K1, P1, K1, P1, K1, S12, hold at front, P2, P2 from cable, p8, S12, hold at back, P2, P2 from cable, K1, P1, K1, P1, K1, P1, K1, P17

Row 6: p64

Repeat pattern for 19 rows. On Row 20, you will cast off for the left sleeve. Row 21, you will cast off for the right sleeve, continue the pattern across until you get to where the left sleeve cast off began, and then knit back and forth for 8 rows.

Row 20: P50 (so purl across needle 1 and needle 2, then purl the first 6 stitches of needle 3), cast off 8 stitches, then P6

Row 21: P6, cast off 8, P3, K1, P1, K1, P1, K1, P1, K1, P2, S12, hold at front, P2, P2 from cable, P4, S12, hold at back, P2, P2 from cable, P2, K1, P1, K1, P1, K1, P1, K1, P3

Return in the opposite direction so that you are knitting on the "right side."

Row 22 (right side): K36

Row 23 (wrong side): P3, K1, P1, K1, P1, K1, P1, K1, S12, hold at front, P2, P2 from cable, p8, S12, hold at back, P2, P2 from cable, K1, P1, K1, P1, K1, P1, K1, P3

Row 24: (right side): K36

Row 25: (wrong side): P3, K1, P1, K1, P1, K1, P1, K1, P4, S12, hold at front, P2, P2 from cable, S12, hold at back, P2, P2 from cable, P4, K1, P1, K1, P1, K1, P1, K1, P3

Row 26 (right side): K36

Row 27 (wrong side): P3, K1, P1, K1, P1, K1, P1, K1, P2, S12, hold at front, P2, P2 from cable, P4, S12, hold at back, P2, P2 from cable, P2, K1, P1, K1, P1, K1, P1, K1, P3

Row 28 (right side): K36

Row 29 (wrong side): P3, K1, P1, K1, P1, K1, P1, K1, S12, hold at front, P2, P2 from cable, p8, S12, hold at back, P2, P2 from cable, K1, P1, K1, P1, K1, P1, K1, P3

Now stop. You should have 12 stitches on a needle in the breast that you left behind 8 or 10 rows ago. Take the fragment of yarn you cut off at the beginning and a spare needle. Pick up the stitch on the "wrong side"—purl-wise—and purl 12, knit back 12, etc., for 9 rows. Now return to needle 3 where we left off on Row 29 above.

Row 29 (wrong side—continued): Your needle 3 should have the K1, P1, K1, p3 from above. Now, cast on 8 stitches and pick up the breast section that you just completed for p6.

Row 30 (wrong side as originally): The remaining 6 stitches of the breast section can now return to needle 1. P6, then cast on 8, then pick up the final 6 stitches of needle 1 on the other side of the sleeve gap for p6. Purl around another 44 stitches until you have completed a full round.

Row 31: P17, K1, P1, K1, P1, K1, P1, K1, P4, S12, hold at front, P2, P2 from cable, S12, hold at back, P2, P2 from cable, P4, K1, P1, K1, P1, K1, P1, K1, P17

Row 32: P64

For the next six rows, you will reduce by 1 stitch on needles 1 and 3. For a wider collar, reduce less.

Row 33: P13, P2tog, P2, K1, P1, K1, P1, K1, P1, K1, P2, S12, hold at front, P2, P2 from cable, P4, S12, hold at back, P2, P2 from cable, P2, K1, P1, K1, P1, K1, P1, K1, P2, P2tog, P13

Row 34: P12, P2tog, p34, P2tog, P12

Row 35: P11, P2tog, P2, K1, P1, K1, P1, K1, P1, K1, S12, hold at front, P2, P2 from cable, p8, S12, hold at back, P2, P2 from cable, K1, P1, K1, P1, K1, P1, K1, P2, P2tog, P11

Row 36: P10, P2tog, p34, P2tog, P10

Row 37: P9, P2tog, p34, P2tog, P9

Row 38: P8, P2tog, p34, P2tog, P8

Row 39: P52

At this point, you can switch to whatever collar pattern you choose. I usually stick with the same pattern I did on the belt. So a P2, K2 rib for 10 rows. Cast off *very* loosely.

For the sleeves, I pick up 8 stitches on each side. If I can't pick up 8, I increase where appropriate for a total of 32 stitches. I purl (wrong side) for four rows, then P2, K2 rib for 4 to 6 rows on each sleeve. Cast off loosely.

Weave in ends.

high-strung knitter

by Elissa Schappell

All this high-strung woman wants is to bliss out with a ball of yarn. Can knitting calm her down?

I WILL ADMIT, YES, I CAN BE A LITTLE HIGH-STRUNG. EVEN SO I was surprised when, during a routine physical six years ago, my doctor announced that I had high blood pressure. It wasn't possible. Me? I was young, I was healthy—okay, *healthyish*—not overweight, okay tense, perhaps I was a little tense. Which isn't a bad thing, right? If you're not tense you're not paying attention. I mean, the world is going to hell in a handbasket. At the time W. was deploying troops like a kid playing with army men; I was in the middle of writing a book, in addition to my monthly book column, and teaching, and picking up work wherever I could—I had children— two children who had become addicted to food and shelter and old enough to not be duped into believing people wore tinfoil shoes, and I had insomnia, and maybe I was grinding my teeth—the headaches weren't new, so okay, maybe yes, yes, my blood pressure was elevated. I suppose if you wanted to get technical about it—and doctors are all about the technical—that wasn't good.

"YOU NEED TO BRING your pressure down," my doctor advised sternly. "If you can't bring it down, then I will have to put you on statins."

"Statins?"

Statins didn't sound like a good drug—it didn't possess the ring of a good drug, like Wellbutrin which promised to make you well, or Effexor which sounded like the name of a superhero. Statins suggested static and statistics, the word itself like the prick of a pin, the opposite of the dreamy-sounding Valium, which was so close to helium.

"Do you exercise? What about yoga?"

"Oh sure," I said, "I've done yoga."

Which was true, where I was misleading was in my tone, which suggested an openness to going back to yoga. Which I could do, but given recent history, it wouldn't help. Yoga made me tense. The girls who'd challenge each other to see who could hop across the mat fastest with a leg tucked behind her head. The last time I'd gone the instructor, clearly exasperated that my downward dog pose suggested a puppy with distemper, whacked me on the back of the head, and told me I had to relax.

"Have you ever tried knitting? It's a great way to relieve stress. A lot of people find it very therapeutic."

GROWING UP, MY SISTER and I were not allowed to watch television unless we were doing something with our hands—drawing, beading, embroidering, making potholders—we had potholders enough for an octopus's soup kitchen—and for a short time, I tried knitting.

BOTH OF MY GRANDMOTHERS and my mother knit. My grandmothers knitted us hats with pompoms and fancy cabled sweaters with intricately designed yokes, patterned with snowflakes, leaves, and flowers. The tag in the back reading always, *Made with Love by* GRANDMA. My mom knit, too, although not with the same zeal. Her sweaters had dolman sleeves or were made out of eclectic yarns, some spun with feathers.

THE FIRST THING I made—the only thing I recall making was a rainbow-colored rug for my dollhouse. Okay, it started out in my mind as a sweater, downgraded to a scarf once I began to drop stitches and add them. My knitting expanding and narrowing, the middle swollen like an anaconda digesting a cow. Until, the physical evidence of my incompetence undeniable, I begged my mother to teach me to cast off.

THE "RUG" LOOKED out of place in the dollhouse which my father had built for us. It was spare and modern and furnished in blond Scandinavian-style furniture that looked like it came from Barbie Ikea. In contrast, the rug like something pulled out of a dumpster.

STILL, SURELY I COULD knit again. After all, wasn't it in my blood? Soon after—in the way that shoplifters start noticing other people sticking turkeys under their sweatshirts, I started seeing knitters everywhere. A sisterhood of flashing needles.

MY DREAM WAS delicate shawls, knit from yarn spun from the fur of a goat that lived high in the Andes fed only on a diet of clover and honey. Delicate lacy wraps that draped around my shoulders, and magically stayed put. I wanted to be that woman, the one who doesn't have to keep adjusting her stole. Who can say when complimented, "Oh this, I made it myself."

I HAD TO ADMIT it, the knitters did look a whole hell of a lot less strung-out than me. Zen. Everyone said that knitting was meditative. And though I'd never know if there was indeed a pose called "The Knitter," there should be. A modified lotus, energized arms at right angles, a look of purpose and bliss.

This was what I wanted. I wanted to bliss out with a ball of yarn, the sound of my needles clicking against each other in a natural rhythm like birds in a bamboo forest tapping their beaks against the trees.

Over Thanksgiving, my mother took me to buy yarn. I'd found some fancy yarn shops in the Yellow Pages. However, my mother very gently suggested we'd find "more appropriate yarn" at the local craft store. Not only would it be much less expensive, it was, as she put it delicately, "more forgiving." Which was what I needed, forgiving. Meaning it could stand up to being tugged and unknotted, it would knit up fast, delivering the gratification I longed for.

·   ·   ·

I WANTED TO LEARN to knit European-style. It possessed the savoir faire and efficiency of eating European-style. However, it quickly become apparent that I was hopelessly American. My mother assured me she preferred the American way, the extra movement, the rhythm, it was almost like Tai Chi. Sure, Tai Chi as practiced by someone being swarmed by bees.

MY MOTHER TAUGHT ME to cast on. With every stitch she'd say, "You see, it's easy." And I'd answer, "Keep going, I'm watching."

My daughter, watching all this, decided it didn't look too hard, and so she too took a set of needles and started to learn. Four, four generations of knitters!

I went slowly, fingers gripping my plastic needles near the tips near the end, white-knuckled like a child learning to hold her pencil. Knitting slowly, shoulders hunched, I kept my fingers on the stitches so they wouldn't slide off, when I knit too tight, fearing they'd slip off, I lifted them off by hand, I counted and recounted each stitch as I inched forward. Gnashing my teeth when I'd see I'd dropped one, or added three—how could I add stitches when I couldn't cast on by myself?

I spent a lot of time with my head in my mother's lap watching her remove my stitches and then catch me up to where I had been. It was like a kid at home trying to figure out a math problem. Maddening and embarrassing.

AT HOME, I FORGOT everything my mother had taught me. How could I forget something like how to cast on? So I watched videos, seeking out the ones made by hippie knitters who smiled a lot, and those who spoke in simple sentences like sedated kindergarten teachers. Steering clear of the folksy pioneer ladies who knit at the speed of a galloping horse and I imagined would knit even if they'd broken both arms, and the cool Teutonic taskmaster who I could almost feel glaring at my incompetence through the screen.

Finally, after a few days I had a strip of knitting that was long enough for me to consider a scarf, although it fell somewhere between an ascot and a scarf (a scarfscot?), in any case I could wrap it around my neck, and I did.

I HADN'T EXPECTED ANYONE to stop me on the street and ask me where I got that bright red five-inch-wide foot-long strip of knitting, but maybe someone might at least acknowledge it. When I announced to friends I'd made it they looked surprised. No, I said, I hadn't been to rehab, but knitting was, for all practical purposes, occupational therapy.

Over the next two weeks, I'd loosen up some, and so would my knitting. I'd knit two more scarfscots. I liked the slip of my stitches on the plastic needles, but the slight resistance of the bamboo—and the fact that they were wood—appealed to me too.

When I went home for Christmas, I showed off my three scarves, and my mother presented me with a family heirloom, a collection of my grandmother's needles. They were glorious-looking, metal and shiny in a rainbow of candy colors—rose and emerald, jade and ice blue. For the most part they were thick as porcupine quills, but there was a pair of 10's. I slipped my stitches on. The metallic click and slide, the idea they belonged to my grandmother, pleased me. I was a third-generation knitter.

·   ·   ·

MY HABIT WAS GROWING. We'd rented the *Lord of the Rings* trilogy and my daughter and I sat and knitted for six hours straight. Only grudgingly getting up, at my mother's pleading, to come and eat. My first knitting bender, a harbinger of what was to come.

During the two *Godfather*'s and a *GoodFellas* I'd knit a scarf for my husband that could double as a hammock. Soon I was bingeing regularly. Looking for excuses to sit and knit, I'd begun watching TV series, old episodes of shows I'd never seen—after all, when I was watching TV I had to be doing something with my hands—so my daughter and I sat and knit for hours in front of *The Gilmore Girls*. And yes, I enjoyed it. Mostly.

I MADE FAT SCARVES, and skinny ones that could work as stylish neckties for hobos. I made a striped scarf, which was fine from a distance—in what I liked to think was a sort of DIY distressed dirty hipster way—up close you could see the places I'd been forced to knot the edges to straighten out the lines. As always it was for the best if you didn't flip the scarf over. The backs of my scarves revealed the myriad surgeries—emergency stitches to patch holes, a web of knotted-together loose ends.

I learned at my daughter's insistence how to purl. It was just going backwards, knitting in reverse. I could do that. I liked how flat purling was, like fish scales; however, I couldn't count, and had no patience for row holders or marking the numbers down, and often it took a few rows before I'd realize my mistake and have to rip it out.

Unlike me, who was tentative and dogged, my daughter was

reckless and creative. Not content to knit forward, she'd outdistance me, learning to purl, she was making cables—the equivalent of learning how to swim butterfly—and then moving on to circular needles and hats. I was knitting strip scarves and she'd moved on to beanies. I tried not to be competitive. Damn her youthful skin, and ability to knit in a circle! Who, though, knit better straight ahead and backwards?

I bought nice yarn and made scarves that curled up and had to be steamed and pinned down like the hides of some sort of animal, which invariably curled up again. I made very thin scarves out of very nice yarn—spring weight, I told myself—perfect for gardening.

I was anxious about knitting in public, but driven by my doctor's admonition and warning about statins, about the threat of having to take yoga again, I began cramming a ball and needles in my bag. Where once I read I now knit on the subway. Indeed a man on the subway asked me, "Will you knit something for me?" I was flattered. "But in a different color."

Occasionally, I locked eyes with other knitters—Hey what's up, sister? Most of the time when they looked at what I was doing, they'd smile, nod encouragingly. Perhaps a flicker of pity crossed their faces.

For my technique was far from perfect, in fact it was lousy and more than once a fellow junkie scolded me for the way I was holding my needles—I was going to hurt myself, and insisted addict-to-addict it would be easier if I scooted my hands down.

There were those who seemed to believe it was their duty, as part of the Sisters of the Needle, to correct me—nay, their right. The way older mothers (or sometimes just domineering women without children) like to give you unsolicited advice on child rearing. Cover the child's ears when the train goes by, make them wear shoes, and not let them walk on top of walls. Sitting in the park, an elderly lady I'd noticed eyeing me from a distant bench had come over and, smiling, taken my hands and corrected me the way a stern ballet teacher corrects the pigeon-toed student's turnout.

I confess that what had begun as a way to unwind now had me in knots. I'd gotten cocky, started buying fancy yarn and sweating over it. Still, I was obsessed, not by a desire to get better, but by the mere action of knitting. I was obsessed.

It got so bad that when we went to the movies, I took my knitting. I had to. How could I sit there in the dark and not do something. I wasn't lazy. Knitting was relaxing me, dammit. It was good for me, and my blood pressure—which indeed I'd been taking every morning—was, if not dropping fast, improving. So I'd sit in the dark, and knit, while the pirates on the screen engaged in swashbuckling swordplay.

Or the needles would slip out of my hand in the middle of a love scene, the ping and skittle breaking the mood, and the person in front of me, picking it up perhaps imagining it was a piece of jewelry, something precious, not a stick. However, it was precious to me, I found I could not sit still unless I was knitting. I bought light-up needles for the car. Who could just sit? If I sat in the dark all I'd do was obsess about all the people I loved come to terrible mortal ends, or worry about my career, global warming, I could fairly hear the sounds of polar bears drowning in the Arctic.

IN NO TIME, it seemed, my daughter went from knitting scarfscots to scarves with cables and patterns, to hats in one sitting, and now a sweater! She knit a sweater. A chunky white fisherman sweater!

Then one day, as the air grew chill and my arms were aching from all the typing I'd been doing to finish a draft of a book,

I wrapped a scarf around my arms, and it clicked. I'd knit hand warmers! Hand warmers, not with any pattern, I couldn't read a pattern, or count. In the beginning I sewed them together in pieces, sometimes one color, sometimes I created stripes, despite their Frankenglove vibe, I loved them. I experimented with dropping a stitch for the thumb hole and imagined them on the mitts of a modern-day Oliver Twist. I knit a pair of opera glove–length arm warmers out of cashmere (which I then promptly lost) and a set of thick wristbands in a manly slate blue for my twelve-year-old son. They were perfect. They were a comfort to me, as I worked. Not only that, outside, they kept my hands and arms warm while allowing me to move my fingers. I stashed them in my bags and in my backpack. Friends started to ask if I could knit them a pair. My daughter wore them when she drummed and my son wore them to bed at night.

STILL, DESPITE MY ANXIETY, my obsession, my fear of circular needles when I went back to the doctor a year later she said, "Your pressure is much better." And it was. "I started knitting," I said.

"Ah, I hear it works," she said.

"You ought to try it," I said with the zeal of the convert, the addict, the next words out of my mouth might have been, *Here, I've got the needles in my bag, let me give you a little taste.*

I bought a bag for my yarn, it says, *I Knit So I Don't Kill People.* And it's true. I'm grateful I discovered knitting, and you should be too.

knitted goods: notes from a nervous non-knitter

by Elizabeth Searle

What is it about knitting that makes it addictively soothing, even as a spectator sport? And what is it about the "knitted goods" her grandmother left behind that still exudes the reassuring calm and goodness of Grandma Price herself?

I AM NOT GOOD WITH MY HANDS. A NON-KNITTER, I AM drawn to knitting as a spectator sport. I love and envy knitters, from my Grandma Price, now gone, to my knitting-whiz friend, who is at my side as I write this. Anyway, she is at my side in my mind. I like to—even "need to"—sit by my friend while she knits. Hypnotized by her rhythmically clicking needles, I am hooked up to an IV of peacefulness.

I rock slightly with the steady soothing rhythms of her knitting the way my Grandma Price used to rock in her oak rocker as she knit. And knit, and knit: a multicolored skein unwinding into the past for me as my friend's needles flash. Sleep "knits up the raveled sleeve of care," my husband likes to quote from the Bard to insomniac me. My mind can get pretty darn raveled.

At the ends of many busy days, I need to retreat and—as my own Bard, my husband, puts it—"just lie on the bed and twitch." In the same way, when my knitting friend is near, whether on her old-fashioned comfy couch in front of the TV or in straight-backed chairs at teacher meetings or events, I need to sit beside her. Once at a student performance, I happily headed toward my accustomed seat beside my busily knitting friend. Only to stop short, finding my knit-watch perch occupied, fully.

I froze. As the rest of the audience settled in place, I faced a tall fellow faculty member who had innocently settled into "my" seat beside Suzanne. I fixed this six-foot-plus man with a stricken, even appalled gaze. I did not say the words aloud: You are in my seat. But the man in question seemed to hear me. As if I'd spoken, he rose up to his full height, towering over me, looking apologetic as he sidestepped away to another seat. I shot him a sheepishly apologetic look in return. And I sank back into my "rightful" seat at my friend's left hand, her needles paused. I caught her understanding glance and I flushed. Sorry to have been mutely rude but happy to be where I needed to be.

Yes, "need" is the word, I realized as the student performance began and Suzanne resumed her knitting, the medicinal powers of the clicking needles doing their work. My spine relaxed and I sank back in my seat, the world restored to its proper order.

What is it about knitting that makes it downright addictive, even to those who merely sit near and watch? Why is the act of knitting so powerfully soothing that even as a "spectator sport," it can offer chemical-level mood-altering calm?

As I watch my friend knit, watch a sweater or scarf grow on her lap, I contemplate these questions—considering, first, my grandmother's legacy of knitted goods. "Goods" in many senses, but I'll start with the ones made of yarn. And made with a care that makes them last.

FROM MATCHING FRINGED AFGHANS in my sister's and my "official" favorite colors—red and yellow, still bright thirty-some years later—to an accidentally sexy olive green sweater I wore night and day through college, including in my long-haired boyfriend's bed; to the "Birds of Happiness" wedding blanket my husband and I still have on our own bed; from a white sweater set for my mother, my sister, and me, embroidered with daisies and delicate green stems; to my mom's "mod" 1970s-style belted blue sweater; to the crocheted tablecloths in four different sizes, culminating in the gravy-stained-yet-still-elegant cloth my mother currently uses when she extends the dining room table to serve twelve— including my son and my siblings' kids—our Grandma Price's lovingly knitted "goods" live on.

Mom's mother was our family's sole knitter. And Grandma Price was also, not coincidentally, our lively, high-strung family's island of calm. Her speaking voice in her later years wobbled as her hands did not. Yet that game shaky voice always had sensible things to say. Grandma gave the problems of the day a comically exaggerated shrug. She used to tell my earnest worry-prone mother, "Whatever is, is best."

My mother says her mother did not begin knitting till later in her life. In Mother's childhood, what she remembers was her mother sewing clothes, not for pleasure but out of necessity. Grandma Price's "good hands" had years of strengthening. Mother and her parents and three siblings lived out the Great Depression in rural Loyal Oak, Ohio, in a white board farmhouse. Grandma milked a cow named Cherry every day. She made butter and blackberry jam—from berries the children picked—for her homemade bread. And she canned the corn, tomatoes, and beans they grew, as well as their neighbor's peaches.

Grandma and Grandpa belonged to a Wesleyan Methodist church, which forbade dancing and bingo and movies. Maybe Grandma's early "lap work" came not only out of the necessity to make clothes for her four children but from a need for entertainment in the evenings. In her later years, Grandma knitted on and on, creating endless new projects for her ten grandchildren by the blue TV light.

I wish I could ask Grandma Price now to put into words what it was about knitting that made it her passion. Gail Donovan, a writer friend of mine, says, "I love taking what is basically a long string and constructing a three-dimensional object. I love thinking about how somebody figured out how to do that!"

The sense of a "created" object, of a blanket where there was once only a ball of yarn, is something even we non-knitters can appreciate. It is part of why some of us love so much to watch knitters and why we treasure their hand-knitted goods. Fingering my grandmother's careful yet not machine-regulated stitches, I can literally "feel the love" that went into each good.

Grandma Price's serene and ceaseless knitting seemed of a piece with her inner peace. Her knitting epitomized Grandma—especially the patient, stoic Zen qualities I wish I had inherited.

Uncomplainingly, Grandma always shuffled about with a lopsided walk due to "bad feet" (maybe the price she paid for such good hands). So she'd collapse in her rocking chair in the evening with a giant sigh she seemed to savor, before grinning good-naturedly and taking up what she called her "lap work."

In the years when we visited Grandma and Grandpa Price's mobile home in Ohio, TV light lit Grandma's flashing needles, her concentration unbroken by the jumpy bright screen images she half watched with a bemused half-smile. As a kid, quiet on the outside but jumpy on the inside, I liked to plant myself near Grandma and her knitting as if near a cozy calming fire.

At our own home in the evenings, my mother too liked working almost ceaselessly while watching TV. She'd iron clothes or grade papers for her high school classes. Knitting was never her forte, but Mom was skilled in creating crafts and displays as a science teacher. She'd poke mini-marshmallows with toothpicks and straws to make model DNA molecules. Like her mother, Mom has to keep her hands busy, though not in a rocking chair.

I AM THE ROCKER—in both the Grandma Price sense and in a decidedly un-grandmotherly musical sense. "Music has charms to soothe a savage breast," my husband John quotes from Congreve when John DJ's our evenings of rock music. Which I enjoy for hours on end in my favorite rocking chair. My own "lap work" involves scribbling in a notebook as I groove to the music.

When Grandma and Grandpa Price moved into my parents' home in Arizona, Mom had a rocker ready for Grandma. But it wasn't quite "right." Soon Grandma, utterly un-fussy in all other ways, found a high-backed light brown oak rocker with soft cushions exactly like the one she'd left behind in Ohio. Soon she was rocking away her evenings by Grandpa's TV, often tuned to professional bowling matches, Grandma's needles moving to the rhythm of her rocking.

I too need to end each day with a period of time rocking, listening not to TV but to our full-blast stereo. "What is the name of your game?" I was once asked out of the blue at a party, as a conversational salvo. My husband answered for me, but I wasn't mad because he got it right.

"Trance," he said for me. And for many creative types, whether knitters or writers or both. We just want what Virginia Woolf called (and deemed necessary for novelists) an "uninterrupted trance." Being "in flow"; or "in the zone"—long before those pop psych terms were popularized, Grandma Price knew how to "go there," without fuss.

On evenings of music with my DJ husband, I often still wear my favorite knitted good from Grandma Price, that thick cable-knit olive green sweater. This is the sweater I wore both asleep and awake all through college, often throwing it on over a T-shirt and my favorite patched-up jeans. I still recall the sexy thrill of stepping out into the fall air with no bra under my T-shirt, feeling through the cotton the snug fit of my warm-wooled sweater. Always half-zipped. When I unzip it, I sometimes recall my then-boyfriend inching down the same zipper, slowly.

That long-haired college boyfriend is now my long-haired gray-haired husband. Another of the knitted goods that has accompanied us through twenty-plus years of marriage is our "Birds of Happiness" afghan, fine cream-colored wool knitted in a pattern of interlocked birds, wing to wing. The cream color is stained now with wine, chocolate, baby vomit, cat hairs, and God knows what else. But it receives an occasional wash and retains a place of honor at the foot of our bed, keeping our feet warm through the winters.

Both Grandma and Grandpa Price died within weeks of each other, in the early eighties, in their mid-eighties. They are buried in adjoining graves in a cemetery near my parents' Arizona home. When my husband and son and I stay in Arizona, we get the "guest apartment" where my mother's parents lived and slept.

I never sleep well anywhere, especially away from home. But when I lie in Grandma and Grandpa's old bed, it helps me drift off to picture Grandma Price sitting in her old-fashioned white cotton nightgown, letting my sister and me watch as she "took down" from its hairnet and pins—her hands moving slowly for once—her long silver-streaked hair.

MEETING MY FRIEND, the knitter, for the first time, I was struck by her long dark hair, streaked with silver. In no other way does my friend resemble full-figured blue-eyed Grandma Price. In fact, she looks more like the "Searle side" of my family, my side: tall and slim with dark brows and an intense dark gaze. But her face and body are more relaxed than the Searle clan tends to be. In an impromptu charade exercise, she was cast as a gently swaying willow tree.

Though she is always warm, friendly, and seemingly at ease, a kinetic nervous energy fuels her. Her hands when she knits move briskly, looping and pulling her yarn with no-nonsense efficiency. Before my friend, I'd assumed all serious knitters were like Grandma Price: naturally calm individuals whom I could love and admire but never hope to be. Yet my friend, I have learned, has her share of stress and worry. Though we are both lifelong "good girls" with longtime marriages, one big difference between my friend and me is that she grew up in a small town. She has a deep connection to rural western Massachusetts.

My childhood was marked by moves. I wound up going to four different high schools. Maybe being more rooted in one place is part of what makes my friend the willow tree be able—like my Grandma Price, steadily and patiently and seemingly endlessly—to sit and knit.

MY MOTHER SAYS her mother's knitting helped "keep her going" through her long and productive old age. Like my mother's, my own middle-aged hands tend to tremble. My mother and I both go shaky when nervous. Which, for us, is fairly often. Grandma would always tell Mom, as Mom would later tell worrywart me: "Today is the tomorrow you worried about yesterday." A quietly mind-bending remark that I still puzzle over, watching my knitter friend loop her yarn round and round.

Maybe knitters can especially appreciate the cyclical nature of life. As I get older, even I am beginning to mellow out. "Have you never been mellow?" my sister and I used to sing, mocking Olivia Newton-John's spaced-out delivery. The answer for me, back then, would be a flat-out "No." In my frenzied twenties, I seldom sat still long enough to do anything except read and write. Even when writing, I'd pace the floor, pound the keyboard, rock in place as I worked.

But later in my life, around the time I became addicted to my friend's knitting as a spectator sport, I began to catch up, too, on the small sewing tasks I used to let pile up, undone. These days, I find my own miniature knitter's trance by sewing on the occasional button. The in-and-out motion of the needle lends itself to contemplation. As I get deeper into middle age, what my husband and I call "muddle age"; as I see the same day-to-day "crises" rise up, then fall back, the same worries looping round and round, I am learning to take peace where it comes.

A few minutes sewing on a button or a few hours sitting by a knitter can—like a waking version of sleep—"knit" my overly raveled sleeves of care. Or at least I can relax a bit, the way I did as a hyper kid sitting near the glow of my knitting grandmother. Grandma Price is by my side again when I darn my son's socks or when I sit by my friend as she knits. And knits and knits. Her deft steady hands never stopping.

what are you making?

by Ann Shayne

That simple and much-asked question: What are you making? saves the day for one knitter.

SOMETIMES, THE IDLE CHAT THAT GOES ALONG WITH KNIT-ting isn't idle at all. Maybe knitting has never literally saved my life, but I recall three perilous moments when my knitting sparked an unexpected conversation that saved the day.

I. BABY SWEATER

I KNEW WHEN I WOKE up that it was going to be a Queasy Challenge Day.

We arrived at the dentist's office at 9:59, figuring that the closer we were to the appointed time, the less my son David would stew while waiting to have his tooth pulled. It was Mother, of course, who was the problem. David was a trouper, nine years old, a pillar of stoic, steely will. He had no clue about what tooth pulling entailed. "Will I be asleep for this?"

"Uh, not really. Numb is the word. You'll be really numb and rubbery."

Kelly the Prettiest Dental Assistant Ever opened the door, beckoned David, and said to me, "You coming?"

I said, "Oh, you go on, David," and he said, "Aw, you come too, Mom." So, against every bit of good judgment in my body, I went. I sat in the corner, knitting furiously on a tiny wool sleeve for a baby sweater, a pattern called Fern.

Dr. Evans breezed in and, with the stealth of a cat burglar, slid big pliers onto his tray, out of David's eyeshot. I went back to my knitting. Rumor had it that Dr. Evans had the elegant ability to stick a big needle in a kid's gum without the child ever knowing it. But I knew better than to watch how he performed his magic. Never in my life had I focused like this on a piece of knitting.

I decided to knit my way through the whole thing. *Fern, Fern, Fern.* Dr. Evans' brilliant patter mesmerized me. He talked in a smooth stream, about anything, and he finally slipped in, "Do you mind if I just wiggle it a little?" which is the Dentist Code Phrase for "I am pulling your tooth now." Unfortunately, at the worst possible moment, I forgot to Fern and glanced over. I caught sight of it: that root-'n'-all tooth, fresh out of the gum, as God never intended a mother to see her boy's tooth. I flopped forward, head between my knees, bracing for impact, hoping they would think I was searching for a lost . . . anything.

I go through life in a vague cloud of queasiness. Weak stomachs abound in my family, with plenty of stories having to do with pulling off into a ditch, or running for the trash can at Grand Central

Station, or other crises involving puking. At this point, it's more perverse and comical than a mere fear of gross things: I have a fear of queasiness, which is the worst of all.

Decades passed while I studied my shoes. If only I hadn't seen that tooth. It looked like the sign for a medieval dentist's shop. It was an iceberg's worth of hidden tooth root. I came up for air and found that David was great, with a wad of gauze in his mouth and one Iron Eyes Cody tear in the corner of his eye. He was the star; nobody was paying any attention to me.

We made it to the waiting room where I lay down full out on the sofa, my Fern sleeve sliding out of my bag onto the floor, the ball of yarn rolling across the carpet. I told him I felt kind of hot and woozy. David said, "Momth. Ah you okay? Weawwy, ah you okay?"

I saw stars and a long tunnel with Jesus at the end. "Okeydokey, we're off," I said, and we made it to the sidewalk in the parking lot. "I think we'll just sit down right *here*," I said, even as drizzle fell around us. I could not look at David's wounded mouth without going into full headspins, so I said to the cement, "I am so *dizzy!*"

He said, "I hink you hath hat viwus thing I had wast week." I suddenly realized that he had not connected my queasiness with what he had just been through, and for that I was grateful.

"You okay?" I opened my eyes to see the pink face of Kelly the Prettiest Dental Assistant Ever above me. She had a ball of green yarn in her hands. She smelled like mint. *I have died,* I thought, *and this is how you are greeted in heaven.* "You dropped your knitting—glad I caught you. Whatcha making?"

Mint is the single most restorative smell to anyone who suffers from the queasies. *Of course,* I thought: *Heaven smells like mint.*

"A sleeve. I'm making a sleeve."

"Pretty!" she said. "I just don't know how you knitters do it. It looks so hard."

Hard? Knitting is hard? She was the one who stuck her fingers into David's gory mouth, not me.

"You did great, David," she said, and patted him on the shoulder. "See ya," she said to me, mercifully ignoring the fact that I was huddled on the sidewalk in the rain. And with that, I sat up. Cured. Retrieved from the cusp by this angel of dentistry.

At dinner, my husband asked David if he had had a shot, and David said, "No, it was just this gel stuff, mostly. Couldn't feel a thing." As I put him to bed, he told me, "I was glad you were there with me, Mom. It made me feel better."

"Piece of cake," I said. "Anytime you get a tooth pulled, I'm your gal. Any. Time."

II. SCARF

IT HAPPENS OFTEN ENOUGH. I'm waiting for a doctor, a dentist, an oil change, and there's another knitter in the waiting room. There is no way I will leave that room without engaging with that knitter. It's downright rude not to give each other at least an acknowledgment that we are both living life to the fullest, while all these losers around us are stuck reading *Parenting* magazine.

Across the room sat a lady who had to be at least eighty, knitting something so tiny that she held it directly in front of her face, about four inches from her thick eyeglasses. Most of what she had finished was balled up in the palm of her hand while she worked, deep in what I call "the zone." She lowered her hands and gave me a look. She saw me cranking away on my scarf, a piece of unremarkable knitting I kept in my car for those moments when I didn't bring something more interesting with me. She nodded the way a farmer raises a finger from the steering wheel in greeting, then returned to her crazy knitting.

I was waiting with my dad for an appointment with his cardiologist. We were there because there was something weird about his aorta, and he had a big procedure scheduled for the following day. He was calm—sanguine!—about the plan. This was just a plumbing job, to hear him talk about it. He was a physician, so he talked about his own health in a matter-of-fact way. I was the opposite: the human body was not something to be messed with. Even a flu shot seemed like a terrible imposition. I didn't know much about aortas except that they are right down there in the thick of a person, and it seemed like a big damn deal to get access to the thing. I was upset that somebody was going in tomorrow to manhandle my dad's aorta. Horrified, actually.

In a nonchalant way, Dad started telling me about his living will and the durable power of attorney that would give me the legal authority to oversee his care should he become incapacitated. I hung in there, pretending to care about the details, trying to match his levelheaded tone. Then I lost it, with no warning, a sudden downpour in a morning of lame jokes about parking garages and hospital elevators. He was sweet as I cried into his shoulder, his arm around me. I stayed huddled against him awhile, younger than I had felt in a long time, hating that oxymoron phrase "living will."

"Excuse me," a voice said. It was the lady from across the waiting room, tapping my shoulder with the corner of a tissue box. "Here," she said, then sat down in the chair across from us. I sat up and took the box. "What are you working on?" she asked.

"Scarf," I said into a tissue. "You?"

"Lace. For a veil. Great-granddaughter." She relaxed her clenched fist, the one that contained whatever it was she had been cranking out, and two yards of gossamer lace unfurled to the ground. Tangled, unblocked, a damp butterfly just out of the cocoon. She took the end and spread it across the dark gray of her skirt, that gesture of stretching that knitters do all the time.

"Beautiful," I said. The intricate fan shapes alternated back and forth, impossible.

"It's my backup knitting," she shrugged. "We're here a lot." She raised an eyebrow toward my dad, who had gone to look for the bathroom. "Your dad?"

I nodded, wobbly.

"Scared?"

I nodded again.

"Not you. Him."

"He never gets scared."

She let out a quick breath, a puff of surprise. "Is that so? I wish you could have seen his face just now."

III. SOCK

IN THE GAME THAT is airplane seat roulette, I watched the passengers coming down the aisle, wondering which one would end up as my seatmate. You can tell by their eyes how far down they're aiming, so when a tiny guy eyeballed my stretch of real estate, I was relieved. A tiny guy meant more room for a knitter to do her thing. No armrest issues, less likely that my pesky claustrophobia would kick in.

From the minute he entered the airplane, he was working the room: he joked with the flight attendant, let out a "whoopsy!" to the woman onto whose head he dropped his baseball cap. "Well hey," he said loudly to me from four rows ahead. "I'm your roommate!"

Oh man. Jovial.

I had no steam for this. I was late to Wisconsin to give a knitting talk with my co-conspirator Kay Gardiner, who was flying out from New York. Bad weather meant that my day's travels had already taken me from Nashville to Cincinnati to Minneapolis. This final leg to Madison felt like Mile 900 of the Iditarod. And I was already jumpy about the prospect of giving a long talk to a group of expert knitters. Public speaking had always been a terror for me, and only with Kay's help did I manage to get through these events.

The little guy's progress was slow. He enlisted the help of a tall man in front of us to hoist his overstuffed carry-on into the compartment. Dropping into the aisle seat beside me, he sighed heavily and wrapped his arms around the heavy backpack in his lap. I recoiled—such a sunburn on that arm: deep red, radiant, like an actual burn.

"Is your arm okay?"

He shrugged. "It's my foot that's on my mind right this minute." He stretched a leg out into the aisle, and I saw why he had moved so slowly: his foot was swollen to the point that his shoelaces were untied, and it was purple. The whole ankle was a blotchy purple. He studied it.

"What on earth?" I asked.

"Portuguese man-o'-war." A wound from a sea monster? My nightmare. "Been in Hawaii. On a job."

"What do you do?"

"Electrician."

"You travel for that?" I thought electricians were local guys.

"I do. Extreme electrician, you could say. I'm not what you call phobic. Heights, water, Antarctica—not a problem. I once spent four months in Mammoth Cave. If you're little, you fit in tight places."

"What were you doing in Hawaii?"

"Volcanoes. You know." He glanced down at the knitting in my lap. "What you making?"

"A sock."

"Making a sock? In this day and age? You're crazy."

"I know. That's not the half of it," I said, and with that, I started talking. Something about this guy was so disarming. He was a leprechaun, or an elf. I told him about my knitting blog, the knitting books Kay and I had written, and the reason I was going to Madison, Wisconsin. I also told him that I was not looking forward to giving a big talk in front of a lot of people.

"Hold on," he said. "You're worried about standing on a stage in front of people who are knitting? This is a problem?"

I said it was.

"Here's what I want you to do. This is cake. When you go up there, and you look out on all those people, and you think, ohmygod I can't do this, I want you to think about me: dangling on a rope, in a gas mask, wiring sensors in a live volcano crater. I'd take your gig any day. Right? Maybe you knit too much," he said. "Get out of your comfort zone?" He shook his head, chuckling.

Comfort zone. I studied the side of his excruciatingly red face, peeling like an onion. I needed to get out of my comfort zone in order to get into my comfort zone. The guy was a walking book of parables.

He winced as he looked down at his foot. "I honest to God hate to ask you this, but would you mind if I elevated my foot a minute? I pretty much can't stand this." He was gazing at the sock in my lap.

But I realized he was actually looking at my lap as a landing zone for his foot.

"Sure," I said, instantly. He shifted to swing his short leg across my lap, his poor, inflated foot now front and center, heavy, right on top of my half-knitted sock. I saw a welt where one of the sea monster's tentacles had wrapped across his shin. On most days, this would have pegged the meter on the queasies, not to mention claustrophobia and my fundamental discomfort at human bodies in distress. It was the purple balloon foot of a guy I didn't even know. But it was okay. It really was. There was no knitting happening for me anyway. I had run out of yarn, and I needed to wind another ball. Reaching gently under his leg, I fished out a fat skein and handed it to him. "You hold. I'll wind."

crafty critters

by Suzanne Strempek Shea

A childhood rule to "not just sit there" leads to a writing and knitting life.

I SIT HALFWAY DOWN THE SHINY GRAY-PAINTED STEPS LEADing from the Bigdas' kitchen to their cellar on what is the most important moment in my life as a Crafty Critter.

The Crafty Critters is my 4-H troop, comprised of my sister and me and eight other girls who assemble in that cellar every Friday night of my grade school years. Led by my mother and Mrs. Bigda, the daughters of whom make up half the club's membership, we begin each meeting by standing and singing with proper anatomical gestures:

"I pledge my head to clearer thinking, my heart to greater loyalty, my hands to larger service and my health to better living, for my club, my community, my country, and my world."

Then we launch into whatever craft we critters are offered in the next two hours.

Over the years, there is plaster. Lots of plaster. Gallons poured into clear plastic molds shaped like trolls or the Blessed Virgin Mary. There are armloads of reeds, long and looping, soaked in buckets to make them pliable for weaving into baskets of unintended shapes. There are piles of fabric to be fed under the foot of a sewing machine, a shift or a pair of culottes magically emerging from the other side. There are skeins of jewel-like embroidery thread and pieces of linen on which a cornucopia or *Be It Ever So Humble, There's No Place Like Home* has been printed in soft blue *X*'s, ready for cross-stitching. And because, on one Friday night when I am in the third grade, there are balls of yarn in every imaginable color, and a tube from which dozens of metal needles spill in a musical clatter, there is knitting, which, for me, turns out to be a lot more than just this week's craft.

At the long table where the lesson is given, I watch my mother cast ten stitches onto a pair of size 4 or 5 needles. She finishes no more than three rows of what she tells us will become a headband before I know this is something I really want to do. I grab the needles and yarn and head to the stairs for the start of something big that to this day is a most constant companion.

On those stairs, everything stills. The older girls' chatter about the cuteness of the guy who leads Herman's Hermits—is he Herman?—fades. All I know is what's happening in my hands—the transformation of synthetic yellow yarn into the rectangle starting to dangle from my needles. Cool at the start, the needles warm as I lean into the right-hand wall of the stairway and work at the simple knit stitch, finishing a row and admiring the hooked U-shapes. I flatten the piece against my similarly polyester pant leg and marvel at how I did all this. I get lost in the process, as I had when slaloming reeds around the vertical pieces sticking from the wooden base of baskets-to-be. I don't know the word yet, but I'm in the same zone

I enter when I color or draw, intent on what's before me, what's happening, what I am able to make—awed by it, even if it is just scrawling. I am in that zone there on those steps, but this is different. I could sit here all night and make this happen. And, I realize, feel it happen. The bargain-basement fiber is far from the homespun woolens and nubby silks I'll one day choose with care, but the feel of it flowing through the palm of my right hand, the pull of it around my index finger as I loop it between the crux of the needle points, the tiny result actually becoming bulk beneath my left hand—is rich. I don't set the work down when punch and brownies are brought out for refreshments. I won't put it down when it's time to pack everything away. But when my mother says I can take my knitting home, I give in. I need to keep working on this. And the truth of that need is a surprise.

I finish the headband the next day. My mother shows me how to cast off and how to sew the ends flat. I hold the resulting circle before me. It becomes a frame through which I see the room where we stand. We call this "the middle room" for its location between our apartment's two bedrooms, but it deserves a better title for being the space in which so much creativity happens in a household headed by two parents who always, always, always are making things—my father in his "shop" two floors down, turning out doghouses, chicken coops, benches, or finishing details for the patio or playhouse he just constructed in the backyard; my mother here in the middle room, where a Stone Age black metal Singer sewing machine stands in a sturdy cabinet in the corner. Across the room is the nook where, in the nascent days of permanent color processing, she hand-colors black-and-white portraits taken by a local photographer with the Hermits-sounding name of Henry Herman. Her easel and canvases are in this room, too, for the painting she does for fun, her oils and her palette and her jars of brushes adjacent. A cabinet holds large jars of spare buttons. A drawer to the right is packed with Simplicity and Butterick patterns. There's another drawer mostly of pencils and scissors, markers and crayons. On the counter stands a tall stack of shiny paper bearing ads for the Uniroyal tires made in the factory where my father works, the backs of each sheet blank and ready for pen or pencil. So many materials, so much possibility. Along with, in the far corner, a television set. One that turns out to be a reason for so much of what my sister and I learn to do and make.

The deal is that we are allowed to watch TV, but only if we are doing something creative at the same time. As with the word "zone," it'll be a while before "multitasking" works its way into my vocabulary, but I'm doing that way back in the mid-sixties, when I join my sister on the couch, the tube snapped on before us. In Mary Ann's hands might be the latest paper dolls under construction. I might have my Spirograph set up on the coffee table for circling new designs in red or blue ink. My mother often is at the Singer, and Mary Ann and I protest each time she runs a line of stitches and somehow fills the TV screen with static.

The rule to do something else while watching TV applies at my grandparents' house, downstairs, where my sister and I sleep over every childhood Saturday night while my parents are out polka dancing. There, whether engrossed in *The Lawrence Welk Show, The Dating Game, Get Smart,* or *Petticoat Junction,* I might be making potholders on a square metal frame, Mary Ann might be sewing a hem on a skirt she hopes to hike. But once I learn to knit, both upstairs and down I knit and I knit and I knit. I long before had been taught that bragging was a sin, but can't help myself from showing a project to others and proudly stating that, yes, I did all this, with just two sticks, a ball of yarn, some simple instructions, and my own two hands.

Around the same time was born another big interest that to this day figures largely in my life. On those Saturday nights in front of the four-legged television in my grandparents' living room, I also began to write, "publishing" *The Nutty News*, a handwritten four- or five-page newspaper featuring stories I wrote and "photos" I drew. It held the news of the day—a bridge collapse, a presidential candidate's speech, the winner of the Kentucky Derby—copped from that night's broadcast of *The Huntley-Brinkley Report*. I'd add a few coupons for invented products, a recipe you'd never want to attempt, and several pages of fashion drawings by Mary Ann. Before bed, I'd run upstairs and leave the copy at our back door. When we climbed the stairs the next morning to dress for church, we'd be greeted with my parents' cheery "The paper's here already—we can't wait for the next one!" I believe the feeling I have to this day—that I can try any creative endeavor and maybe be half good at it, a rare confidence for me—was due to their enthusiasm for a paper-clipped newspaper drawn on the back of tire ads.

While *The Nutty News* was created only on Saturday nights, knitting was done every day of the week, including on school vacation afternoons spent in front of *The Guiding Light*, *The Edge of Night*, *As the World Turns*, and *Another World*. Over the years I also moved my act into the backyard patio, out to the car, and into the world beyond. I became able to knit without looking at the needles, and playing license-plate bingo or studying a road map at the same time was easy. I knit at the trailer my family kept at New Hampshire's Hampton Beach each summer until I left for college. I'd hunker near the fire my father lit every night in a circle of rocks and I'd pretend we were on the prairie somewhere and I had to make the family's clothing or we'd freeze. It was all on me and I sped up the pace of the stitches. I knit at the beach we went to when not at the trailer, the length of my progress a too-warm pile in my lap, but I didn't care. It beat just lying there, like my sister, then so into tanning that on a family trip to Myrtle Beach got sun poisoning, swelled like somebody had inflated her, and was taken to the emergency room while I stayed back in the hotel room, and knitted.

I took my projects on visits to relatives in and around our western Massachusetts hometown. If there were no cousins to run with, I knitted in living room armchairs. It beat just sitting there listening to adults talking, the subjects often a mystery to a kid, and even harder to dissect when they switched to Polish when bringing up the really good stuff.

Around eighth grade, the age at which some kids might search their houses for racier material their parents collect, I began to explore my mother's trove of knitting books stored behind the button jars. The people in those books resembled the actors populating old movies I watched on Sunday afternoons via a Boston channel that in pre-cable days we accessed by directing the giant antennae in the attic in the direction of the state capital seventy-three miles to the east. The women in the knitting books giggled while wearing fitted knitted blazers, matching knitted skirts, and hats with pompoms and earflaps, their hands encased in knitted muffs. The men smoked pipes while showing off ski sweaters across which little knitted people ski jumped, and each guy hiked a leg onto a log to display the matching kneesocks below their knickers. Noting my fascination with the men's pieces that were knitting-as-painting, my mother reached to the top of the hall closet and brought down two V-neck cardigans she'd knitted for my father when they were dating in the early 1950s. Geese flew across the yokes of each, scatterings of stitches made a snowfall of fleur-de-lis across the body. She told me I could make sweaters like these. Intimidated, I found a more boring knitting book, and a picture of a woman in a simple no-frills pullover. I asked my mother for yet another few balls of yarn from the stash that, like her wealth of sewing fabric, seemed to self-propagate in a chest in the attic. I misread the directions and knit three rows of ribbing at the waist, rather than three inches, but the project still was a success. I had learned to read a pattern, to decrease, to increase, and to sew the pieces together. As I had with the headband, I wore the royal blue acrylic slump of a turtleneck nonstop. As I had with the headband, I told anybody who would listen that I had made it myself. With my own two hands.

The five-hour bus ride to the art school that was my college experience meant plenty more time for knitting. I knit through homesickness and through the hard reality of independence, through finals and through roommate tiffs. The college was in Maine, home to many sheep. The yarn store one block up from the YMCA that was my first home in Portland in freshman year 1976–77 offered a section of local wool. I used savings from my weekend job as a hostess at the Maine Mall Pizza Hut to buy six giant skeins of ecru in a fat ply more fitting for rug weaving. The resulting cardigan was nearly bulletproof. But the woman at the funkier yarn store, down in the Old Port, admired it. And she admired the way I'd knitted it, after I of course told her I had. She asked if I'd like to knit for pay—and would I have the time?

THE RED-SHELLED 12-INCH black-and-white I'd received as my First Communion present back in third grade had accompanied me to Maine. Throughout the four years of college, it often kept me company, broadcasting the nightly weather report from Mount Washington by nattily bow-tied and classically accented Marty Engstrom as I knit for pay, picking up a packet of yarn, a Xeroxed pattern and a customer's measurements the same day I delivered a finished product. I received thirty dollars for a sweater that took me roughly thirty days to knit, block, and finish. The store sold it for ninety dollars. Nobody was getting rich, but the customer did receive a gem. Norwegian knits were what I was assigned and what I mastered. Sweaters that reminded me of those worn by the pipe-smoking guys in my mother's catalogues, of the cardigans she'd pulled down from the hall closet shelf. Flying geese. Skiers. Hearts. Flowers. Snowflakes all over.

In and around knitting those, I discovered luxurious Lopi Icelandic wool, and the patterns displayed adjacent to those bins—Scandinavian designs with intricately patterned yokes done on circular needles. I also discovered a boyfriend, who worked on boats. With him I took my act onto the water, knitting in the wheelhouse of a charter boat once we'd anchored and fitted each customer's hook with a writhing sea worm. I knit big bulky and warm Gorton's Fisherman looks for the boyfriend, for his fleet of friends, for their girlfriends. I skipped the yarn store middleman and managed to make a somewhat better profit.

I managed also to graduate, and though I'd studied photography I started work two days later as a reporter at a paper back home, a more polished version of *The Nutty News* where I'd worked part-time since high school. My desk in the features department was across from that of Zedra Aranow, a woman forty-two years my senior for whom knitting was breathing. She consulted with me on projects, shared patterns, and introduced me to her habit of reading while knitting, with the help of a cookbook stand. We became linked by our mutual interest, and though she purchased me stitch holders and daily modeled examples of the wonder of cables, I never learned them. Fittingly, I store in a treasure chest the stunning and extravagantly cabled pullover she made for me in a New Brunswick worsted the color of a live lobster.

At twenty-three, I bought myself a little A-frame on a local lake. There I knitted through the grief over the death of my best friend earlier that year, a you-never-know-when-your-number's-up horror that spurred me to get my own place on the water because, well, you never know when your number's up. Rosemary was killed in a highway crash just weeks after we'd returned from a month driving the California coast, taking turns at the wheel of a rental car. The brown, white, and black mohair cardigan I knitted while in the passenger seat remains my warmest sweater for more than the yarn's ply. The last time I saw Rosemary, she was wearing the tan pullover I'd knitted for her on bus trips to school in a then-favorite pattern that calls for a braided lacing at the neck. It's a gift to have that last picture of her in my head. In the A-frame, I'd light a fire in the hearth and turn on the TV. While the wind blew strongly across the lake, I'd pick up my needles and pretend I was in a cabin on a prairie on a lake somewhere and I had to make all my clothing or I'd freeze. It was all on me. I sped up the stitches.

And life, as it does, outpaced me. I knitted extra fast to keep up, including a big gray turtleneck for the fellow reporter who became my darling husband, conveniently a person also unable to just watch TV, needing a book or newspaper or magazine open before him at the same time. In those early years we anchored ends of the couch, between us a dog taught not to play with a ball that happens to be yarn. A few years later, in the late 1980s, before my shift at the paper began, I tried my hand at writing fiction, breaking to have lunch and knit during *The Young and the Restless* before leaving for work. Upon my return home, I knit to clear my head, to use my hands after using my head all day. I rinsed and repeated many times and in a year had a first novel, and found a godsend of a mentor, a fine and funny novelist admirable for many qualities, including the practice of starting a new book right after completing another, and doing the same thing with her knitting projects.

That first book launched me into many readings—those of others as well as my own. As much as I enjoyed and was inspired by what I heard, it felt strange to just sit there while someone read. I was not taught to just sit there. But that's what I did for the nine years of such events. Then, at a reading in sheep-filled Maine, I spotted a woman several rows up pulling a length of yarn from a bag. I craned my neck. Yes, someone was knitting.

SO FOR THE PAST nine years I have knit at readings, too. I like the combination of taking in a story and taking the yarn through my fingers. I don't do complicated pieces at these events—it would be too much to be consulting a pattern constantly. I will do a garter or a seed stitch, or something with alternating colors. Scarves are naturals because you don't have to check increases. The body of a sweater, past the increases and up to the armholes, works, too. It's a constant for me, and when I'm in Maine twice a year now for ten days of teaching, I have a constant companion for the craft. A dear friend long ago sought out a seat to my left at each of the nightly readings the residency features. She claims the position early and might kindly boot someone who unknowingly occupies "her" seat. In the rush and bustle of our residency days, Elizabeth finds something soothing about watching the motion and progress of my knitting. I can't say I know. I don't watch it. While I'm knitting, I'm normally watching TV. Or watching someone's face while having a conversation. Or watching out the window of a train. Or watching someone who's reading.

I HAVE TWO TEN-YEAR-OLD nieces who love to craft, and who visit my mother-in-law's house with woven blanket or crocheted Easter egg in progress. At my home last summer, Maeve and Grace asked to see the supplies for the knitting I bring to family gatherings. They carried yarn and needles out to the yard and continued from the casting on I'd done. I was back in the Bigdas' cellar, back on childhood visits with relatives as I watched the girls sitting in a circle of adults and attempting the next row. Crafty Critters after my own heart. I wish them a life of making things as a constant companion, I wish them flying geese, skiers, hearts, flowers, snowflakes all over. And I bless my parents for their long-ago edict, which has made my life in so many ways. You never know what you can do if you don't just sit there. You never know what you can do with your own two hands.

found objects

by Anita Shreve

A mother and her daughter discover between them a dozen incomplete projects and set out one weekend to finish them.

"ANTICIPATION." "BEWILDERMENT." "VOWS." "TRIAGE." "Growing Excitement." "Giddy." "Knitting Fools." "Pause for Nourishment." "Mistake." "Renewed Determination." "Joy."

"ANTICIPATION"

ON A WEEKEND THAT my daughter Katherine, who lives in Baltimore, is to visit me in Maine, I ask her to bring with her any unfinished knitting projects. I taught my daughter to knit on the same day I taught her entire Brownie troop (seven girls, ages seven to eight) to knit. I do not recommend this. It's a wonder my love of knitting survived ("Ms. Shreve, I only have fourteen stitches now!" "Ms. Shreve, my yarn is so tight I can't get it off the needles!" "Ms.

Shreve, my scarf is in the shape of a trapezoid!" Precocious kid).
Katherine, to her credit, not only learned to knit that hideously
confusing day, but became an expert knitter in the process (far more
accomplished than the teacher, may I add). At thirty-one, she is a
perfectionist, she reads directions, and she loves challenges. I present
her with a challenge: We will pool all of our unfinished projects, see
which are salvageable, finish them and have entirely new additions
to our wardrobes. Good, no? She loves the idea.

Later, in anticipation of the big weekend, she writes, "I am bringing an off-white sleeveless sweater for which I accidentally did one
sleeve's edging inside out and then gave up rather than fixing it
(would only take eight more rows to be completely finished; this
was nine years ago); a man's argyle sweater that I knit approximately
ten rows per year, but I'm still one hundred percent confident will
be finished one day; Molly's sweater that I was going to alter for
her but ended up just keeping for myself; a blue sock-yarn vest you
made for me that I rediscovered and wore to work all this winter;
a third of a scarf in white and gray that didn't come out looking as
good as I expected."

I personally have, in a large basket, sixteen unfinished items
ranging from an odd-looking red SensuWool bib-type thing that
might have been trying to be a vest before the yarn ran out, to two
pieces of an ochre Rowan Felted Tweed sweater, the back of which
I keep unraveling each time I take it out of the basket to look at
it. I also have nine separate socks made in nine different jacquard
yarns, none of which has a mate, and five pieces of a Blue Sky white
cotton sweater that surely does not require more than four pieces
to put together.

I should point out that Katherine and I have finished many projects, several of which we did together: matching sweaters for two

new babies in the family was one; and a rather astonishing knitted patchwork quilt was another. The latter was knit by the whole family and sewn together by Katherine. I maintain that the colors are Essex green, gray-green and off-white; she swears the colors are black, gray, and white. We will never agree on this. We do agree that the blanket is a tour de force.

"BEWILDERMENT"

KATHERINE ARRIVES, and we empty the basket. What are we to make of the rather large rectangle of ribbed Ecological Wool, shade brown? A baby blanket? No, the yarn is far too scratchy for a baby. A piece of a larger blanket? No, for the same reason. The beginning of a sweater for my husband? In the recesses of my mind, a dim bulb is sparking. Yes, I remember now. I was going to knit my husband a simple sweater, shade lavender-brown, for Christmas last year; I had been promised that the yarn would soften up once I had washed it. Reason for quitting? I did not believe what I had been told, and my husband is too big for an experiment.

(And while we are on the subject of knitting for men, I will repeat here a true story. I have a good friend who once knit a camel-colored cashmere Aran sweater in size 1 needles—I kid you not—for her tall boyfriend. She gave it to him, he put it on, they went to dinner in Manhattan, he took it off because he was hot, he draped it over his chair, he walked out of the restaurant without the sweater. It was never found. And, get this: She *married* him.)

And what was I thinking, Katherine sweetly asks me, as I line up the nine single socks with no mates, all in jacquard patterns? "Ah," I say. The year these astonishing patterned yarns came out from Opal, I was so excited that I learned to knit socks, was thrilled with the different patterns, and decided to knit every single Opal sock yarn going. The only way to do this, of course, was to knit one sock instead of two, or else I'd never get to every pattern. Hence my large pool of singles. I pondered for a long moment last November whether it would be cool to give family members two unmatching handmade socks, and decided that it was not, since each sock swore violently with the others.

"VOWS"

T HIS IS SILLY, Katherine and I say to each other that rainy, cold weekend in Maine (perfect for knitting as such a weekend is good for nothing else). We need to do something about the absurd pile. We vow to finish at least two projects each that weekend and not start anything new until we have completed everything salvageable. (The fact that I am knitting a rust-colored cowl while we make these vows is more or less ignored.) Okay, agreed. But which projects?

"TRIAGE"

A S FIELD NURSES treat soldiers based on which of the wounded can be saved, so do we select knitted items that can conceivably be worn or given away as a gift to someone in the future. Katherine picks a lime green cashmere sweater that appears to have four pieces already knitted. Great choice then, because all that is needed is a seamstress. But on closer inspection, Katherine discovers that one raglan sleeve is about an inch longer than the other. Why? she nicely asks. I cannot account for the mistake, although it is obvious to both of us that I did surely realize my error since I did not sew the sweater together myself. (In my defense, I will just say that it is, in a small way, difficult, not to say a pain in the ass, to reshape a raglan sleeve cap.) Never mind, Katherine is a good sport. She sets about sewing up one sleeve to its front and back, the task made only slightly complicated by the cabled edges all around. My heart is warmed by my daughter's generosity.

She also vows to knit together a simple brown tweed sweater I have made. We agree that since she is doing the finish work, the sweater will be hers when completed. I am happy with this notion since it's obvious that it won't fit me anymore. (Have I mentioned that I am five feet eight inches tall and that my daughter is five feet four inches tall? And this is without even considering our respective weights? Needless to say, she is petite, and I am not.)

I vow to sew together a simple vest of sock yarn in, of course, a blue and white jacquard pattern and to finish knitting a Berroco Trilogy sweater in a sort of rust and gold yarn that I have been warned I won't like when it's finished. Obviously, I do not believe the woman who told me this.

"GROWING EXCITEMENT"

W E ESTABLISH OUR places on the couch. Katherine finishes sewing up one side of the raglan-sleeve, cable-edged, lime green sweater. Voilà! We're geniuses for deciding to do this. One more sleeve, and an actual garment will have emerged from the overstuffed basket of orphans. I can now wear the lime green sweater, jewel-tone colors having made a recent resurgence. I am already planning a cowl to go with it. (On the subject of cowls, may I just say that they are a godsend to lazy knitters. They don't require the length of a regular scarf, they are easier to wear, they look good, and they make acceptable last-minute gifts. They are especially useful when considering three balls of wool left over from a sweater made a decade ago. Wait long enough, and even pink looks good.)

"GIDDY"

W E ARE DELIGHTED with ourselves. A couple of days, and we could have as many as a half dozen new garments! I might even be able to save the red bib-like thing by knitting an underlayer of thin black yarn so that the bib will grow to become a vest. Katherine points out that I could just wear a long black T-shirt underneath, but I am pretty certain the red bib will look ridiculous that way. I suspect that the red bib will look ridiculous no matter what I do with it.

"KNITTING FOOLS"

K ATHERINE AND I HAVE truly lost it; we are knitting fools. We knit, we talk, we laugh. We decide to learn how to knit from the top down, since nearly all of our problems would be solved if we could just rip out the bottom edges of the bodies and sleeves of the sweaters and lengthen or shorten them. Once, in my early days, realizing the sweater I had knit was too short, I attempted to unravel it from the bottom because the sleeves had already been sewn in. I would just like to report that the results were not good, and I had to throw away the sweater. I am not saying that it is not possible to do this difficult task. I am simply saying I cannot do it and would not try again, even for a large sum of money. Tears were involved.

"PAUSE FOR NOURISHMENT"

N ATURALLY, we get hungry.

"MISTAKE"

W E RETURN FROM the kitchen, nicely sated. We pause to stare at the plethora of orphans that have escaped the basket. Both reasonable and smart, we simultaneously realize that we cannot possibly fulfill our commitment to finish even four projects this weekend, never mind the half dozen we insanely considered just before lunch. We have an additional realization: there is a reason there are so many orphans in the room. Projects don't get finished because (1) the sweater one is making goes out of style by the time the garment is finished; (2) the many children who used to be excited when receiving handmade gifts have wised up, and there are no longer recipients for pairs of jacquard-patterned socks, mismatched or otherwise; or (3) no one can sustain, for more than the front and the back of the sweater, the belief that a hot pink and cool blue variegated yarn will look good on anyone.

"Wow," I say quietly.

"Yeah," says Katherine.

"RENEWED DETERMINATION"

O NE OF US ACTUALLY says, "Rome wasn't built in a day."
It might be me, since I'm the mother figure.

Actually, I'm the mother.

Chastened, we take another look at our pile of unloved objects. The lime green sweater will get finished this weekend. The brown sweater that needs only to be sewn together will get taken home by Katherine and completed. This much she vows. I vow to studiously consider the five white pieces and decide which is the superfluous one, and complete the garment. Perhaps in the very near future, I will also think about the red bib-like mystery that should or should not be salvaged. We are to keep each other apprised of our progress. If we hold true to our vows, we agree that we can then take a look at my gargantuan stash of unused yarn, enough to take up an entire cedar closet, and ponder new projects that, of course, we will finish.

Katherine presents me that weekend with a finished lime green sweater. I present her with precious little. She takes the brown sweater home with a promise that it soon will be done. In the meantime, I explain to Katherine how easy it is to make a cowl, and we raid my oversized stash for a yarn she likes. At the airport, we hug and kiss and say what fun the weekend was, and how we'll do it again soon. I notice that before she even boards the plane, she is already a foot into the cowl.

"JOY"

I GO HOME AND BEGIN to put the orphans back into the basket. Before I do, however, I notice a white shirt box at the bottom.

I take it out and open it. Inside the white shirt box are twenty-six completed miniature sweaters, each three inches by three inches, that I knit two years ago to use as Christmas ornaments on our tree and then forgot about. Each sweater is different, each uses a unique yarn, and each has its own pattern. More important, each is finished! Twenty-six completed sweaters!

Oh joy!

I can hardly wait to tell Katherine.

why bother?

by Jane Smiley

The writer discovers what knitting and writing novels have in common, and why she enjoys doing both.

D ID MY GRANDMOTHER TEACH ME TO KNIT? I VAGUELY remember her casting on a row of stitches—no doubt the needles were 10's—and then myself sitting slumped at one end of the couch, the needles maybe four inches from my face, laboriously pushing the point of the right needle between the yarn and the left needle, pausing to loop that disobedient strand I held in my right hand, then trying to figure out how to get that strand back through the space and onto the right needle (a conundrum not presented by, say, crochet. A crochet hook was a hook, you aimed, you caught, you pulled). I also vaguely remember abandoning my knitting needles after very few rows, but those rows were enough—my brain was imprinted with the English method.

I did crochet for a long time. It was easy, it was quick, so what if I could only produce doilies and collars? But crocheting also produced pain, and, for my cousin, who crocheted backstage waiting for her cues in dramatic productions, it produced carpal tunnel syndrome. I took heed. Back to knitting. Somehow, over the years, I had imbibed my grandmother's other way of doing things, which was, Figure it out yourself. I never saw my grandmother open a cookbook. I never saw her buy a dress pattern. Over and over, I saw her putting together the pot roast, pressing out the spritz cookies, overseeing the divinity (she loved sweets). A prom dress for my aunt? A flower girl's dress for me? A black pillbox hat for herself? She would sit at her sewing machine on the enclosed porch of her house, the sunlight filtering around her as she bent toward the seam she was stitching, her hands precise by the presser foot, the fabric flowing over her lap onto the sheet covering the linoleum. Evenings, my grandfather would watch the news or boxing or *Lawrence Welk*, while my grandmother would turn out another pair of booties for one of my cousins, most of whom were younger than I was.

My mother and aunts didn't knit or sew. My mother made boeuf bourguignon out of *Gourmet* magazine and prowled the aisles of our local department stores looking for the New Look at a reasonable price. She edited the women's section of the local newspaper and put on fashion shows. She went to New York twice a year to see what was current. Her job was to be a conduit of the up-to-date, bringing to our extremely self-satisfied but curious community the next good thing. Woolly knitted afghans weren't that thing. Of how delicious my grandmother's cooking was, my aunt said (I think with a sniff), "Well, that's just because she adds butter to everything."

When I went back to knitting, I did it my grandmother's way, making it up as I went along, sitting in front of some TV show or other listening to the dialogue and half paying attention to the screen. I also made my stitches the English style, right-hand loop, even though I had been to Iceland and seen firsthand the other method—how a woman outside our language class, waiting for the session to begin, plucked plucked plucked her way through the entire left front of a child's sweater in ten minutes. Or there was the woman who ran the knitting shop in Ames, Iowa, where I bought my yarn. She knitted as the Icelandic woman had, standing, holding her skein of yarn under her arm, the strand running out of it to her hands, smiling, talking—zippity doo dah, she could knit a sweater in a few days. I felt I couldn't change, but what I think is really true was that I didn't want to—I wanted to soldier on in my tortoise-like way, scratching my head, enjoying my fiber, keeping to myself.

I THINK THE FIRST time I realized that I really didn't know what I was doing was when I saw in the mirror that the cotton hip-length cardigan (trellis with moss stitch) that I had been working on all winter hung around me like a horse blanket. I'd been knitting it so long that I didn't remember what I'd imagined, but surely it was not this—the only way I could achieve any sort of shape was to wrap the two halves of the front all the way across. However, shape was achieved by sacrificing the neckline, which went from a V to what looked like the collar of a straitjacket. And then there was the shade—medium blue. I'd liked it while I was working with the yarn, but why had I not bothered to consider if it flattered my complexion? I did understand the design flaw—when I concocted the pattern, I'd remembered a rule from eighth grade sewing class—the front has to be larger than the back to accommodate "the bust." Except—not. Not when you are tall and thin and the front is the front of a sweater.

I made myself like it. I gave it a double-breasted look with two rows of buttons and some fiddling to make them work. I wore it around the house and when I happened to pass a mirror, I focused my gaze on the pattern, which was, indeed, complicated and well done. But it didn't work—my labor of love found its way to the back of the closet, where, two years later, it was unearthed by my daughter, who was living in a colder climate than I was. She took it and brought it back a year later. She didn't have to say a word—I knew what she was thinking.

Three years after that, it appeared again, and I tricked my husband into putting it on. It fit perfectly. The V-neck opened attractively across his chest; the sleeves were the right length, and the color did, in fact, flatter his rosy complexion and gray hair. He walked around in it for a minute or two, and looked in the mirror. He said that he would consent to wear it after he died, for the cremation. Not till then. We laughed. After all those years, I was inured to the insult.

I gave it to my sister last Christmas. Until Christmas Eve day, I thought that our gift exchange was only going to be for the children, but she dropped a hint—she really liked what she'd found for me. We scrambled in the wine closet for something we knew her husband would like, and the cable sweater fell out onto the floor, a little dusty. I wiped off the dust and wrapped it. I said, "We'll tell her it's a joke present. At least it'll be out of the house."

She loved it. It looked good on her. I came up with a hurried lie—been working on it all fall, so glad you like it, perfect for the cold weather. And the color was great on her, I have to admit that. The only other thing I said was, "If you don't like the buttons, I'm happy to—"

If only the blue sweater were the one misadventure.

I love to knit. I love to buy yarn and sit in my chair watching movies at night and adding row upon row. I love to look at pattern books, especially *A Treasury of Knitting Patterns* by Barbara G. Walker, page after page of color change, slip stitch, cable, eyelet, and lace patterns. Stitch patterns inspire me and excite me, but garment patterns bore me. If you know what it's going to look like when you are finished, why bother? Well, because you know what it's going to look like when you are finished.

MY DAUGHTERS LIKE to knit, and one of their aunts is an expert—she has a knitting shop and conducts classes. For years she sold handmade felt bags. A rumor was floated that you couldn't successfully make your own felted garment. I took this rumor personally, and I made a jacket. My finding is that you *can* make your own felted garment, that the way to do it is to do a sort of patchwork design, and to make and felt one piece at a time. If you have plenty of yarn and plenty of time, you can construct a felt garment. It will stand on its own, because in addition to the thick felted panels, you will have to line it with a sturdy material so that you can stand to wear it. At that point, it will be so hot and make you so sweaty every time you put it on that you will have to find a relative who lives in Canada to take it off your hands. She might object to the odd eighteenth-century-style stand-up collar you couldn't resist adding because you hated to leave out any of the felted pieces, but if she's far enough away, then you will never see that she put it in the doghouse and dogs enjoy it very much. It holds up like iron, too.

There have also been successes, a few more than random chance would predict, which I find encouraging. I often wear the off-white bamboo sweater I made, also cable. Once I realized that if I crocheted a rim around the collar, it would stop expanding every time I wore it, it remained stable and attractive. Bamboo is a seductive fiber. It is silky and allegedly "antiseptic"—you can wear it when you have a cold, and it will cure you. Every skein is endless. It takes color beautifully. But it stretches. The first time I tried lace (feather and fan stitch), I made myself a bamboo vest. It was so determined to expand and expand that I finally had to rip it out and remake it into a much stricter and more circumscribed vest, with white boundaries and everything sewn together with small, authoritarian stitches.

My favorite Hollywood story is about Joanne Woodward, who sewed her own dress to wear to the Oscars—and she was presenting! With her as my inspiration, I have made public appearances in my own knitwear. My most ambitious outfit was also knitted from bamboo, a sweater and skirt in a black and white mosaic Barbara G. Walker pattern, called Mosaic #19, "Basketweave." I knitted the sweater first. In fact, I only ever intended to knit the sweater. But it was so busy when I tried it on that it looked like an optical illusion, and, I admit, gave me a headache, so I ordered more yarn, on the principle of doubling down, and made myself a gored skirt with an elastic waist. The gores alternated patterned panels with plain white. In many ways, it was a mathematical nightmare, but I kept up my spirits by thinking about the mathematician at MIT who crocheted multidimensional objects that had never been produced before—she used the very fine mathematical calculations of crochet to embody the equations. Thus I remembered to subtract my stitches in spite of the complexity of my pattern, and thus the skirt, once put together, not only fit but had an insouciant way of moving as I walked. Nevertheless, it would not do, I thought, to roll it out in New York City. The perfect opportunity presented itself when I was asked to give a speech at an awards ceremony for a group of geriatricians in Omaha. They loved it. Next stop, Los Angeles—but the book festival, not the Oscars. No red carpet at the book festival.

About two years ago, I decided that I was sweatered up, but the knitting had to continue, so I looked around for targets. Fortuitously, I discovered that babies were being born to three women I knew (one only slightly, but I figured I could force it on her). Hats! This time, I bought soy fiber, color "Napa," an alluring mix of lavender, green, and yellow dyes. Soy is drier and stiffer than bamboo, but the product has an attractive drape. I of course decided to complicate my task by continuing my lace education. I did not begin with anything mechanical, like faggoting, but the stitch I chose looked simple enough—Flemish block lace, from *Vogue Knitting*, fourteen stitches by twelve rows, and half of those rows were just purling! I would knit a few inches of simple ribbing, then about four inches of the lace, then garter-stitch for the decrease around the crown. Easy as pie.

It is possible that I have some spatial or mathematical deficiency in my brain, because as I was knitting in my usual tortoisey way, I could not make those fourteen stitches and those twelve rows work out. The lace is geometric—it looks like rectangles defined by eyelets, interlocking diagonally up the garment. I would sit in the vicinity of Turner Classic Movies, knitting patiently, only to discover at the end of my fourteen rows that I had introduced a square into the rectangles, or that the right end was fine, but the left end made no sense at all. Would a baby notice this? Especially since the Napa color had proved to make the whole project look like an optical illusion? I soldiered, or I should say, I grandmothered on, ripping and reknitting, aiming for, if nothing else, a Zen-like degree of self-acceptance. The hats slowly formed themselves, and then, of course, I liked the yarn so much that I ordered enough for a sweater, and now I knew that Flemish lace, what could go wrong, and the only thing that did was the shaping of the neck and collar, so that the shoulder seams slip severely off my shoulders, and I did know a woman once who would rip out the seams and the entire upper portion of the garment and do it properly, but all I did was take a tuck in the middle of the back and you can hardly see it if I remember to keep my hair neatly arranged on top of it. It is lace; I consider it formal wear.

My daughter decided to get married. I looked over her wedding registry—blender, sheets, comforter. Nowhere on that registry was there any mention of hand-knit place mats. I floated the idea, hypothetically of course, linking my email to a website where there were 148 colors of cotton yarn made in Greece. She chose one. I miscalculated the amount I would need, and saw that I would need two colors. She chose another. Having learned my lace lessons from both the Flemish block lace and the ever-expanding feather and fan stitch, I chose vine lace, nine stitches by four rows, according to Ms. Walker, "very pretty results for very little effort." Indeed. Row 1—knit 3, y/o, knit 2, etc. Row 2, knit 2, y/o, knit 2, etc. It took me three whole place mats not to learn to count, but to learn to pay attention to where I was in the design. Probably, since it is a wedding present, I *will* rip out number 3 and do it over again.

I love writing novels and I enjoy playing solitaire. Both appeal to my pleasure in seeing how something turns out—I imagine a character, or even just a moment; I lay out my cards. Some little thing—say, a particular word—attaches itself to that moment, and the moment begins to take on idiosyncrasy. Another character walks into the room, and mentions that it is going to snow, and my character does something. As he does, the novel comes alive, the tiniest seed issuing the tiniest shoot. Or that 6 turns up to vary the wall of 7's I'd thought were going to end my game. What I like about solitaire is that no two games are alike, that my moves and my thought processes take different paths with every turn of the cards. If there is a win, it is different from all previous wins. A novel, too, is always original. Even if it isn't always interesting, it always reflects the idle connections the author's thoughts happened to make on certain days, in certain moods, in certain places. The author certainly comes back, certainly smooths and sorts those connections, but the randomness remains, the author's unique handprint on the story. Knitting isn't supposed to work this way. Knitting is mapped—here is the sweater you are headed for, and here is how to get there, and if you follow the map, you will have something that suits you, something to enjoy. Knitting is neither as quick as solitaire nor as revisable as a novel, but I draw that same pleasure from it—the "what will happen next" pleasure, the sense of surprise at what is being, has been made. I don't mind if in the end it makes me laugh or wince—it was fun while it lasted.

"fisher" lacy wrap

by Helen Bingham

This elegant, lacy wrap is created in three sections yet it is seamless. The provisional cast on allows the stitches to remain live even after the body of the wrap is complete. The edging design is created by casting off the stitches as you make the decorative edge. This piece is named after Peggy Fisher, my great-aunt, who was an avid knitter and who taught me what love is all about and how to give a strong hug.

MATERIALS:

5 skeins Heichi by ShiBui (100% silk with 105 yards)
Color: Chestnut #14

OR

5 skeins Captia by Berroco (60% cotton/23% polyester/17% acrylic
    with 98 yards)
Color: #5515 Laurel
US 10.5 needles or size needed to obtain gauge
Waste yarn for provisional cast on
Size J hook

SIZES: one size

FINISHED SIZE: 20″ × 60″ prior to blocking

GAUGE: 16 sts = 4″ in garter stitch; 12 sts = 4″ in lace pattern

PATTERN NOTES & ABBREVIATIONS:

YO = yarn over

Sl1 = slip one purlwise

K2tog = knit two stitches together

Psso = pass slipped stitch over

Tbl = through back loop

Provisional cast on = Using a crochet hook and waste yarn, chain 64 stitches. Look closely at the chain and notice that the front side looks like V's and the back has little bumps. Insert US 10.5 needle into first bump from front to back, wrap the yarn around the point of the needle and pick up a stitch. Continue in this manner till you have 61 stitches on your needle.

Cable Cast on = Put your needle in between the two stitches closest to the needle tip on your left-hand needle (LHN), wrap the yarn around the needle and knit the stitch, but don't take the stitch off the LHN, instead insert the LHN into the stitch (on the RHN) under its loop and slip the loop off the RHN and onto the LHN. Continue this process till the stated number of stitches have been cast on.

DIRECTIONS:

WRAP BODY:

—With straight needles, provisional cast on 61 sts

—Work the following rows:

Foundation Row: P2, K2, Purl 53, K2, P2

Row 1 (RS): K2, P2, K4 (yo, sl1, K2tog, psso, yo, K3)8 times, K1, P2, K2

Row 2 (WS): P2, K2, Purl 53, K2, P2

Row 3 (RS): K2, P2, K1 (yo, sl1, K2tog, psso, yo, K3)8 times, yo, sl1, K2tog, psso, yo, K1, P2, K2

Row 4 (WS): P2, K2, Purl 53, K2, P2

—Repeat Rows 1 through 4 till piece measures 40" from cast on edge, end with a Row 4.

—Leave stitches live to work the edging.

WRAP EDGING:

—Even-numbered rows, work the edging toward the shawl body (the right side will be facing when you work these rows).

—Odd-numbered rows, work away from the shawl body (the wrong side will be facing when you work these rows).

—Slip as if to purl with the yarn in front when the pattern asks you to slip a stitch.

—With RS facing and using the needle that holds the 61wrap-body sts, cable cast on 20 sts.

—Work the following rows:

Foundation Row: K19, K2tog tbl (the first cable cast on stitch with the last of the shawl-body sts)

Row 1: sl1, K3, (yo, K2tog)7 times, YO, K2

Rows 2, 4, 6 & 8: Knit till one st remains before the wrap-body stitches, knit this last st with the first stitch appearing on the wrap body **through the back loop (tbl).**

Row 3: sl1, K6, (YO, K2tog)6 times, YO, K2

Row 5: sl1, K9, (YO, K2tog)5 times, YO, K2

Row 7: sl1, K12, (YO, K2tog)4 times, YO, K2

Row 9: sl1, K23

Row 10: Cast off 4 sts loosely, K18, K2tog tbl

—Repeat Rows 1 through 10 a total of 11 times.

—Work Rows 1 through 9 once more.

—On the very last Row 10 cast off all edging stitches till 2 sts remain on your needle (the last edge st and the last wrap-body st). Knit these two sts together tbl, then cast off this last stitch.

—There will be 12 edge points.

—Once this edging is complete, undo the provisional cast on, put live stitches on the needle, and repeat the process for the second edge.

—Weave in all ends and steam lightly.

For pictures of this pattern, please go to www.helenbingham designs.com.

contributors

ELIZABETH BERG is the *New York Times* bestselling author of many novels, including *Open House*, which was an Oprah's Book Club selection in 2000.

HELEN BINGHAM has been knitting since she was twenty and working as a freelance knitwear designer for the last eight years. Helen has designed for companies such as Classic Elite, Nashua, Misti International, Sheep Shop Yarn, Swarovski, Skacel, and *Vogue Knitting*. You can follow Helen on Ravelry.com under "needlerunner," on Twitter under "HBinghamDesigns," and on her website: helenbinghamdesigns.com.

LAN SAMANTHA CHANG learned to knit from her grandmother. She lives in Iowa City, where she teaches at and directs the Iowa Writers' Workshop. She is writing a new book of short stories.

ANDRE DUBUS III is the author of seven books, including the *New York Times*'s bestsellers *House of Sand and Fog*, *The Garden of Last Days*, and his memoir, *Townie*. Dubus has been a finalist for the National Book Award and has been awarded a Guggenheim Fellowship, the National Magazine Award for Fiction, and two Pushcart Prizes. He is a 2012 recipient of an American Academy of Arts and Letters Award in Literature. He teaches full-time at the University of Massachusetts, Lowell, and he lives north of Boston with his wife, Fontaine, a modern dancer, and their three children. His new book, *Dirty Love*, was published in October 2013.

JOHN DUFRESNE is the author of two short story collections, two books on writing fiction, and five novels, most recently *No Regrets, Coyote*. He's also written for stage and screen. He lives in South Florida and teaches at Florida International University in Miami.

HOPE EDELMAN is the author of six nonfiction books, including the bestsellers *Motherless Daughters, Motherless Mothers* and *The Possibility of Everything*. She teaches at Antioch University–Los Angeles and lives in Topanga Canyon, California, with her husband and two daughters.

JANICE EIDUS has twice won the O. Henry Prize, and is the author of numerous books including the novels *The War of the Rosens* and *The Last Jewish Virgin*, and the story collections *The Celibacy Club* and *Vito Loves Geraldine*. She lives in Brooklyn, New York, with her husband and daughter.

MARTHA FRANKEL is the author of the memoir *Hats & Eyeglasses: A Family Love Affair with Gambling*, and the executive director of the Woodstock Writers Festival. Knitting is just one of the many things she's been addicted to in her life.

SUE GRAFTON entered the mystery field in 1982 with the publication of *A Is for Alibi*, which introduced female hard-boiled private investigator Kinsey Millhone, operating out of the fictional town of Santa Teresa (a.k.a. Santa Barbara), California. *B Is for Burglar* followed in 1985, and since then she has added twenty novels to the series, now referred to as the "alphabet" mysteries. The publication date for *V Is for Vengeance* was November 2011. The projected publication date for *W* is November 2013.

JESSI HEMPEL covers technology and the Internet as a senior writer at *Fortune* magazine. She has written extensively about digital media, online advertising, and social networking. She is a graduate of Brown University and received a master's in journalism from the University of California at Berkeley.

ANN HOOD is the author of the bestselling novels *The Knitting Circle*, *The Red Thread*, and *Somewhere Off the Coast of Maine*. Her memoir *Comfort: A Journey Through Grief* was a *New York Times* Editors' Choice and was chosen as one of the top ten nonfiction books of 2007 by *Entertainment Weekly*. The winner of two Pushcart Prizes and Best American Spiritual, Travel, and Food Writing awards, her most recent novel is *The Obituary Writer*.

KAYLIE JONES is the author of five novels, including *A Soldier's Daughter Never Cries,* which was made into a Merchant Ivory film starring Kris Kristofferson and Barbara Hershey; *Celeste Ascending,* published by HarperCollins; the memoir *Lies My Mother Never Told Me,* published by William Morrow; and most recently she edited the anthology *Long Island Noir*. She has been teaching creative writing for almost twenty-five years and is chairman of the annual $10,000 James Jones First Novel Fellowship.

BARBARA KINGSOLVER is the award-winning author of fourteen books of fiction and nonfiction, including *The Poisonwood Bible* and, most recently, *Flight Behavior*, a novel that involves climate change, sheep farmers, and British yarn bombers. She lives with her family on a farm in southern Appalachia where, with the help of her Icelandic sheep, she knits from the ground up.

JENNIFER LAUCK is the *New York Times* bestselling author of *Blackbird, Still Waters, Show Me the Way,* and *Found.* Her work has been translated into twenty different languages and she has been a bestseller in Spain, Ireland, and England. She has an M.F.A. in creative writing from Pacific Lutheran University and is an Associate Fellow for the Attic Institute in Portland, Oregon. She is at work on her first novel.

Former journalist and radio broadcaster ANNE D. LeCLAIRE is the bestselling author of eight novels, including *Entering Normal* and *The Lavender Hour,* and one memoir, *Listening Below the Noise: An Exploration of Silence.* She has led writing workshops in France, Ireland, Italy, and Jamaica, has been on the faculty of the Maui Writers Conference, and has taught creative writing to women in prison. Anne lives on Cape Cod. She is a Distinguished Fellow of the Ragdale Foundation.

MARIANNE LEONE is the author of the memoir *Knowing Jesse: A Mother's Story of Grief, Grace, and Everyday Bliss* (Simon & Schuster), and has written essays for the *Boston Globe,* WBUR's *Cognoscenti* blog, and *Bark* magazine. She is an actress who had a recurring role on HBO's *The Sopranos* as Joanne Moltisanti, the mother of Christopher (Michael Imperioli), and has appeared in films by John Sayles, Martin Scorsese, and Larry David. She is married to actor Chris Cooper and lives on Boston's South Shore with two rescue dogs, Lucky and Frenchy. She is working on a coming-of-age novel, *Christina the Astonishing.*

ELINOR LIPMAN is the author of ten novels, most recently *The View from Penthouse B,* and a collection of personal essays, *I Can't Complain.* Her book of political poems, *Tweet Land of Liberty: Irreverent Rhymes from the Political Circus,* was published in August 2012.

ALISON LURIE is the author of ten novels, including *Foreign Affairs* (Pulitzer Prize, 1985) and *The Truth About Lorin Jones* (Prix Femina Étranger, 1989). She has also published *Women and Ghosts,* a book of supernatural tales, and *The Language of Clothes,* a study of the

meaning of fashion, and two collections of essays on children's literature. She is married to the writer Edward Hower and lives in Ithaca,
New York, and Key West, Florida.

JOYCE MAYNARD is the author of the bestselling memoir *At Home
in the World*, and eight novels, including *Labor Day*, just adapted as a
film starring Kate Winslet and Josh Brolin. Her latest novel, *The Little
Sister*, has just been published.

BERNADETTE MURPHY has published three books of narrative
nonfiction, including the bestselling *Zen and the Art of Knitting*. She
recently completed a first novel, *Grace Notes*, and is at work on a nonfiction book about women and motorcycling: *Don't Call Me Biker Chick:
Embracing a Love Affair with Risk*. She teaches creative writing at the
Antioch University Los Angeles M.F.A. program, is the mother of
three nearly adult children, and makes her home in Los Angeles.

ANN PATCHETT is the author of six novels and three books of nonfiction. She is the co-owner of Parnassus Books in Nashville, Tennessee.

TAYLOR M. POLITES' first novel, *The Rebel Wife*, was just published
by Simon & Schuster. It was selected as a Top Read by *O* magazine
and an Okra Pick.

ELISSA SCHAPPELL is the author of *Blueprints for Building Better Girls,*
which was a *San Francisco Chronicle*, *Wall Street Journal*, *Boston Globe*,
Newsweek/Daily "Best Fiction Books of 2011," and one of *O* magazine's
"Top 5 Fiction Books of the Year," as well as a *Chicago Tribune* and
New York Times "Editors' Choice." She is also the author of *Use Me*,
which was a finalist for the PEN/Hemingway award, a *New York Times*
Notable Book, and *L.A. Times* "Best Book of the Year," and coeditor
with Jenny Offill of the two anthologies *The Friend Who Got Away* and

Money Changes Everything. Her essays/stories/criticism have appeared in numerous magazines and newspapers, and anthologies such as *The Bitch in the House, The Mrs. Dalloway Reader,* and *Cooking and Stealing.* She is also a contributing editor at *Vanity Fair,* coeditor, now editor-at-large, of *Tin House,* and a former senior editor of *The Paris Review.* She lives in Brooklyn.

ELIZABETH SEARLE is the author of four books of fiction: *My Body to You, Celebrities in Disgrace, A Four-Sided Bed* (which is being developed for film), and most recently the novel *Girl Held in Home* (2011). Her theater work *Tonya & Nancy: The Rock Opera,* based on the ice skating scandal, has been produced on both coasts and has drawn national media attention.

ANN SHAYNE is the author of *Bowling Avenue: A Novel,* and coauthor of two books with Kay Gardiner: *Mason-Dixon Knitting* and *Mason-Dixon Knitting Outside the Lines.* She was born in Birmingham, Alabama, and lives in Nashville with her husband and two sons.

SUZANNE STREMPEK SHEA lives in Bondsville, Massachusetts, and writes and knits wherever she goes. The author of nine books, she just published *This Is Paradise,* the story of Mags Riordan, an Irish mother who has been saving lives daily in the nine years since starting a clinic in the remote African village where her son drowned while on holiday. www.suzannestrempekshea.com

ANITA SHREVE is the author of seventeen novels, including *The Pilot's Wife,* which was selected for Oprah's Book Club in March 1999. She divides her time between Boston and Maine.

JANE SMILEY is the author of many works of fiction and nonfiction, including *A Thousand Acres, The Man Who Invented the Computer,* and the Abby Lovitt series for middle schoolers.